PEACH PIT CORAZÓN

PEACH PIT CORAZÓN

A Judith Ortiz Cofer Reader

Edited by Rafael Ocasio

The University of Georgia Press
Athens

Published with the generous support of the Georgia Writers Hall of Fame

Permission credits for previously published works appear on pages 241–242, which constitute a continuation of this copyright page.

Athens, Georgia 30602
www.ugapress.org

Designed by Mary McKeon
Set in Garamond Premier Pro by Mary McKeon

Most University of Georgia Press titles are available from popular e-book vendors.

Printed digitally

EU Authorized Representative
Easy Access System Europe—Mustamäe tee 50, 10621 Tallinn, Estonia, gpsr.requests@easproject.com

Library of Congress Cataloging-in-Publication Data
Names: Cofer, Judith Ortiz, 1952–2016 author | Ocasio, Rafael editor
Title: Peach pit corazón : a Judith Ortiz Cofer reader / edited by Rafael Ocasio.
Description: Athens : The University of Georgia Press, [2025] | Includes bibliographical references and index.
Identifiers: LCCN 2025017156 | ISBN 9780820374109 hardback | ISBN 9780820374116 paperback | ISBN 9780820374123 epub | ISBN 9780820374130 pdf
Subjects: LCSH: Cofer, Judith Ortiz, 1952–2016—Criticism and interpretation | American literature—Puerto Rican authors
Classification: LCC PS3565.R7737 P43 2025
LC record available at https://lccn.loc.gov/2025017156

DEDICATION

A mentor is a sounding board who gives you direction and guidance, and who asks you questions for you to work out on your own. We all need mentors. We stand on the shoulders of those who came before us.

—*John Lewis 8*

This anthology pays homage to my professional and personal relationship with Judith Ortiz Cofer, whom I met in 1989 when I began a teaching position at Agnes Scott College. Freshly out of graduate school, I was ignorant of any cultural referents pertaining to my new surroundings in Atlanta, where a Southern Latino culture was growing. As someone culturally and linguistically inscribed as a proud Puertorriqueño, born and raised on the Island, a hybrid *Latinidad* both resonated and clashed with my own ethnic identity. Judith became my lifeline to navigating biased Southern stances toward Latinos and served as my compass in handling the complexities behind the tenure and publishing procedures for scholars of color.

This is my humble tribute to a mentor whose influence and friendship impacted my professional career and my life experiences in the most unexpected ways. Descansa en paz, querida amiga.

CONTENTS

CHAPTER 3

CHAPTER 4

ACKNOWLEDGMENTS

I am indebted to the technical assistance of the Agnes Scott College students who transcribed the literary texts: Sheriefa Braswell '25, Joy Tidwell '24, Faith Lockhart '24, Aubrey Deas '22, Stella John '22, Isabella Gonzalez '24, Samia Shire '22, and Maddy Wasky '25. As always, muchas gracias to former student and rising poet Paige Sullivan for her careful copyediting. At University of Georgia Press, this project would not have been possible without the continued support of Lisa Bayer, director; Elizabeth Adams, assistant to the director/rights and permissions coordinator; and Bethany Snead, acquisitions editor.

Thank you to Oscar Ortiz and Dr. Elena Olazagasti-Segovia for their kindness in commenting on their professional relationship with Judith Ortiz Cofer.

I recognize the late John Cofer, Judith Ortiz Cofer's widower, who took time during a difficult transitional period to make sure that manuscripts and books made it safely to the Special Collections at the University of Georgia. He also granted me access to his personal collection of photographs and memorabilia.

PEACH PIT CORAZÓN

INTRODUCTION

"The Infinite Variety of the Puerto Rican Experience"

Judith Ortiz Cofer Within the Development of Latino, Latina, and Latinx Literatures

> I would like to use Shakespeare's phrase to describe Cleopatra; he said that people found her attractive, not because she was beautiful, he never said that she was beautiful, but because of her "infinite variety." This phrase reflects my idea of the infinite variety of the Puerto Rican experience. It may not be infinite, but it is certainly varied and ever changing. There used to be a time when the Puerto Rican experience was the experience of the people on the island; then it became the experience of people in New York City. Now it is the experience of people like me, who started out in New Jersey, and now I am in Georgia and it is a different reality.
>
> —*Judith Ortiz Cofer, qtd. in Ocasio, "The Infinite Variety of the Puerto Rican Reality" 735*

Latinx literature is defined here as writing in English published in the United States by cisgender or LGBTQIA+ individuals who identify as either Latin American–born or who claim any aspects of the socioeconomic, racial, or linguistic elements expressed in modern Latinx identities. As Ilan Stavans argues, the post–Vietnam War era gave rise to a "new wave" of Latino writers: "[They] are revolutionizing the status of Hispanic letters in English by revamping the approach of those who came before them. Their characters often see themselves as fashionable citizens proud of a life at the margin—divided selves whose identity is nurtured by Latin America's magical exoticism and by a hyper-realism a la Raymond Carver" ("The New Latino" 2). Early writers such as Cuban American Oscar Hijuelos (1951–2013); Dominican American Julia Álvarez (1950); Chicanas Gloria Anzaldúa (1942–2004) and Sandra Cisneros (1954); and Puerto Ricans Esmeralda Santiago (1948) and Judith Ortiz Cofer (1952–2016) stand out as foundational voices. Their testimonial writings document their diasporic experiences and are written from their specific gender and sexual orientation vantage points as Latinos and Latinas.

These earliest Latino and Latina writers continue to be household names among college students; they are widely read in interdisciplinary programs such as Latinx, Chicano, Puerto Rican, or ethnic studies. In drawing literary connections between mainstream U.S. cultures and their ancestral Latin American homelands—often countries with a history of U.S. economic or political intervention—these writers dared to raise their voices in a convoluted sociopolitical arena, not unlike today's continued fights for women's rights and gender and racial equality. More important, earlier Latino and Latina writers set the tone for contemporary Latinx literature, a production that has broadened conceptual formulations of what were previously labeled "Latino" or "Latina" identities, expanding on a diversity of socioeconomic and ethnic backgrounds while often challenging traditional binary concepts pertaining to gender and sexual orientations as prescribed in their Latinx communities.

Born in the small town of Hormigueros on February 24, 1952, Ortiz Cofer arrived with her family in Paterson, New Jersey, at age two as part of a large aerial displacement of Puerto Ricans destined to work in U.S. urban centers and agrarian areas. Facilitated in part by the Puerto Rican government, this uprooting process, commonly referred to as "*la guagua aérea*," underscores the ease of air travel. Large numbers of Puerto Ricans traveled on "air buses" to cities in the Northeastern United States as part of a significant historical event that has been described as "the first set of migrants to the United States who arrived mostly via airplane" (Morales 48).

The settlement arrangements for the Ortiz family in Paterson were, however, extremely peculiar. While her father's active military duties as a U.S. Navy boiler engineer took him abroad for extended periods of time, the family, including a younger brother, regularly traveled back to Puerto Rico on their mother's wishes. "Our annual migration," as Ortiz Cofer referred to their frequent travels back to the Island, became the inspiration for numerous creative nonfiction essays (*Cruel Country* 30). In Hormigueros they lived at Ortiz Cofer's maternal grandparents' house, which she often endearingly referred to as *casa*, where "I learned how powerful storytelling can be, it can change lives" (Bartkevicius 61). Mamá, the grandmother, also provided little Judith with family stability as the matron of a rather large family: "[W]hereas other people who come to the U.S. may go to Puerto Rico as visitors, we really went as part of an extended family. My mother would literally pack us up and take us to her mamá's house and Mamá would make room for us. [. . .] So I think I got a taste of the real life in Puerto Rico, even though it was for maybe three months or six months at the time" (Ocasio, "Words" 28). Constant trips back and forth, as Ortiz Cofer traced in several creative nonfiction essays, forced her to relearn English several times.

While in Hormigueros, she received elementary and secondary education in Spanish, first at a local public school and later in a reputable Catholic school in a nearby city. Through her family's practices, she maintained a close connection with a deeply ingrained devotion to Hormigueros's patron saint, Nuestra Señora de la Monserrate (Our Lady of Monserrate), a local Marian apparition dating back to the mid-seventeenth century. She was also immersed in popular religious devotions such as *espiritismo*, or scientific spiritism, a counter-Catholic practice that had surreptitiously arrived from France in the mid-nineteenth century.

Although her father had been stationed in Brooklyn Yard, the family settled in Paterson, where he had relatives. He was only available to spend time with his family during weekend passes. The care of the household was under the complete control of Ortiz Cofer's mother, who as a monolingual individual came to depend on her daughter as her "interpreter of language and culture—my role during her *exilio*" (*Cruel Country* 16). The reversion of roles, Ortiz Cofer observed, prompted her future career as a scholar and a writer: "Reading and research have been for me the route to power ever since my early days as translator for my mother, reinforced when I turned myself into a scholarship kid who would, with education and a mastery of English, break through the boundaries between languages and cultures that imprisoned my parents" (*Cruel Country* 148).

At age fifteen, her father moved the family to Augusta, Georgia, where he intended to continue his military career and where he also had relatives. The Ortiz family was seeking refuge from the rather convoluted racial strife in Paterson, which had first imploded in street riots on August 11–14, 1964 (Mack). Their move to Augusta, four years later, coincided with the Woodstock Festival (August 15–18, 1969), as Ortiz Cofer underscored in her essay "First Class Back to the Summer of Love," which draws parallels between the most iconic event of the hippie era and her parents' decision to uproot their family yet one more time: "the year when my family's hopes for peace and prosperity in America began to give way to the dark months of senseless assassinations, riots, and a war that was dividing and subdividing us; there was dissent between the leaders and the people, parents and children, the races, men and women, gays and straights. Everyone had a fight to pick. My parents feared losing their tenuous claim to a life in this country, and they feared losing control on us" (164).

After her father's early retirement for medical reasons that a sixteen-year-old Ortiz Cofer vaguely remembered as "[having] something to do with his nervous breakdowns," the family's frequent and long trips to Hormigueros stopped (*Cruel Country* 45). A geographical stability allowed her to complete high school in Augusta; however, the transition was the source of yet another traumatic cultural shock. In "First Class Back to the Summer of Love," Ortiz Cofer recalled her new Southern coordinates: "In Georgia we had to explore a different landscape and we had to relearn spoken English with new inflections, acquaint ourselves with another set of customs and boundaries. We became aware that there are many Americas, and Georgia is as different an America from New Jersey as a peach is from a mango, and that saying we were from New Jersey and thus Yankees was at times a more socially awkward admission than explaining our ethnicity" (169). She also witnessed the desegregation of the public school system, at its core a rather violent demonstration of the South's historical handling of race: "Race in the South is a subtle system little understood by outsiders, and it was with a mixture of dismay and relief that I found myself neither in the center nor quite on the margins of turmoil and tensions of the Civil Rights era in the Deep South. There were not enough brown people here to make us players of any significance. I could stay silent and invisible until I knew if I wanted to remain in this America" (169–170).

She went on to attend Augusta College, today Augusta University, where she received a bachelor's degree in 1974. It was the culmination of her father's immigrant dream, an occasion that brought joy to an often deeply depressed man: "He smiled when I got accepted to college. I remember that day clearly. He stood almost at attention as I read the letter of acceptance. He smiled and nodded. Yes, this is what he wanted for us" (*Cruel Country* 45). Ortiz Cofer completed a master's degree in English, including a summer program at Oxford University, at Florida Atlantic University in 1977.

After her father's death by suicide in 1976, Ortiz Cofer's mother permanently returned to Puerto Rico, where she settled in her own home near Hormigueros's historic downtown. The mother-daughter bond remained strong, with Ortiz Cofer making yearly trips to her beloved hometown. Those visits as an adult and as a rising Latina writer became subjects for her creative nonfiction essays, which explore her mother's "twenty-five years of her exilio" as that of "Rip Van Winkle, waking from a decades-long dream to a changed world" (*Cruel Country* 82).

INITIAL LITERARY WORK: EARLIEST IMAGES OF PUERTO RICAN AND BORICUA CULTURES

Ortiz Cofer's avid love of learning fueled her initial literary career as a poet. In 1981, she was granted residency fellowships from the Florida Fine Arts Council and the Bread Loaf Writers' Conference. Her connection with the Bread

Loaf Writers' Conference was enduring and included receiving a John Atherton Scholarship in Poetry in 1981 and again in 1987. The chapbooks *Latin Women Pray* (1980), *The Native Dancer* (1981), and *Among the Ancestors* (1981) indicate her interest in mapping an iconography associated with popular Puerto Rican traditions. These chapbooks involve her earliest archiving of foundational childhood anecdotes in "this country," as she refers to the United States in "A Partial Remembrance of Our First Year in This Country," a poem in *The Native Dancer.*

Ortiz Cofer was billing herself, according to a biography in *The Native Dancer*, as a "native of Puerto Rico who, as the daughter of a Navy Man, traveled from the Island to the United States regularly during her childhood" (30). She also maintained a busy academic career as an adjunct English instructor at Broward Community College and Palm Beach Junior College. Her public image, as a short biography in *Latin Women Pray* highlights, was a "featured poet at many poetry readings, and at cultural and community events in the South Florida area, including *The Florida Arts Gazette*'s Poetry-in-a-Pub series, The Women of the Eighties program at Broward Community College, The Miami Earth Chapter of F.S.P.A. Library Readings, The Women's Advocacy Majority/Minority Meeting, The National Organization for Woman (NOW) Reception for Gloria Steinem, and others" (qtd. in cover page). She also served as the poetry editor for *The Florida Arts Gazette* (qtd. in cover page of *Among the Ancestors*).

Ortiz Cofer won her first national recognition in 1985, when Linda Pastan (1932–2023) chose *Peregrina* (1986) as the winner in the Riverstone International Chapbook Competition. She had also published poems in several journals, including *Kansas Quarterly*, *New Mexico Humanities Review*, *South Florida Poetry Review*, *SEZ: A Multi-Racial Journal*, and *Reading Journal* (*Native Dancer* 30). In 1989, she received the National Endowment for the Arts Fellowship in Poetry.

More national acclaim followed with the poetry collections *Reaching for the Mainland* (1987) and *Terms of Survival* (1987). As their titles suggest, Ortiz Cofer continued her exploration of the migration processes of Puerto Ricans while underscoring the effects of such geographical displacement. *Terms of Survival* is a reference to *la lucha*, a common label in Puerto Rican jargon that Ortiz Cofer succinctly defined as "life's challenges" (*Cruel Country* 46). Those struggles, as Ortiz Cofer experienced as a newly arrived monolingual individual, included learning a new language and adapting to mainstream traditions while satisfying cultural expectations, such as maintaining various Puerto Rican traditions and speaking Spanish as the family's language.

Ortiz Cofer's initial literary production was focused on the socioeconomic factors that shaped urban Puerto Rican communities in the United States. An homage to Borikén (Borinquén), the island's original Indigenous Taíno name, the term "*Boricua*" used here describes the rather unique presence of Puerto Ricans in the United States, given the island's political connection as a U.S. territory. By extension, *Boricua* encapsulates the cultural heritage that defines those experiences of Puerto Ricans either as new arrivals in the United States or as part of established communities, whether inscribed (or not) into a so-called mainstream American lifestyle.

ORTIZ COFER AS A *GEORGIA RICAN* AND A LATINA WRITER

Ortiz Cofer was among the first Boricua writers in the United States published by university and mainstream publishing houses. Her initial work in particular explores the peculiarities of her family's constant displacement, which defined her childhood as a frequent traveler of la guagua aérea. Her first novel, *The Line of the Sun* (1989), explores her memories of growing up in Paterson, funneled through the character Marisol, a teenage girl who also finds herself caught as interpreter of two colliding worlds.

The Line of the Sun was also the first novel published by the University of Georgia Press. This association with the University of Georgia Press was significant. It not only catapulted Ortiz Cofer as a "Georgia Rican" writer, a label that was a common subject of our conversations, but it also placed her work outside the publishing houses that had traditionally published Boricua writers. It was named one of the "Twenty-Five Most Memorable Books" of 1989 by the New York City Library System.

With the nomination for the Pulitzer Prize for *The Line of the Sun*, hailed as "storytelling as transgression" (Socolovsky 97), Ortiz Cofer brought Boricua literature to a wider audience. Ilan Stavans has underscored that the book "pushed the Puerto Rican novel into new, lyrical areas not dependent on urban crime for plot and style" ("New Latino" 6). Furthermore, Ortiz Cofer commented on her intention to document the peculiarities of her transculturation experiences as an immigrant:

> I felt that it was important to make my life as a bilingual person and a Puerto Rican woman the subject of a lengthy work. The reason I use so much autobiographical material in the novel is not so much that I think my life is important. I feel it is sort of an obligation. As a Puerto Rican immigrant my key experience was growing up bilingual and bicultural. Therefore, I felt a need to share that with others, before I could go on. Perhaps you can call it a rite of passage or something similar. But I felt that I had to

> get that straight in my mind. In writing *The Line of the Sun*, I was recreating my past in a way that I could understand it myself. It was a kind of training for myself both as a thinking person and a writer to get my life straight. (Acosta Belén qtd. in "*MELUS* Interview" 84–85)

Ortiz Cofer continued to explore key autobiographical events in *Silent Dancing: A Partial Remembrance of a Puerto Rican Childhood* (1990), her debut short story collection. Through poems, nonfiction essays, and short stories, *Silent Dancing* encompasses critical and celebratory commentaries on Puerto Rican social and cultural practices as they adapted (or not) to the urban setting of Paterson. Moreover, she drew attention to the strong connection between her earliest works as part of a well-thought-out literary project: "And so, *Silent Dancing* and *The Line of the Sun* are both based on those years when the two cultures were intermingled in a truly bicultural and bilingual way" (Ocasio, "Words as Cultural Bridges" 27). *Silent Dancing* received the 1991 PEN/Martha Albrand Award Special Citation for Nonfiction and was selected for the New York Public Library's 1991 Best Books for the Teen Age. Pregones/Puerto Rican Traveling Theater, based in New York City's Bronx, successfully adapted the opening story, "Silent Dancing," as "The Wedding March," which remained on stage for over six years in the Bronx and around the country.

Puerto Rico's complex migrant history has been the subject of critical discussions. Marisel Moreno delineates the island's political peculiarity as such: "Puerto Rico's colonial status as an unincorporated territory of the United States has had a profound impact on its migration history and has also marked a significant contrast to the histories, patterns, and conditions faced by other Latina/os" (1223). The myriad economic and often dire social reasons for the Puerto Rican migration is the focus of *The Latin Deli* (1993). Moreover, by gathering short stories, creative nonfiction essays, and poetry, Ortiz Cofer undertakes an exploration of her and other Puerto Ricans' migrant experiences, which ultimately involve trading one's familiar, yet conflicted, native island surroundings for the uncertain settings of an urban barrio. *The Latin Deli* received multiple awards, including Georgia Top 25 Reading in 2005 by the Georgia Center for the Book; the Anisfield-Wolf Award, which praises books that have made important contributions to the understanding of racism and diversity; and a National Book Award nomination.

Yet, in positioning herself as a Georgia writer published by a mainstream academic press, Ortiz Cofer purposely removed her work from long-established literary circles, commonly known as *Nuyorican*, named after the inhabitants of urban Boricua barrios in New York City. Claiming independence from the aesthetics of Nuyorican literature implied that she did not live in New York and that she wrote in mainstream English. As we often discussed, Puerto Rican literary critics on the island continued to resist literature written in English, or in Spanglish, as part of a larger concept of "Puerto Rican literature." She fervently spoke about her preference to write in English:

> I was born in Puerto Rico and the first language I heard was Spanish; it remained my home language all throughout my childhood into my early youth. I don't think it was ever replaced by English, only that I added English. Since most of my education was in English it became the language of my literary expression. It has become my functional language, that's why I write in English. It will be very difficult for me to write in Spanish since I have lost a lot of the intimacy with the language required to make metaphors and to do certain types of abstract thinking in that language. But, of course, I still speak Spanish with my relatives. ("Puerto Rican Literature in Georgia?" 44)

Nonetheless, in the use of certain Spanish words as signifiers of peculiarities in Puerto Rican cultural practices, Ortiz Cofer was mindful of previous linguistic experimentation: "The greatest works often contain many other languages: Greek in *The Waste Land* [by T. S. Eliot], Italian with [Ezra] Pound, French with many people. I just assumed if I couldn't grasp the meaning in context, if the work was important enough and we were interested enough, that we would go find a dictionary and look things up" (Shea 101). In her innovative intermingling of English and Spanish while chronicling Puerto Rican or Boricua characters, she forecasted linguistic changes already taking place at the global level: "Am I corrupting the language when I use my own Anglicisms because that's what I grew up with? Or is the language simply evolving and changing to reflect a global society? So before I get too philosophical or 'global' in my perspective, I'd just like to say that I relish and enjoy the thought that language does not dominate us, but that we dominate language" (qtd. in Ocasio, "Infinite Variety" 736).

Full recognition as a Georgia writer came in 2007 as *The New Georgia Encyclopedia Companion to Georgia Literature* listed Ortiz Cofer as a notable writer from "contemporary Georgia" (Ruppersburg 9). On March 23, 2010, in recognition of her literary contributions, she was inducted into the Georgia Writers' Hall of Fame, an accolade that she fully appreciated in her unpublished acceptance speech: "I will now speak words never spoken before at a Georgia Writers' Hall of Fame induction: Muchas gracias. Gracias for making su casa mi casa."

Ortiz Cofer indeed felt at home in Georgia. She had put down roots in Louisville, known as Georgia's first permanent capital, proudly billing itself as a closely knit "Capital Community" ("Capital Community"). Her husband, John Cofer, had built a quaint house on a former farm that had belonged to his family for several generations. Her loving relationship with Southern ways of being was deeply felt and, most important, another sentimental connection with Georgia: "I have lived most of my life in the United States but never left my connection to the island behind [. . .] to my present situation, which is that I live in Georgia. I consider this my home. I have a family and a love story here" (Shea 96). She became, as John affectionately called her, a "Georgia-mango," which Ortiz Cofer further explained at the Twelfth Annual Calhoun Community College Writers Conference in 2013 as "a fruit that cannot exist in nature, you have to imagine it."

Beginning in 1984, she became an instructor in the English Department at the University of Georgia, where she gained tenure in 1992. Throughout her many years at the University of Georgia, Ortiz Cofer was the recipient of numerous awards: Outstanding Teacher by the Student Government Association (2000), Outstanding Teaching Faculty Recognition (2000), Love of Learning Award by the Honor Society of Phi Kappa Phi (2003), and a Faculty Research Grant (2004). In 1999, she was named the Franklin Professor of English and Creative Writing. She retired from teaching on January 1, 2014.

THE CHILDREN AND YOUTH EXPERIENCE IN BORICUA URBAN CENTERS

Although stories about children and adolescent characters acquiring culture and language are clearly important in her earlier works, *An Island Like You: Stories of the Barrio* (1995) is Ortiz Cofer's first narrative collection specifically written as young adult literature. It centers around young and teenage characters, such as children born in Puerto Rico who find themselves in the United States with little preparation (in terms of English-speaking skills or facilities to adapt to U.S. ways of life) or children born in the United States expected to culturally behave like Puerto Rican children. These urban Boricua youth often experience clashes with Puerto Rican traditions: for example, their family's expectation that they speak fluent Spanish or that they maintain rather dated social customs while they also face increased peer pressure to adapt to mainstream U.S. values. Boricua youth frequently face microaggressions and openly racist attitudes as they venture into mainstream urban settings. Ortiz Cofer was particularly proud of this collection. One of her teenage characters, Arturo, openly questions his queer identity, which, according to Ortiz Cofer, "refrained the book from being adopted in some very traditional schools" (qtd. in Ocasio, "Words" 30). *An Island Like You* was the winner of several awards, including the American Library Association's inaugural Pura Belpré Prize in 1996, *Kirkus Review*'s Editors' Choice, and *School Library Journal*'s Best Book of the Year List; it also appeared in Italian and Dutch translations in 1997.

Ortiz Cofer returned to the format of short stories and poems gathered as a collection in *The Year of Our Revolution: New and Selected Stories and Poems by Judith Ortiz Cofer* (1998). It highlights young female characters struggling against imposed gender roles prevalent in Puerto Rican and Latinx communities. One such character is María Sabida, the fictional protagonist of a well-known Puerto Rican fable, whose ingenuity manages to not only tame the bloodiest of road thieves but to end his criminal career—by marrying him. However, the valiant wife must endure a rather unusual precaution, drawing from a popular Puerto Rican saying: to sleep every night with one eye open.

An Island Like You was followed by a sort of sequel, *If I Could Fly* (2011). It highlights Puerto Rican youth struggling and thriving within the physical and social constrictions of el barrio. The opening story, "If I Could Fly," is a literal translation of a Puerto Rican phrase, "si pudiera volar," commonly used to express the yearning to metaphorically fly to the island of Puerto Rico, thus avoiding the physical limitations of traveling by means of a guagua aérea.

Two other outstanding works for youth audiences are the novels *The Meaning of Consuelo* (2003) and *Call Me María* (2004). They feature Puerto Rican girls and Boricua teenage girls as protagonists of deeply moving coming of age stories. Ortiz Cofer boldly introduced *The Meaning of Consuelo* at the Library of Congress and Laura Bush Book Festival on October 4, 2003, as a book written "to try to understand how one becomes an American woman; I wanted to explore the concepts of gender and language" ("Judith Ortiz Cofer at 2003 National Book Festival"). Indeed, Ortiz Cofer daringly explored rather taboo subjects in Puerto Rican culture, such as a small girl's sexual molestation, mental health (in this case, schizophrenia), and gay sexual orientation. The novel was included on the New York Public Library's Books for the Teen Age list in 2004.

In *Call Me María*, the protagonist, not unlike many young people of the guagua aérea generation, is caught between two worlds and must choose which life story to pursue: staying in Puerto Rico with her mother or joining her father's dream of financial success in a tough urban barrio environment. Similar to *Silent Dancing* and *The Latin Deli*, *Call Me María* returns to genre-merging as indicated in its subtitle, *A Novel in Letters, Poems and Prose*. María discovers her new U.S. environment from the basement apartment of a *bildin'* while writing in different genres, as Ortiz Cofer underscored: "She comforts herself in her initial loneliness by trying to construct the world" (Shea 99). The novel was selected as an Honorable Mention for the 2005 Americas Awards, sponsored by the National Consortium of Latin American Studies Programs.

Continuing her interest in reaching youth audiences, *Animal Jamboree:*

Latino Folktales (2012) is a bilingual collection of updated fables for children and youth readers. Ortiz Cofer often credited her passion for storytelling to her grandmother, whom she often presented as a prime literary mentor: "The stories I heard from my grandmother became the basis for my imaginative life" (qtd. in Ocasio, "Infinite Variety" 733). By reinterpreting popular folk stories that draw from common popular associations of an abundant Latin American fauna and flora, Ortiz Cofer intended to appeal to young Boricua and Latinx readers.

A standout publication in her writing for young readers is *The Poet Upstairs* (2012). It is a fictional story of a Puerto Rican girl living in el bildin' who wonders about the identity of a neighbor, a mysterious woman poet who lives in the apartment above her. As the story unfolds, the reader eventually comes to understand that the woman was Julia de Burgos (1914–1953). Although she is well known today as a poet and early Puerto Rican feminist activist, de Burgos spent the final years of her life in solitude in New York City fighting abject poverty and an alcohol addiction that eventually led to her untimely death. The book is also striking because of the beautiful illustrations by Puerto Rican artist Oscar Ortiz. In an email (April 8, 2022), he described to me his experience of producing the illustrations that serve as a visual narrative for *The Poet Upstairs*: "Interpretar el texto mediante ilustraciones resultó ser una tarea absorbente donde, además de darle al lector claves visuales de lo que leía, también intentaba entregar una dimensión atmosférica, cuasi surrealista. Esto se logró a través de imágenes superimpuestas de índole casi transparente" (To interpret this text through illustrations became a profound experience, besides giving the reader visual cues about what they were reading, I was also creating another atmosphere, an almost surrealist dimension. I managed to do just that through almost transparent, over imposed images).

A GEORGIA RICAN WRITER IN SPANISH TRANSLATION

There is yet another aspect of Ortiz Cofer as a Boricua writer that is often unexplored. Her works were frequently published in Spanish translations. *The Line of the Sun* appeared as *La línea del sol* (1996) by the prestigious University of Puerto Rico Press. The publication of this translation by Puerto Rico's premier university is of notable importance. Its translator, Dr. Elena Olazagasti-Segovia, a Puerto Rican and at the time professor of Spanish at Vanderbilt University, wrote to me about the significance of this publication in an email dated April 11, 2022: "Translating *The Line of the Sun* was a major undertaking and a challenge because it would be the first work written by a Puerto Rican author writing in English to be published by the University of Puerto Rico Press." Indeed, Ortiz Cofer was hopeful that *La línea del sol* could improve her connection with monolingual Puerto Rican readers on the island who would otherwise not read *The Line of the Sun.*

The University of Georgia Press maintained an interest in publishing Ortiz Cofer's works in Spanish translations, including *Woman in Front of the Sun* as *Mujer frente al sol* (2005) and *The Latin Deli* as *El deli latino* (2006). Speaking about the translation of *Woman in Front of the Sun*, Ortiz Cofer described the press's decision as "very courageous" (Shea 102). Her long association with UGA Press concluded with the 2016 release of her memoir *The Cruel Country.*

The Spanish translations of Ortiz Cofer's work also had international appeal. Her YA short story collection, *An Island Like You: Stories of the Barrio* (1995), was published in 1997 in Spanish as *Una isla como tú: Historias del barrio* by the prestigious Mexican publishing house Fondo de Cultura Económica. She was extremely proud of the Spanish translations, several of them performed by Olazagasti-Segovia, her preferred translator. They had been working closely together for years, an experience that grew into a long friendship. Olazagasti-Segovia felt that Ortiz Cofer intended her publications to serve as an activist vehicle for expressing and celebrating different accounts of Boricua culture: "Judith Ortiz Cofer devoted her literary work to foregrounding the history and traditions of her native culture, so I felt privileged to help her reach out to Spanish-speaking readers, particularly Boricuas" (personal email dated April 11, 2022).

The international impact of Ortiz Cofer's Spanish translations is also reflected in one special recognition. The Federico García Lorca Foundation selected some of her poems to be read as part of an international traveling exhibit in observance of the reputable poet's one hundredth birth anniversary in 1997. As part of these events, Ortiz Cofer read Spanish translations of her poems in Madrid, Granada, and Alcalá de Henares. Indeed, Ortiz Cofer was extremely honored to be a part of this recital, listing her participation in it on her curriculum vitae as "[o]ne of five Latin American writers" invited to it. She maintained an interest in reading her poetry in Spanish. At a Poetry@Tech event on November 29, 2005, she read "Del libro de los sueños," a poem from *The Latin Deli.* This is perhaps indicative of her growing desire to connect more with a Spanish-speaking audience and, I dare say, indicative of her plans to start writing in Spanish.

"I FIND MYSELF A LATINA WRITER" AND A GEORGIA RICAN WRITER

Ortiz Cofer was an active guest speaker at academic and writers' conferences and literary festivals. She frequently appeared in other public forums and interviews, such as 1998 and 2003 segments on National Public Radio. As I came to experience so many times, her readings mesmerized her audiences, who were captivated by the funny and sincere passion of a consummate storyteller. In 1993, she was the first Latina guest speaker at Agnes Scott College Writers' Festival, where she highlighted her ongoing literary production in a presentation titled "I Find Myself a Latina Writer." She boldly introduced herself to the audience: "[T]oday I do not speak to you as a scholar in the field of Latino literature, but rather as a writer of books written in English whose main subjects and settings often reflect the author's emigrant background, and with issues pertaining to her ethnicity" (25).

Her final public presentation took place at the West Carolina University Writers' Festival in 2016. It was an outstanding lecture, despite her frail health. In her introduction to her reading, she billed herself a "Southern Latina writer" and announced her ongoing work in progress: "I am interested in the intersection of time, place, and self; that is, when does a writer belong to a place and a place belongs to a writer? It did not happen to me about Paterson until I was away from New Jersey, and it did not happen about the South until recently. When I started thinking that it was time to write about Georgia. I shouldn't be the tourist" ("Judith Ortiz Cofer at WCU's 2016 Literary Festival").

She had started conceptualizing a more complex Southern literary project much earlier, however. As part of a promotion of a forthcoming reading at the University of Georgia, on February 20, 2008, Ortiz Cofer spoke briefly about a "new multi-genre work in progress, 'The Peach Pit Corazón,'" which she briefly described in these terms: "The peach pit is the hardest thing you can find, according to an old, Southern saying. This collection is going to be about Georgia, and finally, after 20 years, I feel that I can write about it. This is going to be about making this place home, without giving up the other part of me" (Oberst).

Months later, on May 26, she described in an email to me an ongoing piece, "Georgia Apparition," as "a lyrical essay [. . .] one of a series of witnessing poems and essays I am writing, many of them about Latinos in the South." A day later, during our formal interview, she expanded on the lyrical article, which had a sad genesis pertaining to the rising number of Latinos in urban Atlanta:

> I had read in an article in the *Atlanta Journal-Constitution* that most of the pedestrian deaths now in Atlanta are of Latinos. The reason they gave is that it is hard for illegal immigrants to get licenses, or they may be too poor to own a car. There was also an indication that people just don't see these people crossing the roads. It was a particularly tragic situation. A young Mexican mother with her two babies was crossing a road to get to a phone to call her mother, and she was struck and one of her boys was killed. I was just haunted by that image, not only so much about the facts, but also about the

> invisible person syndrome. We are all guilty of making others invisible, those who are not necessarily to be seen. ("Latina Writer" 2).

She also offered a more detailed account on the tentative title of the collection, *Peach Pit Corazón*, which she noted had a more concrete meaning: "The title came from the fact that I heard a Southern woman say, 'That man of mine has a peach pit heart,' and I said, 'What does that mean?' She said, 'Don't you know, honey, the hardest thing next to a rock is a peach pit.' I wrote that down in my journal, and when I decided to write essays, stories, and poems about my time in the deep South, I said, I'd love to blend the cultures by calling the book 'Peach Pit Corazón'" ("Latina Writer" 2).

THE CRUEL COUNTRY: A FAREWELL TO HER "ISLAND OF MY DREAMS"

Shortly after her retirement from teaching responsibilities at the University of Georgia in 2014, Ortiz Cofer started undergoing experimental clinical treatment for cancer while writing her testimonial work, *The Cruel Country* (2015). It was her last work published by the University of Georgia Press, and "The Latino Author.com" named it a Top Ten Best Non-Fiction selection that year. The memoir traces her mother's final days as a victim of an aggressive lung cancer and documents the death of her father-in-law, which occurred a few days before Ortiz Cofer left for Puerto Rico to take care of her dying mother. Ortiz Cofer's husband also became ill while she was in Puerto Rico. Ultimately, death becomes a marker for the painful, although inevitable, passing of generations, Ortiz Cofer's recognition of her new role as repository of family lore and Puerto Rican cultural practices.

Her mother's cancer takes center stage as the result of many years of heavy smoking, the last ones unbeknownst to her dutiful daughter, who had been traveling annually to the island to ascertain her mother's medical condition in her old age. The memoir documents Ortiz Cofer's rather impromptu return to her native Hormigueros, where she laboriously facilitated the best medical care for her dying mother. The memoir is, above all, a loving ode that praises the strong influence of her mother, and it is with this praise that she leads her mother to her final resting place.

The Cruel Country continued to explore the feelings of uprootedness so often experienced by Boricuas, whether they have recently arrived or have been in the United States for several generations. As she details in *The Cruel Country*, she referred to herself as being "*de afuera*," a label that is frequently applied to Puerto Ricans who have left the island for a considerable amount of time and are thus considered outsiders by island Puerto Ricans: "When does one stop being de afuera and become one with a culture? Within the inner circle of a family and close friends, things like appearance and accents matter less and less over time and are rendered psychologically invisible by affection. My Latina appearance and the accent I can no longer hear in my voice inspire questions in both my cultures: 'Where did you come from?' Puerto Rico, New Jersey, points in between, and Georgia" (167). Her answers to the questions about her allegiance to Puerto Rico and New Jersey were clearly given in her extensive literary production. Unfortunately, her untimely death precluded her literary explorations of Georgia as a sentimental geography.

Because of her debilitating physical condition, Ortiz Cofer did not engage in an active promotional tour of *The Cruel Country*. True to her superstition of not commenting about her work in progress, our copious correspondence pertaining to *The Cruel Country* dealt with her drafting of the rather specific funeral arrangements and proper etiquette during the formal wake, including her hosting of *la novena de muertos*, nine rosary sessions following the burial, expected of her as the only daughter of her deceased Roman Catholic mother. It would also be her last trip to Hormigueros, her hometown that often appears as a source of literary inspiration and an iconic representation of a rich Puerto Rican cultural identity.

Our last email exchange was her proof of my requested "payment" for my fact-finding services while drafting *The Cruel Country*. I had asked for a passage highlighting my native Old San Juan. It was not an easy task, since the action of the memoir takes place solely in Hormigueros, so far removed historically and geographically from the capital city. She did agree, although she gave me some grief in her characteristic sense of humor: "I feel like the genie in the bottle (I don't see you as Barbara Eden, however). I promised you a gift and now you have asked me for one, I must try to find the magic to realize. I will have to refresh my memory of Old San Juan, watch some YouTube videos and look at photographs. Let me see what I can do, hijo" (email dated May 19, 2013).

She rendered an aerial view of my beloved Old San Juan, set as part of her return trip to the United States, starting in Mayagüez, the city nearest to Hormigueros with a small airport, where an *avioneta*, a propeller plane, flew to the international airport outside San Juan. The beginning leg of her guagua aérea route, an annual trip completed for so many years, these bird's eye views from a low-flying propeller plane were still a source of admiration of the outstanding beauty of the Island:

> Here is the revised Old San Juan passage. I thought it'd be appropriate to send it to you as you leave your beloved old city. Gracias por todo.
> —Judith

> I board the tiny propeller plane in Mayagüez, and I look down at that vast azul sea of variegated blues, I see at the green eye of my Island looking at me, fixing me with the vision of place that I will take to my grave. In half an hour we are on the other side of the Island. There is the old city of San Juan on whose blue cobblestone streets fortune-seekers from all over the world have walked. There are the narrow alleys lined with old warehouses that once stored rum and spices and are now stores that sell trinkets to the tourists. There are the imposing condominiums and hotels, and there the cruise ships disgorging the masses whose dollars keep the island afloat. And just below us, as the avioneta dips and descends towards the airport in Isla Verde, is the Spanish fort built by the Spaniards to defend their rich port, there is El Morro. I watch it recede in the distance like a mirage, until it disappears. When it does, I look forward toward the horizon, letting my heart lift at the thought of home. (email dated May 31, 2013)

Ortiz Cofer died peacefully on December 30, 2016, at her home in Louisville, Georgia. She had been bravely fighting an uphill battle against an aggressive bile valve cancer, which John Cofer described to me as "a cholangiocarcinoma in the ducts in the liver caused by a genetic mutation, and only less than 1% of the 5% of cancer patients have this deadly cancer and life expectancy is six months" (email dated August 30, 2017). She was buried in Louisville.

Her literary legacy as an intersectional Puerto Rican, Georgia Boricua, and Latina writer still resonates strongly for a new Latinx generation as they continue to explore the complexities behind today's expanding racial and gender orientations. She plainly stated to me her heartfelt mission: "I would like to be remembered perhaps as someone whose words bridged cultures. Someone who allowed through her poetry and her words for there to be some new understanding of what it's like to live in between cultures. So, perhaps as a sort of facilitator, a bridge between cultures and a light into the concept that it isn't a negative thing to own two cultures" ("Words as Cultural Bridges" 34–35).

UPDATING ORTIZ COFER'S BORICUA AND LATINA LITERATURE: SHORT STORIES AND CREATIVE NONFICTION ESSAYS

Ortiz Cofer's work appeared in both academic and commercial publishing houses, often "specialty publishers," which Christopher González has identified as mainly Latinx publishing houses with an established Latino/a readership (5). As González posits, although breaking away from traditional Latinx publishing houses did create a new phase in Latino and Latina literatures, the switch to mainstream publishing houses also prompted "major publishing houses [to be] selective in the Latino/a novels they publish[ed]" (5). More frequently, her short narrative and creative nonfiction essays were published in Latino and Latina literary anthologies that highlight her role as a founding mother of a Latina literature, a role she understood as such: "If my stories have serious lives being lived, that is, lives that are not being recounted for the sake of mere entertainment, then I am a writer of political intent. I am not an ideologue, have never been one. If I put ideas into my books, it is simply because my characters reflect things that are of interest and importance to me. But if I write about a woman's hard life, I make it as interesting as possible, because I want other women to read it, not as sociology or history, but as a story, like my grandmother's stories" (qtd. in Ocasio, "Infinite Variety" 739).

Ortiz Cofer's strong women characters document and discuss events that recall her life story as part of a guagua aérea generation, as a New Jersey–raised Boricua, a Southerner, and a self-proclaimed Georgia Rican. Ortiz Cofer was extremely proud of this cultural intersectionality, which she began to underscore toward the end of her literary career as an example of an "infinite variety of the Puerto Rican experience."

The subject of Puerto Rican–born individuals who relocate to the United States as immigrants has been heatedly discussed. Take, for instance, the nationwide controversy surrounding the statement by Kimberly Guilfoyle, the national chair of the Trump Victory Finance Committee, made at former President Trump's reelection rally on August 24, 2020, claiming immigrant ancestry as a first-generation American citizen: "My mother, Mercedes, was a special education teacher from Aguadilla, Puerto Rico. My father, also an immigrant, came to this nation in pursuit of the American dream" (qtd. in Acevedo, par. 3).

Just as widely discussed and contested in Puerto Rico were claims made during the 2021 Olympic Games in Tokyo by diasporic (second-generation) Puerto Ricans born in the United States that they were proud holders of a Puerto Rican identity. Olympic gold medalist Jasmine Camacho-Quinn, a track and field athlete born in the United States, for example, qualified to compete as a full-fledged athlete of the Puerto Rican delegation based on her claims of Puerto Rican ancestry through her Puerto Rican–born mother. The news of Camacho-Quinn's first-place run at the women's hundred-meter hurdles on August 1, 2021—the second gold medal in Puerto Rican Olympic history—sparked controversy on the Island, given that Camacho-Quinn was born in the United States and, as pointed out by her detractors, does not even speak Spanish. Perhaps anticipating such heated debate, Camacho-Quinn received the gold medal proudly wearing a "*flor maga*" (a hibiscus bloom, the national flower of Puerto Rico) in her afro (Castillo).

This anthology brings together selected short stories, creative nonfiction, and academic essays as illustrations of Ortiz Cofer's varied explorations of the sociopolitical and economic components that inform Puerto Rican and U.S.

Boricua cultures. Four themes in Ortiz Cofer's narrative production stand out and are the subjects of the following chapters. First, there is the Puerto Rico that she recalls as a child of the guagua aérea generation. Indeed, her family's personal circumstances, which prompted them to leave their native Hormigueros, intersect with key events in Puerto Rican migrant history after World War II. Furthermore, as a second literary interest, Ortiz Cofer was among the first Boricua writers to gain mainstream attention for her documentation of an urban Boricua identity, as reflected in her multifaceted images of el barrio in Paterson, New Jersey.

A third exploration highlights Ortiz Cofer's groundbreaking incursion into multiple Latinx identities. She was among the founding writers of a mainstream Latina literature movement, and most important, she was also a Georgia Rican who, while solidly grounded in Southern traditions, brought to the forefront another type of Puerto Rican migrant experience. Last, a fourth subject is Ortiz Cofer's celebration of Puerto Rican culture through her documentation of the Island's rich oral folklore. With her reinterpretation of short narrative pieces, "fábulas criollas with lots of creative license involved," as she described them to me, Ortiz Cofer joined a number of Puerto Rican and Boricua researchers who have found in these popular stories early evidence of a strong Puerto Rican identity. They are connections to multiracial Latinx communities, a recognition and enjoyment of shared cultural values.

The first chapter, "A Deeply Felt *Añoranza*: A Remembrance of *La Isla* through Puerto Rican Culture," brings into focus Ortiz Cofer's detailed archiving of native Puerto Rican cultural traditions. This type of documentation, as William Luis has underlined, has served a vital function: "Latino literature tends to narrate a familiar and personal experience, mainly from a first-person perspective. The author provides insight into the life of the protagonist, who has undergone a significant experience or come to terms with a particular moment in the past" (vii). The readings underscore Ortiz Cofer's documentation of Hormigueros as an iconic pueblo, particularly for its opposing popular religious practices: the devotion to Nuestra Señora de la Monserrate, a Marian apparition associated with memorable ritualistic performances, and Kardecian spiritist sessions, as Ortiz Cofer witnessed them in her grandfather's *centro espiritista* home. In other articles, Ortiz Cofer records the cultural peculiarities of Hormigueros as a small town, specifically how traditions impacted her development as a bicultural and bilingual child.

Ortiz Cofer's experiences as a newcomer struggling with a new language and cultures are similar to other Latinx writers, as Falconer and López suggest, as a creator who "often appears on the scene as a mediator, translator, or insider ethnographer bearing literary artifacts from the native culture to enlighten and entertain members of the dominant culture" (1). Her in-depth documentation of Puerto Ricans in U.S. urban centers, and particularly her adaptation to an urban Puerto Rican experience in Paterson, is the theme of chapter 2, "In the Midst of the Puerto Rican Barrio: A Facsimile of the Island." The resilience of Boricuas, who had started to reclaim dilapidated downtown settings in the second half of the twentieth century, was certainly noteworthy. Against all odds, they created a vibrant community, reflective of their strong desire to overcome racist barriers while at the same time adapting iconic Puerto Rican cultural traditions to the new city surroundings. It was not, however, an easy transition to urban living, as Ortiz Cofer herself experienced: Monolingual children recently arrived from the Island were subjected to persistent microaggressions from individuals in positions of power.

Ortiz Cofer was also highly critical of the sexist and homophobic aspects of Puerto Rican and Boricua traditions that were often left uncontested. At the heart of Ortiz Cofer's narrative is her exploration of women characters, whether on the island or in urban Boricua settings, who struggle against openly sexist cultural viewpoints. Chapter 3, "Boricua Women and Latinas: Facing Gendered Categorization and Stereotypes," groups short stories and creative nonfiction essays that highlight strong-willed female characters—Puerto Rican, Boricua or Latina women of various age groups who opposed gender-based, sexist traditions, whether on the island or in urban Boricua, Latinx, or mainstream settings. Additionally, Ortiz Cofer wrote critical essays that archived her own life experiences and conceptual feminist approaches to fighting sexism as a Latina writer and college professor.

The tradition of telling oral stories was an area of increasing interest for Ortiz Cofer, both as the grandchild of a reputed storyteller and as an admirer of Puerto Rican folktales. Chapter 4, "Revamped Puerto Rican Fables as Repositories of Cultural Legacy," takes a twofold approach to highlighting the impact of oral folk literature in Ortiz Cofer's overall narrative production. First, akin to "*échate un cuento*," a popular phrase in Puerto Rico that celebrates the innate gifts of certain individuals as storyteller entertainers, this chapter underscores Ortiz Cofer's familiarity with a rich repertoire of Puerto Rican oral folktales, often connected with key characters who are well known throughout the island or in her native Hormigueros or colorful individuals related to her family histories. Second, I bring to the forefront her revamped oral stories, highlighting the way in which she modernized Puerto Rican folk characters, settings, and motifs to accommodate a new Puerto Rican, Boricua, and Latinx readership while also promoting reading habits among children and youth.

This project of cultural recuperation reflects a long narrative tradition among Latinx writers who underscore shared social and cultural identities. Whether it is a quinceañera, a baptism, a wedding, or Christmas festivities, Latinx groups find solace in the celebration of social events because they are expressive of a deeply felt sense of cultural belonging that often transcends national and ethnic boundaries to incorporate elements from other Latinx cultures. In short, as Chicana writer Lorraine M. López has posited, visual representation does matter: "Growing up in the age of television, I rarely encountered representations that informed my quest for cultural identity in a helpful way. I am old enough to remember the Frito Bandito, Speedy Gonzales and a host of slumbering, sombrero-wearing Mexicans in westerns who were as significant as cacti to the gun-slinging white hero" (40).

Finally, in my critical commentaries, I draw heavily from our enduring personal and professional relationship, which began on October 7, 1989, at Ortiz Cofer's reading of *The Line of the Sun* in Atlanta at the iconic, now-closed Oxford Bookstore. Until her untimely death, we frequently met in person to discuss issues related to our "migrant life experiences" while living so many hundreds of miles away from "the island of our dreams." In spite of the differences in our upbringings, Puerto Rico's many cultural referents were the object of the many questions turned into my published interviews and also our personal connections as longtime Georgia Ricans who embody "the infinite variety of the Puerto Rican experience."

CHAPTER 1

A Deeply Felt *Añoranza*

A Remembrance of La Isla *Through Puerto Rican Culture*

I'm no longer the same kind of puertorriqueña that my mother is. I refuse to be politically correct and say that I'm a pure, unadulterated, native puertorriqueña. No. I've undergone an evolutionary process as has everyone who has ever left their homeland.

—*Judith Ortiz Cofer, "The Poetic Truth" 123*

In her first interview in Spanish for a Puerto Rican newspaper, shortly after the publication in 1989 of her novel, *The Line of the Sun*, Ortiz Cofer stated her heartfelt sentimental connection with the island of her birth: "Puerto Rico es la isla de mis sueños; es la que facilita mis poemas y todo lo que yo escribo. Esa idea que llevamos dentro la Isla de Puerto Rico es lo que nos hace individuos en este mundo tan complejo" (Trelles 22; Puerto Rico is the island of my dreams; it inspires my poems and everything else I write. The idea that we carry inside the Island of Puerto Rico is what makes us individuals in this complex world). The interview, which accompanied a positive review for the newly published novel, introduced Ortiz Cofer as "una puertorriqueña que vive en los Estados Unidos desde la infancia" (Trelles 22; a Puerto Rican who has lived in the United States since childhood). It was a rather oversimplified characterization that Ortiz Cofer challenged as part of a poetic description of her perceived Puerto Ricanness: "Aunque escribo en inglés, yo vivo a Puerto Rico y pienso siempre en él" (Trelles 22; Although I write in English, Puerto Rico lives within me and is always on my mind). She continued to underscore her goal as a writer, which she contextualized within the hardships that her generation experienced in the United States: "Yo pienso que uno hace política viviendo la vida. La vida misma es política; el arte puede usar la vida para tomar una posición. Si escribo sobre los sufrimientos de mis compatriotas, de alguna manera hay una perspectiva política en lo que escribo" (Trelles 22; I believe that by living one engages in politics.

Life itself is political; art can draw from life in order to make a point. If I write about the sufferings of my fellow Puerto Ricans, in a certain way there is a political perspective in my writings).

Ortiz Cofer often addressed my questions about *añoranza*, an overwhelming yearning for something left behind, a sentiment of sadness common among immigrants displaced from their place of birth, regardless of the years living in their adopted country. Often expressed in English as homesickness, she often referred to it as *tristeza*, particularly while speaking about her mother's acutely felt sadness during her years living in the United States: "My mother did ache for Puerto Rico. I have come to the conclusion that there are some people who attach themselves to a particular place, and if they are not there, they suffer anguish. My mother was one of them. Many women of her generation lived only to go back to *la isla*. Her deal with my father was, 'When you retire, we are going back to Puerto Rico.' Always Mamá, *la casa*, *la isla*. She did not expect to die in this country" (unpublished interview). In contrast, Ortiz Cofer had fully assumed her condition as a first-generation Boricua: "That is the *nostalgia* that you are talking about, that calls you back and makes you sad if you are not there. Mine is not like that. I have never felt that I need to live on the island. I feel a debt of gratitude to have been enriched by the Spanish language, and by the culture, and by the fact that I can always make that necessary comparison between cultures." In short, as she expressed in her memoir *The Cruel Country*, she had managed to escape what had overwhelmingly affected her mother: "Grief over the loss of family and friends, over the loss of the mother tongue, over the loss of culture; grief over the loss of the homeland, over the loss of contact with your ethnic group, over the fear of physical danger; grief over the loss of the original dream, and the grief of no possible return" (172).

Ortiz Cofer was born in 1952 in Hormigueros, an iconic small town located near the Island's western coast, known for colorful and deeply rooted religious practices. Although officially recognized as a town in 1874, Hormigueros was formed years earlier as a village at the footsteps of a primitive hermitage, or a chapel, a tribute to the miraculous apparition of Nuestra Señora de la Monserrate (Matías 54). Popularly known as the "Black Madonna," her devotion as a miraculous Lady had inspired enduring religious traditions beginning in 1640, including crowded peregrinations to her shrine (Toro Sugrañes 193). Today a Minor Basilica (the second on the island), the church boasts distinctive architecture and is Hormigueros's center of great cultural importance (Albino Plugues 75).

Hormigueros appears barely disguised as Salud, a rural town in *The Line of the Sun*, a novel that has been hailed as a highly complex novel "layered with transgressions, addressing the limits between history and the present moment, the narrative of U.S. mainland and the island, fiction and autobiography" (Socolovsky 96). Although Ortiz Cofer told *The San Juan Star*, Puerto Rico's only English newspaper at the time, "I tried to avoid a biography of Hormigueros" (Turner n.p.), Hormigueros's city hall public functionaries thought otherwise. In 1990, Ortiz Cofer was recognized with a plaque as a "*Hormiguereña ausente*" (Turner n.p.; a distinguished expatriate). She came to share honors with another notable local personality, Segundo Ruiz Belvis (1829–1867), an abolitionist and patriot who in the nineteenth century actively promulgated the pro-independence movement under the Spanish central government.

Hormigueros's overwhelming religious cultural fabric is an integral component of *The Cruel Country*, which details her childhood witnessing of the town's enduring Marian devotion: "I grew up with the invoked Holy Mary hovering over our days and nights. . . . This goddess worship—a term that would cause outrage here if I spoke it aloud—shaped my imagination, as I spent part of my formative years in a town that was formed around the supposed apparition of the dark-skinned Virgin of Monserrate" (71). On her last trip to Hormigueros, the presence of La Monserrate was an important part of a farewell visit to the iconic church, where she had gone seeking a Marian blessing prior to her return to the United States. She goes on to describe that moment with the imagination of a poet: "The church does seem to float above us like an apparition as we sit in the darkened car. I feel like I did as a student when I looked at the stars through a telescope and was told that what I was seeing was in the past: the configuration of the stars, the nimbus of colors surrounding them—none of it existed in real time; it had already happened thousands or maybe millions of years ago. It had taken the light that long to reach us. I am seeing what my mother may have imagined, looking out the windows of the many places that she would not call home: a view from the past, suspended in time—one she could come back to" (180). Although not a practicing Catholic, Ortiz Cofer kept a simple framed photo reproduction of la Virgencita Negra as a visual aid on her writing desk.

Espiritismo, or scientific spiritist practices, also influenced Ortiz Cofer's childhood. The teachings of French spiritist practitioner Allan Kardec, pen name for Hippolyte Léon Denizard Rivail (1804–1869), had given rise to a type of "Spiritist doctrine" in Puerto Rico (Román-Odio 18). After the publication of Kardec's *The Book of the Spirits* (1857), the first of a series of seminal books, espiritismo surreptitiously arrived on the Island in the early 1860s and was practiced underground (Román-Odio 20). In 1871, however, the first spiritist center opened in Mayagüez (Romeu Toro). A major urban center near Hormigueros, Mayagüez became an important location for the dissemination of Kardecian practices throughout Puerto Rico.

In *The Cruel Country*, Ortiz Cofer documented her profound knowledge of espiritismo through the practices of her maternal grandfather, Papá Basi. A kind and soft-spoken man, as she described him in several of her creative nonfiction essays, Papá Basi was a reputable head practitioner of "*a mesa blanca*"; he oversaw various types of spiritual consultations for neighbors at a table covered with a white cloth. At mesa blanca casas, homes turned into meeting centers, spiritist heads often consecrate medals, rosaries, or other religious objects such as ex-votos, which are charged with powers to repel curses (Romeu Toro 70–71). Papá Basi's spiritist exercises were heavily ingrained in Ortiz Cofer: "Growing up with this daily exposure to Espiritismo meant that I did not find it strange to overhear discussions about ghosts visiting someone or about restless spirits causing trouble for a neighbor; as a rebellious teenager, however, I was infuriated to hear my actions discussed in terms of the restless spirit that was my constant companion" (76). Papá Basi had identified his granddaughter, the rebellious teenager who once had cut her long hair short as a sign of contestation for the frequent trips to the Island she was forced to endure, as a potential spiritist practitioner and encouraged her to develop her *facultades*, or gifted spiritist skills. In particular, Papá Basi attributed to Ortiz Cofer an uncanny ability to see beyond the physical realm, which years later the mature writer equated to her ability to write: "I want to believe that my grandfather was not so much a clairvoyant medium as he was a sensitive, perceptive man—a poet. Perhaps what he saw in his book-obsessed granddaughter was potential, and so he took on the guise of the seer to grant me permission to see myself as a potential seer too. I understand that this is an interpretation made in hindsight. In my medium, I can grant myself the right to find, in the significant moments of my life, **the continuous threat of revelation**" (emphasis in the original 77).

Papá Basi also wrote *décimas*, a popular type of poetry associated with the *jíbaro*, the inhabitant of the Puerto Rican countryside. As an adult, Ortiz Cofer maintained a rich correspondence with him, and he transcribed many of his décimas for his emerging poet granddaughter. In return, Ortiz Cofer shared her earliest poetic production, which frequently drew from Puerto Rican cultural iconography.

This chapter underscores Ortiz Cofer's role as a cultural historian of "el pueblo de Hormigueros," the hamlet of her childhood and early teenage years. A strongly knit family is the subject of "More Room," which remakes her maternal grandparents' casa, the first classroom where she witnessed compelling cultural patterns. It was an ancestral home that Papá Basi had built following the specifications of his wife, adding a room on the occasion of the birth of each new child. The last addition of one "more room," however, represents an unexpected turn of events and a savvy way that Mamá managed to challenge oppressive gender roles.

"Talking to the Dead" is a tribute to Ortiz Cofer's Papá Basi as a well-known mesa blanca spiritist practitioner and composer of décimas. As a sequel to "More Room," this creative nonfiction essay features Ortiz Cofer as a curious child spying on her grandfather's private spiritual consultations. The religious activities took place in his special room, the "more room" of the previous creative nonfiction essay, located at the back of the house and away from the disappointed look of Mamá, who was a strict Roman Catholic practitioner. Mamá remained a nonbeliever until Papá Basi's visions came to resolve the whereabouts of one of their sons, who had been recruited to work in the Northeast United States. He and a group of Puerto Ricans were eventually held incommunicado and against their will on a fruit farm, where they were forced to work in horrible living conditions. As a reward, Mamá handmade an elaborate white tablecloth, a mandated object in Papá's mesa blanca spiritist practices. Embroidery was both Mamá's and their daughters' pastime and a well-known local tradition.

Popular Roman Catholic religious traditions as practiced in Hormigueros are the subject of the creative nonfiction essay "The Black Virgin." The piece highlights rather unusual Marian devotional practices, such as *promesas* as prepayments for desired, and highly expected, divine favors. For instance, women would slowly and painfully climb the seventy steps to reach the entrance of Monserrate's sanctuary on their knees or wore *hábitos*, crude robe-like habits designed to castigate the flesh, as they were made of rough fabrics. The true setting of this essay is Ortiz Cofer's paternal grandmother's casa, a household where her pregnant mother waited for the return of her newly married husband, who had been deployed abroad. It was a remarkable household; in the absence of men serving in the U.S. Army, women were left to fend for themselves. This essay also offers a striking look at Ortiz Cofer's father's childhood, a subject that she rarely explored given the severity of his increasingly debilitating depression.

In "The Aging María: On the Value of Talismans and Amulets," published during her aggressive cancer treatment, Ortiz Cofer takes a detailed look at the funeral practices following her mother's death in Hormigueros, which was also the focus of her memoir *The Cruel Country*. This creative nonfiction essay explores the wearing of protective religious objects, such as medals, as a tenet known as *resguardos*, a practice shared by Roman Catholic and spiritist practitioners. Indeed, those who knew Ortiz Cofer well would remember her wearing a medal, Nuestra Señora de los Milagros; Our Lady of the Miracles, that had belonged to her grandmother.

The last two essays, "Primary Lessons" and "¿La Verdad?: Notes on the Writing of *Silent Dancing*, a Partial Remembrance of a Puerto Rican Childhood (A Memoir in Prose and Poetry)," illustrate Ortiz Cofer's reinterpretation of creative nonfiction essays as "the strange morphing of fictional technique and nonfiction writing" ("¿La Verdad?"). "Primary Lessons" memorializes her first day at school in Hormigueros, a traumatic event that goes beyond the common childhood fear of leaving home for the first time. It admonishes the colonial imposition of the use of English in the public school system. It also reflects on key "*moments of being*" ("¿La Verdad?") that introduced Ortiz Cofer to the racial tensions at play in Hormigueros. Indeed, as she wrote in "¿La Verdad?," a theoretical essay on the craft of memoir writing, other such life lessons came from her unusual (for a Latina writer) literary mentors, such as Virginia Woolf.

MORE ROOM

My grandmother's house is like a chambered nautilus; it has many rooms, yet it is not a mansion. Its proportions are small and its design simple. It is a house that has grown organically, according to the needs of its inhabitants. To all of us in the family it is known as *la casa de Mamá*. It is the place of our origin; the stage for our memories and dreams of Island life.

I remember how in my childhood it sat on stilts; this was before it had a downstairs. It rested on its perch like a great blue bird, not a flying sort of bird, more like a nesting hen, but with spread wings. Grandfather had built it soon after their marriage. He was a painter and housebuilder by trade, a poet and meditative man by nature. As each of their eight children were born, new rooms were added. After a few years, the paint did not exactly match, nor the materials, so that there was a chronology to it, like the rings of a tree, and Mamá could tell you the history of each room in her *casa*, and thus the genealogy of the family along with it.

Her room is the heart of the house. Though I have seen it recently, and both woman and room have diminished in size, changed by the new perspective of my eyes, now capable of looking over countertops and tall beds, it is not this picture I carry in my memory of Mamá's *casa*. Instead, I see her room as a queen's chamber where a small woman loomed large, a throne-room with a massive four-poster bed in its center which stood taller than a child's head. It was on this bed where her own children had been born that the smallest grandchildren were allowed to take naps in the afternoons; here too was where Mamá secluded herself to dispense private advice to her daughters, sitting on the edge of the bed, looking down at whoever sat on the rocker where generations of babies had been sung to sleep. To me she looked like a wise empress right out of the fairy tales I was addicted to reading.

Though the room was dominated by the mahogany four-posters, it also contained all of Mamá's symbols of power. On her dresser instead of cosmetics there were jars filled with herbs: *yerba buena*, *yerba mala*, the making of purgatives and teas to which we were all subjected during childhood crises. She had a steaming cup for anyone who could not, or would not, get up to face life on any given day. If the acrid aftertaste of her cures for malingering did not get you out of bed, then it was time to call *el doctor*.

And there was the monstrous chifforobe she kept locked with a little golden key she did not hide. This was a test of her dominion over us; though my cousins and I wanted a look inside that massive wardrobe more than anything, we never reached for that little key lying on top of her Bible on the dresser. This was also where she placed her earrings and rosary at night. God's word was her security system. This chifforobe was the place where I imagined she kept jewels, satin slippers, and elegant sequined, silk gowns of hearth-breaking fineness. I lusted after those imaginary costumes. I had heard that Mamá had been a great beauty in her youth, and the belle of many balls. My cousins had other ideas as to what she kept in that wooden vault: its secret could be money (Mamá did not hand cash to strangers, banks were out of the question, so there were stories that her mattress was stuffed with dollar bills, and that she buried coins in jars in her garden under rosebushes, or kept them in her inviolate chifforobe); there might be that legendary gun salvaged from the Spanish-American conflict over the Island. We went wild over suspected treasures that we made up simply because children have to fill locked trunks with something wonderful.

On the wall above the bed hung a heavy silver crucifix. Christ's agonized head hung directly over Mamá's pillow. I avoided looking at this weapon suspended over where her head would lay; and on the rare occasions when I was allowed to sleep on that bed, I scooted down to the safe middle of the mattress, where her body's impression took me in like a mother's lap. Having taken care of the obligatory religious decoration with a crucifix, Mamá covered the other walls with objects sent to her over the years by her children in the States. *Los Nueva Yores* were represented by, among other things, a postcard of Niagara Falls from her son Hernán, postmarked, Buffalo, N.Y. In a conspicuous gold frame hung a large color photograph of her daughter Nena, her husband and their five children at the entrance to Disneyland in California. From us she had gotten a black lace fan. Father had brought it to her from a tour of duty with the Navy in Europe (on Sundays she would remove it from its hook on the wall to fan herself at Sunday mass). Each year more items were added as the family grew and dispersed, and every object in the room had a story attached to it, a *cuento* which Mamá would bestow on anyone who received the privilege of a day alone with her. It was almost worth pretending to be sick, though the bitter herb purgatives of the body were a big price to pay for the spirit revivals of her story-telling.

Mamá slept alone on her large bed, except for the times when a sick grandchild warranted the privilege, or when a heartbroken daughter came home in need of more than herbal teas. In the family there is a story about how this came to be.

When one of the daughters, my mother or one of her sisters, tells the *cuento* of how Mamá came to own her nights, it is usually preceded by the qualifications that Papá's exile from his wife's room was not a result of animosity between the couple, but that the act had been Mamá's famous bloodless coup for her personal freedom. Papá was the benevolent dictator of her body and her life who had had to be banished from her bed so that Mamá could better serve her family. Before the telling, we had to agree that the old man was not to blame. We all recognized that in the family Papá was as an *alma de Dios*, a saintly, soft-spoken presence whose main pleasures in life, such as writing poetry and reading the Spanish large-type editions of *Reader's Digest*, always took place outside the vortex of Mamá's crowded realm. It was not his fault, after all, that every year or so he planted a baby-seed in Mamá's fertile body, keeping her from leading the active life she needed and desired. He loved her and the babies. Papá composed odes and lyrics to celebrate births and anniversaries and hired musicians to accompany him in singing them to his family and friends at extravagant pig-roasts he threw yearly. Mamá and the oldest girls worked for days preparing the food. Papá sat for hours in his painter's shed, also his study and library, composing the songs. At these celebrations he was also known to give long speeches in praise of God, his fecund wife, and his beloved island. As a middle child, my mother remembers these occasions as a time when the women sat in the kitchen and lamented their burdens, while the men feasted out in the patio, their rum-thickened voice rising in song and praise for each other, *compañeros* all.

It was after the birth of her eighth child, after she had lost three at birth or in infancy, that Mamá made her decision. They say that Mamá had had a special way of letting her husband know that they were expecting, one that had begun when, at the beginning of their marriage, he had built her a house too confining for her taste. So, when she discovered her first pregnancy, she supposedly drew plans for another room, which he dutifully executed. Every time a child was due, she would demand, *more space, more space*. Papá acceded to her wishes, child after child, since he had learned early that Mamá's renowned temper was a thing that grew like a monster along with a new belly. In this way Mamá got the house that she wanted, but with each child she lost in heart and energy. She had knowledge of her body and perceived that if she had any more children, her dreams and her plans would have to be permanently forgotten, because she would be a chronically ill woman, like Flora with her twelve children: asthma, no teeth, in bed more than on her feet.

And so, after my youngest uncle was born, she asked Papá to build a large room at the back of the house. He did so in joyful anticipation. Mamá had asked him special things this time: shelves on the walls, a private entrance. He thought that she meant this room to be a nursery where several children could sleep. He thought it was a wonderful idea. He painted it his favorite color, sky blue, and made large windows looking out over a green hill and the church spires beyond. But nothing happened. Mamá's belly did not grow, yet she seemed in a frenzy of activity over the house. Finally, an anxious Papá approached his wife to tell her that the new room was finished and ready to be occupied. And Mamá, they say, replied: "Good, it's for *you*."

And so it was that Mamá discovered the only means of birth control available to a Catholic woman of her time: sacrifice. She gave up the comfort of Papá's sexual love for something she deemed greater: the right to own and control her body, so that she might live to meet her grandchildren—me among them—so that she could give more of herself to the ones already there, so that she could be more than a channel for other lives, so that even now that time has robbed her of the elasticity of her body and of her amazing reservoir of energy, she still emanates the kind of joy that can only be achieved by living according to the dictates of one's own heart.

TALKING TO THE DEAD

My grandfather is a *Mesa Blanca* Spiritist. This means that he is able to communicate with the spirit world. And since almost everyone has a request or complaint to make from the *Other Side*, Papá once was a much sought-after man in our pueblo. His humble demeanor and gentle ways did much to enhance his popularity with the refined matrons who much preferred to consult him than the rowdy *santeros* who, according to Papá, made a living through spectacle and the devil's arts. *Santería*, like voodoo, has its roots in African blood rites, which its devotees practice with great fervor. *Espiritismo*, on the other hand, entered the island via the middle classes who had discovered it flourishing in Europe during the so-called "crisis of faith" of the late nineteenth century. Poets like Yeats belonged to societies whose members sought answers in the invisible world. Papá, a poet and musician himself when he was not building houses, had the gift of clairvoyance, or *facultades*, as they are called in spiritism. It is not a free gift, however: being a Spiritist medium requires living through *pruebas*, or tests of one's abilities.

Papá's most difficult *prueba* must have been living in the same house with Mamá, a practical woman who believed only in what her eyes recorded. If Papá's eyes were closed that meant that her lazy man was sleeping in the middle of the day again. His visionary states and his poetry writing were, I have heard, the primary reasons why Mamá had, early in their married life, decided that her husband should "wear the pants" in the family only in the literal sense of the expression. She considered him a "hopeless case," a label she attached to any family member whose drive and energy did not match her own. She never changed her mind about his poetry writing, which she believed was Papá's perdition, the thing that kept him from making a fortune, but she learned to respect his *facultades* after the one incident that she could not easily dismiss or explain.

Although Papá had been building a reputation for many years as an effective medium, his gifts had not changed his position in Mamá's household. He had, at a time determined by his wife, been banished to the back of the house to pursue his interests, and as for family politics, his position was one of quiet assent with his wife's wise decisions. He could have rebelled against this situation: in Puerto Rican society, the man is considered a small-letter god in his home. But, Papá, a gentle, scholarly man, preferred a laissez-faire approach. Mamá's ire could easily be avoided by keeping his books and his Spiritist practice out of her sight. And he did make a decent living designing and building houses.

In his room at the back of the house he dreamt his dreams and interpreted them. There he also received the spiritually needy: the recent widows, the women who had lost children, and the old ones who had started making plans for the afterlife. The voices were kept low during these consultations. I know from having sat in the hallway outside his door as a child, listening as hard as I could for what I thought should be taking place—howlings of the possessed, furniture being thrown around by angry ghosts—ideas I had picked up from such movies as *Abbot and Costello Meet the Mummy*, and from misinterpreting the conversations of adults. But, Papá's seances were more like counseling sessions. Sometimes there were the sounds of a grown person sobbing—a frightening thing to a child—and then Papá's gentle, persuasive voice. Although most times I could not decipher the words, I recognized the tone of sympathy and support he was offering them. Two or more voices would at times join together in a chant. And the pungent odor of incense seeping through his closed door made my imagination quicken with visions of apparitions dancing above his table, waiting to speak through him to their loved ones. In a sort of trance myself, I would sometimes begin softly reciting an *Our Father*, responding automatically to the familiar experience of voices joined together in prayer and the church-smell of incense. What Papá performed in his room was a ceremony of healing. Whether he ever communicated with the dead I cannot say, but the spiritually wounded came to him and he tended to them and reassured them that death was not a permanent loss. He believed with all the passion of his poet's heart, and was able to convince others, that what awaits us all after the long day of our lives was a family reunion in God's extensive plantation. I believe he saw heaven as an island much like Puerto Rico, except without the inequities of backbreaking labor, loss and suffering which he could only justify to his followers as their *prueba* on this side of paradise.

Papá's greatest *prueba* came when his middle son, Hernán, disappeared. At the age of eighteen, Hernán had accepted a "free" ticket to the U.S. from a man recruiting laborers. It was a difficult time for the family, and reluctantly, Mamá had given Hernán permission to go. Papá, on the other hand, had uncharacteristically spoken out against the venture. He had had dreams, nightmares, in which he saw Hernán in prison, being tortured by hooded figures. Mamá dismissed his fears as fantasy-making, blaming Papá's premonitions on too much reading as usual. Hernán had been a wild teenager, and Mamá felt that it was time he became a working man. And so Hernán left the island, promising to write to his parents immediately, and was not heard from again for months.

Mamá went wild with worry. She imposed on friends and relatives, anyone who had a contact in the U.S., to join in the search for her son. She consulted with the police and with lawyers, and she even wrote to the governor, whose secretary wrote back that the recruiting of Puerto Rican laborers by mainland growers was being investigated by the authorities for the possibility of illegal practices. Mamá began to have nightmares herself in which she saw her son mistreated and worse. Papá stayed up with her during many of her desperate vigils. He said little, but kept his hands on his Bible, and would often seem to be speaking to himself in a trance. For once, Mamá did not ridicule him. She may have been too wrapped up in her despair. Then one night, Papá abruptly rose from his chair and rushed to his room where, with his carpenter's pencil, he began drawing something on the white cloth of his special table. Mamá followed him, thinking that her husband had gone mad with suffering for their child. But seeing the concentration on his face—it seemed to be lit with a light from within, she later told someone—she stood behind him for what seemed a long time. When he finished, he held a candle over the table and began explaining the picture as if to himself. "He is in a place far north. A place without a name. It is a place that can be found only by one who has been there. Here, there are growing things. Fruit, maybe. Sweet fruit. Not ready to be picked yet. There are lights in the distance. And a tall fence. Hernán sleeps here among the lights. He is dreaming of me tonight. He is lonely and afraid, but not sick or hurt."

Mamá began to see the things Papá described in the rough pencil lines on that tablecloth. Her mind turned into a map of memories, scraps of information, lines from letters she had received over the years, Christmas cards from strange places sent by a dozen nephews, or the sons of neighbors—young men for whom she had been a second mother—until she remembered this: a few years before Hernán's departure, Alicia's (Mamá's older sister) son, had also been "recruited" as a laborer. Like Hernán, he had not been informed as to exactly where he was going, only that it was in another Nueva York, not the city. Unlike her own son, her nephew had written home to say that he had been picking strawberries and did not like the job. Soon after, he had moved to a city near the farm where he had worked for a season. There he had married and settled down. Alicia would know the name of the place. But Papá had said it was a place without a name. Mamá decided to follow up on the only premonition she had ever allowed into her practical mind.

At that early hour, not quite dawn, the two of them set out for the country where Alicia lived; Papá was armed with his Bible and the symbol of his calling: a mahogany stick he had carved into a wand. Every Spiritist must make one and take it with him on house calls. It is hollow and sometimes filled with Holy Water in order to keep "evil influences" at a distance, but Papá had put a handful of dirt from his birthplace in his, perhaps because his calling as a medium was more than anything a poet's choice of missions: a need to accept mortality while struggling for permanence. Anyway, that earth-filled stick was the only weapon I ever knew Papá to carry. That morning he and his wife walked together in silence, a rare occurrence: to Mamá, long silences were a vacuum her nature abhorred. They came home with hope in the form of a telephone number that day.

After sending for the high school English teacher to interpret, they called the city of Buffalo, New York. Mamá's nephew told them that he would start looking for Hernán at the farm right away. He said, everyone just called it "the farm." It turned out that Hernán was at the farm. The situation was very bad. The workers had been brought there by an unscrupulous farm worker who kept them (most of them very young and unable to speak English) ignorant as to their exact whereabouts. They lived in tents while they waited for the fruit to be ready for picking. Though they were given provisions, the cost was deducted from their paychecks, so by the time they were paid, their salary was already owed to the grower. The workers were told that mail was not picked up there and it would have to be taken to the nearest city after the harvest. Though Hernán and many of the other men protested their situation and threatened to strike, they knew that they were virtual prisoners and would have to wait for an opportunity to escape. Mamá's nephew had connections in Buffalo and was able to convince a social worker to accompany him to the farm where he found Hernán eager to lead the exodus. It was not as easy as that, though. Many days passed before an investigation was started which revealed the scheme behind the farm and many others like it based on the recruitment of young men under false pretenses. But Hernán had been found. And Mamá learned to respect, if not quite ever to publicly acknowledge, her husband's gift of clairvoyance.

She paid her tribute to him in her own way by embroidering a new cloth for his *mesa blanca* in a pattern based on his drawings of that night. She did it with white thread on white cloth, so that to see it one had to get very close to the source; something, that as a writer, I am still trying to do today.

THE BLACK VIRGIN

In their wedding photograph my parents look like children dressed in adult costumes. And they are. My mother will not be fifteen years old for two weeks; she has borrowed a wedding dress from a relative, a tall young woman recently widowed by the Korean war. For sentimental reasons they have chosen not to alter the gown, and it hangs awkwardly on my mother's thin frame. The tiara is crooked on her thick black curls because she had bumped her head coming out of the car. On her face is a slightly stunned, pouty expression, as if she were considering bursting into tears. At her side stands my father, formal in his high-school graduation suit. He is holding her elbow as the photographer has instructed him to do; he looks myopically straight ahead since he is not wearing his wire-frame glasses. His light brown curls frame his cherubic, well-scrubbed face; his pale, scholarly appearance contrasts with his bride's sultry beauty, dark skin and sensuous features. Neither one seems particularly interested in the other. They are posing reluctantly. The photograph will be evidence that a real wedding took place. I arrived more than a year later, so it was not a forced wedding. In fact, both families had opposed the marriage for a number of reasons only to discover how adamant children in love can be.

My parents' families represented two completely opposite cultural and philosophical lines of ancestry in my hometown. My maternal relatives, said to have originally immigrated from Italy, were all farmers. My earliest memories are imbued with the smell of dark, moist earth and the image of red coffee beans growing row after row on my great-grandfather's hillside farm. On my father's side there is family myth and decadence. His people had come from Spain bringing tales of wealth and titles, but all I was aware of as a child was that my grandfather had died of alcoholism and meanness a few months before my birth, and that he had forbidden his wife and children ever to mention his family background in his house, under threat of violence.

My father was a quiet, serious man; my mother, earthy and ebullient. Their marriage, like my childhood, was the combining of two worlds, the mixing of two elements—fire and ice. This was sometimes exciting and life-giving and sometimes painful and draining.

Because their early marriage precluded many options for supporting a wife, and because they had a child on the way, father joined the U.S. Army only few months after the wedding. He was promptly shipped to Panama, where he was when I was born, and where he stayed for the next two years. I have seen many pictures of myself, a pampered infant and toddler, taken during those months for his benefit. My mother lived with his mother and learned to wait and to smoke. My father's two older brothers were in Korea during the same period of time.

My mother still talks nostalgically of those years when she lived with Mamá Nanda, as her grandchildren called her, since her name, Fernanda, was beyond our ability to pronounce during our early years. Mamá Nanda's divorced daughter, my aunt Felícita, whom I am said to resemble, also lived with us. The three women living alone and receiving Army checks were the envy of every married woman in the pueblo.

My mother had been the fourth child in a family of eight, and had spent most of her young life caring for babies that came one after the other until her mother had exiled her husband from her bed. Mamá Pola had been six months pregnant with her last child at my parents' wedding. My mother had been resentful and embarrassed about her mother's big belly, and this may have had some effect on my grandmother's decision.

Anyway, my mother relished the grown-up atmosphere at her mother-in-law's house, where Mamá Nanda was beginning to experiment with a new sense of personal freedom since her husband's death of alcohol-related causes a couple of years before. Though bound by her own endless rituals of religion and superstition, she had allowed herself a few pleasures. Chief among these was cigarette smoking. For years, the timid wife and overworked mother had sneaked a smoke behind the house as she worked in her herb garden where she astutely grew mint to chew on before entering the house. Occasionally she would steal a Chesterfield from her husband's coat pocket while he slept in a drunken stupor. Now she bought them by the carton, and one could always detect the familiar little square in her apron pocket. My mother took up the smoking habit enthusiastically. And she, my aunt Felícita and Mamá Nanda spent many lazy afternoons smoking and talking about life—especially about the travails of having lived with the old man who had been disinherited by his father at an early age for drinking and gambling, and who had allowed bitterness for his bad fortune to further dissipate him. They told family stories, stories which moralized or amused according to whether it was Mamá Nanda or the New York–sophisticated Felícita who told them. They were stories my mother would later repeat to me to pass the time away in colder climates while she waited to return to her island. My mother never adopted the U.S., she did not adapt to life anywhere but in Puerto Rico, although she followed my father back and forth from the island to the mainland for 25 years according to his tours of duty with the Navy. She always expected to return to *Casa*—her birthplace. And she kept her fantasy alive by recounting her early years to my brother and me until we felt that we had shared her childhood.

At her mother-in-law's, Mother learned the meaning of scandal. She considered the gossip created by Felícita's divorce in New York and subsequent return to the conservative Catholic pueblo yet another exciting dimension in her new adventure of marriage. After her young husband had left for Panama, she had had trouble sleeping, so Aunt Felícita had offered to sleep in the same bed with her. Felícita had desperately wanted a child of her own, but her body had rejected three attempts at pregnancy—one of the many problems that had helped to destroy her marriage. And so my mother's condition became Felícita's project; she liked to say that she felt like the baby was hers too. After all, it was she who had felt the first stirrings in my mother's belly as she soothed the nervous girl through difficult nights, and she who had risen at dawn to hold her up while she heaved with morning-sickness. She shared the pregnancy, growing ever closer to the pretty girl carrying her brother's child.

She had also been the one to run out of the house in her nightgown one night in February of 1952 to summon the old midwife, Lupe, because it was time for me to make my entrance into the world. Lupe, who had attended at each of Mamá Nanda's twelve deliveries, was by that time more a town institution than an alert midwife. That night she managed to pull me out of my mother's writhing body without serious complications, but it had exhausted her. She left me wrapped up in layers of gauze without securing my umbilicus. It was Felícita, ever vigilant of her babies, my mother and myself, who spotted the blood stain soaking through my swaddling clothes. I was rapidly emptying out, deflating like a little balloon even as my teenage mother curled into a fetal position to sleep after her long night's work.

They say that until my father's return, the social pariah, Felícita, cared for me with a gentle devotion that belied all her outward bravura. Some years before my birth, she had eloped with a young man whom her father had threatened to kill. They had married and gone to New York City to live. During that time, all her letters home had been destroyed in their envelopes by the old man who had pronounced her dead to the family. Mamá Nanda had suffered in silence, but managed to keep in touch with her daughter through a relative in New York. The marriage soon disintegrated and Felícita explored life as a free woman for one year. Her exploits, exaggerated by gossip, made her legendary in her hometown. By the time I could ask about such things, all that was left of that period was a trunk full of gorgeous party dresses Felícita had brought back. They became my dress-up costumes during my childhood. She had been a striking girl with the pale skin and dark curly hair that my father's family could trace back to their ancestors from northern Spain.

Piecing her story together over the years, I have gathered that Felícita, at the age of sixteen, had fallen madly in love with a black boy a little older than herself. The romance was passionate and the young man had pressed for a quick marriage. When he finally approached my grandfather, the old man pulled out his machete and threatened to cut Felícita's suitor in half with it if he ever came near the house again. He then beat both his daughter and wife (for raising a slut), and put them under house-arrest. The result of his actions was an elopement in which half the town collaborated, raising money for the star-crossed lovers and helping them secure transportation and airline tickets to New York. Felícita left one night and did not return for many years, after her father's death.

But the tale is more complex than that. There was a talk at the time that the groom may have been fathered by the old man, who kept mistresses but did not acknowledge their children. For his pleasure, he nearly always chose black women. There was no way to prove this awful suspicion one way or another. Felícita had been struck and blinded by a passion that she could not control. The marriage had been tempestuous, violent, and mercifully short. Felícita was a wounded person by the time I was born; her fire was no longer raging, but smoldering—just enough to keep me warm until my mother came out of her adolescent dream to take charge of me.

The three women and a baby girl then spent the next two years waiting for their soldier to come home. Mamá Nanda, a deeply religious woman, as well as superstitious, made a *promesa* for the safe return of her three sons. She went to early mass every day at the famous Catholic church in our town, the site of a miraculous appearance by the Black Virgin during the Spanish colonial period. Mamá Nanda also climbed the one hundred steps to the shrine on her knees once a week, along with other women who had men in the war. These steps had been hewn out of a hillside by hundreds of laborers, and a church had been constructed at the top, on the exact spot where a woodcutter had been saved from a charging bull by the sudden vision of the Black Lady floating above a treetop. According to legend, the bull fell on its front knees in a dead halt right in front of the man paralyzed by fear and wonder. There is a fresco above the church altar depicting this scene. Pilgrims come from all over the island to visit the shrine of the Black Virgin. A statue imported from Spain representing the Lady sits on a portable ark, and once a year, during her *Fiestas Patronales*, she is taken on her dais around the town, followed by her adorers. She is said to have effected many miraculous cures, and her little room, off to the side of the nave, is full of mementos of her deeds, such as crutches and baby garments (she can induce fertility in barren women). It was to her that Mamá Nanda and other women prayed when their men were in wars and during domestic crises. Being a woman and black made Our Lady the perfect depository for the hopes and prayers of the sick, the weak and the powerless.

I have seen the women dressed in black climbing the rough steps of *La Escalinata* to the front portals of the church and I have understood how the act itself could bring comfort to a woman who did not even know exactly where on earth her son or husband was, or even the reasons why he was risking his life in someone else's war. Perhaps God knew, and surely Our Lady, a woman, wife, and mother herself, would intercede. It was a man's world, and a man's heaven. But mediation was possible—if one could only get *His* attention. And so there were *promesas*, ways to make your requests noticed. Some women chose to wear *hábitos* until their prayers were answered, that is, a plain dress of the color that represented their favorite saint, such as light blue for the Holy Mother or red for the Sacred Heart. The *hábito* was cinched at the waist with a cord representing Christ's passion. The more fervent would wear sackcloth underneath their clothes, a real torment in the tropical heat. The promesa was only limited by the imagination of the penitent and her threshold for pain and discomfort. In many households women said rosaries nightly in groups, and this brought them together to share in their troubles. Mamá Nanda did it all, quietly and without fanfare. She wore only black since the death of her husband, but mourning and penance had become an intrinsic part of her nature long before; of her twelve children only six had survived; the other six died in infancy from childhood diseases which were prevented a generation later by a single vaccine or simple antidote. She had buried each little corpse in the family graveyard with a name and a date on the headstone—sometimes the same date for birth and death—and she had worn black, kept *luto* for each. The death of her babies had made her a melancholy woman, yet one who was always ready to give God another chance. She lobbied for His favors indefatigably.

At Mamá Nanda's house, my young mother and her baby were treated like royalty. Having served a demanding husband and numerous children, the older woman now found herself in a practically empty house with a new grandchild she could dote on and a daughter-in-law that was no more than an adolescent herself. My mother's only job was to play with the baby, to take me for strolls in fancy clothes bought with Army checks, and to accompany Mamá Nanda to mass on Sundays. In the photographs taken of my mother and me during this period, I can see the changes wrought on the shy teenage bride in the short span she was taken care of by Nanda and Felícita: she is chubby and radiant with good health, she seems proud of the bundle of ruffles and bows in her arms—her baby doll—me.

By the time Father returned from Panama, I was out of diapers and ambulatory, Mother had regained her svelte figure, and Mamá Nanda had thick calluses on her knees which kept her from feeling the pain she thought was necessary to get results from heaven. The safe homecoming of her son was proof that her sacrifices had been worthwhile, and she applied her fruitful mind to even greater penances toward credit for the other two who would both be wounded in an ambush while traveling in a jeep in Korea and would soon be back in Puerto Rico—slightly damaged, but alive. Nanda's knees bore the scars like medals received in many wars and conflicts. Aunt Felícita found herself suddenly displaced as my "other parent," and returned to her own life. All changed.

My first memory is of Father's homecoming party and the gift he brought me from San Juan—a pink iron crib like an ornate bird cage—and the sense of abandonment I felt for the first time in my short life as all eyes turned to the handsome stranger in uniform and away from me in my frilly new dress and patent leather shoes, trapped inside my pink iron crib, screaming my head off for *Mami, Tía, Mamá Nanda*, anybody . . . to come lift me out of my prison.

When I ask about the events of that day, my mother still rolls her eyes back and throws her hands up in a gesture of dismay. The story varies with the telling and the teller, but it seems that I climbed out of my tall crib on my own and headed for the party in the backyard. The pig was on the spit and the beer was flowing. In the living room the Victrola was playing my father's Elvis Presley records loudly. *I may have imagined this.* My mother is sitting on his lap. She is gorgeous in the red silk dress he has given her. There is a circle of people around him. Everyone is having a good time. And everyone has forgotten about me. I see myself slipping through the crowd and into flames. Immediately, I am pulled out by a man's strong hands. No real damage: my abundant hair is a little singed, but that is all. Mother is crying. I am the center of everyone's attention once again. Even his. Did I sleep between them that night because my mother had finally realized that I was not a rubber dolly but a real flesh and blood little girl? When I ask, she says that she remembers only staying awake listening to me breathe on the night of "the incident." She had also been kept up by the unaccustomed noise of my father's snoring. She would soon get used to both facts of life: that every one of her waking hours would belong to me from then on, and that this solemn stranger—who only resembled the timid young man she had married two years before—would own her nights. My mother was finally coming of age.

THE AGING MARÍA

On the Value of Talismans and Amulets

And so it is with our own past. It is a labor in vain to attempt to recapture it: all the efforts of our intellect must prove futile. The past is hidden somewhere outside the realm, beyond the reach of intellect, in some material object (in the sensation which that material object will give us) which we do not suspect. And as for that object, it depends on chance whether we come upon it or not before we ourselves must die.

—Marcel Proust, *Remembrance of Things Past*

During my time away from the hospital, I struggle to sleep and instead spend hours wandering around the rooms of her house. I begin identifying the objects I remember from my early life, the days when I was growing new skin so I could rush out of my nest in the sand and plunge into the bountiful American sea. I see the store-bought, massively reproduced (seen in countless Puerto Rican homes) print of a handsome young Jesus knocking on a door. It is now on her bedroom wall, though in New Jersey and Augusta it used to hang somewhere more prominent. I see the painted conch shell from Capri that my father sent her during one of his tours. I am dismayed to see that there is a little ash in it—a late-night cigarette in bed? There are ceramic dogs with gold chains on their necks and an elephant with raised trunk (for good luck); there is a Madama, a black woman cloth doll, no doubt a gift from a Santera—my mother saw no contradiction in keeping these symbols of other religious practices and her Catholic faith. In the extra bedroom she used as an office, library, and catch-all there is a worn Bible and other religious books on a little desk, and a bookshelf with a collection of my books and several scrapbooks of family accomplishments from birth announcements to graduation programs and wedding invitations. In her backyard is a plaster statuette of Mary that had been a permanent fixture in her mother's yard. It was moved from my grandmother's yard to my mother's backyard after my grandmother's death. Year after year I have watched it sink into the soft earth that my mother watered constantly for the sake of her many plants. The badly deteriorated statuette is now in the middle of some home repairs. Her husband, Angel, has spray-painted her mantle blue and her robe white, but her face is discolored and chipped, and she is missing some digits. "Tenemos que salvar a la Santa Madre," my mother had joked last year—we have to try to save the Holy Mother. I now see Mary-in-repair as symbolic of my mother's reinvention, not as the Holy Mother, for she was anything but a saint, but as the fragile woman with a steel frame who rose above the pull of others' designs and expectations, and who managed to find her true self once she was back in her own soil. Over many long months she oversaw the transformation of her little plot of land into her dream of home. How could any of us know that a clock was already ticking? I wrote about her in a lyric piece I called "The Aging María."

> She stands in my mother's front lawn, forbearing the elements, the yearly tropical depressions, and occasional hurricanes, calm blue gaze cutting through time just as she had in my grandmother's jardín, where she stared perpetually at the avocado tree. Santa María, sole witness to the mature fruit's mysterious plunging off the branches in the night, explosions on the zinc roof of my first bedroom; the abrupt starts of my awakenings on the Island. The paint on her plaster face is now cracked so that she seems wiser, somehow marked by lines of pain and laughter. Her blue and white gown is worn through to the raw material of her making, as if she had been neglected by busy offspring in her waning years, living on a fixed income; no daughters checking in on her from time to time, no new robes or sandals on Mother's Day. Now in direct contact with the ground, her naked feet have yellowed. The cloud she once stood on is half buried in the fertilized soil where my mother grows her high-maintenance roses. The Queen of Heaven is aging on a Caribbean Island, sustained only by the collective memory of her one year of living dangerously, and the still popular assumption that glory clings to her presence. Her new smile may be the irony created by loss, the real revelation: she is beyond repair. Yet year after year a tiny crèche is placed before her in December, as if her arms could still hold a child, although it is plain to see that her fragile fingers are chipped at the tips and broken at the joints. In fact, all that is unsustained by cast or mold has begun to fall away. Still, year after year, she stands firm in my mother's garden. In crepuscular light, her still regal form acquires a certain luster, the yellow patina of age briefly turning to a luminous gold, as though she were lit, as she is, from within.[1]

After her death, I put on my finger the ring my mother had never taken off since I gave it to her for Mother's Day when I was fifteen. On the day of her funeral, I closed my hand around it until my fingers cramped. I had paid $14.95 for it at the Fort Gordon's post exchange. It cost me most of my weekly salary for my after-school job at a bakery in Augusta, Georgia: my first earned money. It is an onyx oval with a chip of a diamond in the center, set on a thin gold-filled band. She had much better rings to wear, but I never saw her without the one I gave her. I have been wearing it, cradled in between my wedding rings since her death. What is this impulse? Maybe I'm a fool for thinking that I am keeping her with me by wearing this object she kept close to her living flesh for so many years. I claim to be free of such superstitious belief. I have often made a joke of the many talismans and amulets in her house, but now that she's gone, I have become attached to certain objects she imbued with meaning, and meaning is being transferred from them to me as if I were wearing a medicinal patch. I feel the thin circle of gold on my finger; I twist it around unconsciously during the day. I am practicing magical thinking.

I have made the ring into a talisman. I have taken a symbolic object, an amulet, and charged it with meaning and power to suit my needs and desires.

To be honest, I have always been a magical thinker, and now, despite my skepticism and devotion to science, I am reverting to a former self that believed what the adults around me believed; especially the women, who surrounded themselves with amulets, talismans, and totems. They were in the shapes of Catholic religious objects: prints of The Sacred Heart, The Immaculate Heart, the crucified Christ, bottles of Holy Water, palm fronds that had been blessed by the priest on Palm Sunday, plaster statuettes of the Holy Mother in yards; mixed with these one could also find in certain homes, the paraphernalia of Santería: black dolls you were not allowed to touch, certain syncretized saints that could be representations of an African god, an *Oricha*. And everywhere, the azabaches—small charms in the shape of a fist carved from onyx—protected against *mal de ojo*, the maleficent envy of the evil eye. *La envidia* was to be deflected from the vulnerable with a blessing. If an infant received a compliment without citing the name of God, someone had to rush in with a "Que Dios lo bendiga." While I see these symbols and rituals as quaint and perfunctory, did I not baptize my baby girl in the Catholic church when my mother began to worry about her soul, should something (Por Dios, no) have happened to her without the sacrament, she'd be confined to Limbo for eternity. There with the other Inocentes, she would not suffer, but she would not be reunited with the baptized, or see the face of God. I had given up my active participation in the church soon after I left home for college. But the pull of the magical solution is held in reserve in my psyche.

When Tanya was hospitalized with pneumonia as a toddler, my mother sent me a rosary she'd had the priest bless to pray at my sick child's bedside, and did I not do it? Yes, yes. In spite of my self-professed disdain for prayer as a cure-all, I repeated those Ave Marías and Padre Nuestros until I was in a hypnotic trance. Then of course, I gave all the credit for her full recovery to her brilliant pediatrician and the miracle of modern antibiotics.

I still have those beads, I keep them in the same dresser drawer where I put the other magical objects I brought back from my mother's house after her funeral: a worn out abanico, a hand-painted fan my father had sent her from Spain and which she used daily, keeping it on the table in her living room by her box of embroidery threads and needles. I brought back a black lacquered lace fan I had sent her from my trip to Spain, the one she took to Sunday mass. I sent myself a box of objects that I have taken out one at a time because the weight of all that accumulated hope and the vortex of meaning she injected into them, would, I'm certain, be too big a shock to my heart and mind, if I had them before me all at once. I am a fool for symbol and metaphor.

If something matters so much to you that you must hold it close, never part with it, then it has power. It has all the power of your faith and this power is driven by your will. If I say to the ring, bring back my mother's voice; it does. My mother's spirit can possibly be summoned without her ring, and my little girl would have healed without the rosary and my obsessive vigil, but these objects have the power because they accompanied me in the dark hour: souvenirs from difficult times, reminding me that I can overcome the odds; they absorb my worries, growing heavy with my needs.

Another talisman I hold close to my heart is a porcelain medallion encased in woven circle of gold depicting Mary, Queen of Heaven, floating on a cloud; from her hands pour gold rays of light. The image within the medallion is tiny, the size of a dime, and it hangs from on my neck on a gold chain; a pendulum marking the movements of my day. I never take it off—only for my medical procedures or surgeries, when the order to remove all jewelry is given. This medallion belonged to Mamá, my maternal grandmother, the proto-feminist of my family, whose story-telling sparked my imagination and triggered much of my early work, and whose strong character I wanted to imitate.

This version of Mary was proclaimed "La Milagrosa" in an inscription on the back of the medallion, and I know she believed in its power. When she led her grandchildren in prayer before bed, she often fingered it. I suspected she went over the heads of the hierarchy of the Catholic heaven, no gold crucifix around her neck—she chose the "Wonder Woman" Mary, The Queen of Heaven, as her patron, forgoing the sweet but powerless young Madonna, and the Suffering Mother collapsed at the foot of the Cross. Mary, after her Assumption to her throne in the Heavenly Kingdom that would have more closely reflected Mamá's idea of maternal rule. She commanded. We obeyed. She was the Magna Mater. She had invisible rays of power at her fingertips. When she died, I was still a young woman trying to be a mother, wife, a new academic and writer, and when she bequeathed the medallion to me, I saw it as my Excalibur; I had inherited her symbol for female power. And when I was asked about it, I explained away its religious connotations because they did not suit my feminist sensibilities—it had been blessed by a priest for Mamá, I'd say, and she treated it with reverence, but I wore it in remembrance of a remarkable woman, a memento mori. I shifted its meaning; I transformed it onto it my needs and desires.

The belief that certain objects can carry the spirit of their previous owners seems to be ingrained into our psyches. There's the hunter that carries the arrowhead used by his renowned ancestor, the bride that borrows her mother's necklace, all the mementoes we keep in our homes, or guard as sacred patrimony in museums. This is where we came from—each pottery shard, each quilt, or handmade piece of furniture says to us: this is how we became who we are; this was touched by a human hand, and when I touch it, I travel through time back to the beginning and forwards to me and mine. These evocative objects strung together through time connect us to one another like beads in a necklace.

And when we don't have the amulet, the thing that already contains the magic, we create the talisman, we inject our consciousness into the representative object; magic is in what we wish it to stand for: the wedding band is nothing in the store; it is power-charged, symbolized, only after the words are spoken over it. All things mean nothing until they are consecrated by us in the recurring secular ritual of making meaning. It is what I do as a writer: I collect the shards and I try to re-create the artifact. Every day when I face the blank page and say my incantation, I am indulging in magical thinking. This is also why I can't claim to be a person driven only by reason. I know this now, but not when I was in the throes of separating my young arrogant self from the binding threads of family and culture in order to become my individual self; I know this now: our lives are enriched by allowing a small, controlled amount of magic into our days. Athletes who rely on the latest technologies to improve their skills will still wear that lucky cap, touch that lucky statue on their way to the playing field, or say those magic words before they perform.

This is not to say that all magical objects evoke only positive feelings. Among the things I brought back from my mother's house is a seashell painted with an idyllic scene of boaters on a calm sea. My father sent her this gift from Capri during one of his interminable U.S. Navy tours of duty. She smoked heavily during his long absences, and at some point, she started using this beautiful shell as an ashtray. She put out her cigarettes over the painted scene until it lost its center; the lovers on the boat burned out, the calm sea splotched with black ashes depicted a ravaged scene, more Pompeii after the volcano, than Capri. I saw her carry this shell from room to room, along with her pack of cigarettes and matches. She rose before everyone so she could have that first cup of coffee and a smoke before everyone noticed. In the end, she claimed that she smoked only twice a day at the beginning and the end. By the time she died of lung cancer, my father had been dead for thirty-five years. She had carried that shell, defaced as it was, with her from place to place until she had her own casa. Then she placed it by her chair, by her side. I have it now, pulsing with secret meaning. Anger. Amor. Loneliness. Amor. It is heart-shaped; I can wrap my palm around it. It becomes warm with my body heat, seems to be beating like the heart of a tiny creature. But it is my own pulse reflected, my own currents of blood I feel coursing through it, mine and hers and its maker's, and the shore stroller or fisherman who found it on the beach, the creature who inhabited it before human hands touched it. I am plugged in, connected.

My earliest memories were of attending mass with my mother and abuela, my senses awakened by the ritual: the brilliant colors of an ornately dressed priest, chanting his spells in Latin over a magical chalice and plates of gold, turning ordinary wine and bread into the body of Christ, the slightly salty taste of sanctified wafer in my mouth, the heady intake of incense from censers swung over us by the altar boys, entering my nostrils, filling my head with the smell of sanctity. God went into my body and my imagination through my senses, not as an idea. Poetry does the same for me now.

The museum of us contains the keys, postcards, vinyl albums, photographs, trophies, old textbooks and report cards, your mother's rosary, your father's army tags, your baby's receiving blanket, and it contains clues to who you are and how you came to be; your identity shaped by the acceptance or rejection of what each object represents. Most of us have our memory closets. Sometimes these are real places that are either neatly organized or chaotic; the storage places for the ineffable are invisible to others—they are in us and locked; this is where the magical objects with which we are most intimate become memories: kept in that area of the brain reserved for symbols and miscellany—the things you go looking for at births and deaths and inexplicable events, when we must make meaning or at least find solace in what we have left. We catalogue the totems, the talismans, the souvenirs of past joy and pain to use as we need them throughout our lives. These objects and memories attach us to our former selves through time, reminding us of how we became who we are. At some point, as during my mother's painful separation from her extended family and her native country, we are in an active relationship with these evocative objects; they define us and help us cope. In our times of need we chant the words of the recalling spell—the "I remember when" and the "this reminds me of the time," activating the magic in the amulet or talisman to comfort us, or at least begin the release from pain and grief.

I wish I could have transported the plaster statue of Mary to our yard in Georgia. But she would not have survived the crossing. I can always imagine her, though, sinking into the soft, red clay, weathering the seasons with dignity, forbearing.

Notes

Excerpted from: *The Cruel Country*, 2015, University of Georgia Press.
1. "The Aging María." *Image* 56 (2007): 56. Reprinted in: *The Best Spiritual Writing.* Edited by Pico Iyer. Penguin Books, 2010.

PRIMARY LESSONS

My mother walked me to my first day at school at La Escuela Segundo Ruiz Belvis, named after the Puerto Rican patriot born in our town. I remember yellow cement with green trim. All the classrooms had been painted these colors to identify them as government property. This was true all over the Island. Everything was color-coded, including the children, who wore uniforms from first through twelfth grade. We were a midget army in white and brown, led by the hand to our battleground. From practically every house in our barrio emerged a crisply ironed uniform inhabited by the savage creatures we had become over a summer of running wild in the sun.

At my grandmother's house where we were staying until father returned to Brooklyn Yard in New York and sent for us, it had been complete chaos, with several children to get ready for school. My mother had pulled my hair harder than usual while braiding it, and I had dissolved into a pool of total self-pity. I wanted to stay home with her and Mamá, to continue listening to stories in the late afternoon, to drink *café con leche* with them, and to play rough games with my many cousins. I wanted to continue living the dream of summer afternoons in Puerto Rico, and if I could not have it, then I wanted to go back to Paterson, New Jersey, back to where I imagined our apartment waited, peaceful and cool, for the three of us to return to our former lives. Our gypsy lifestyle had convinced me, at age six, that one part of life stops and waits for you while you live another for a while—and if you don't like the present, you can always return to the past. Buttoning me into my stiff blouse while I tried to squirm away from her, my mother attempted to explain to me that I was a big girl now and should try to understand that, like all the other children my age, I had to go to school.

"What about him?" I yelled, pointing at my brother who was lounging on the tile floor of our bedroom in his pajamas, playing quietly with a toy car.

"He's too young to go to school, you know that. Now stay still." My mother pinned me between her thighs to button my skirt, as she had learned to do from Mamá, from whose grip it was impossible to escape.

"It's not fair, it's not fair. I can't go to school here. I don't speak Spanish." It was my final argument, and it failed miserably because I was shouting my defiance in the language I claimed not to speak. Only I knew what I meant by saying in Spanish that I did not speak Spanish. I had spent my early childhood in the U.S., where I lived in a bubble created by my Puerto Rican parents in a home where two cultures and languages became one. I learned to listen to the English from the television with one ear while I heard my mother and father speaking in Spanish with the other. I thought I was an ordinary American kid—like the children on the shows I watched—and that everyone's parents spoke a secret second language at home. When we came to Puerto Rico right before I started first grade, I switched easily to Spanish. It was the language of fun, of summertime games. But school—that was a different matter.

I made one last desperate effort to make my mother see reason: "Father will be very angry. You know that he wants us to speak good English." My mother, of course, ignored me as she dressed my little brother in his play clothes. I could not believe her indifference to my father's wishes. She was usually so careful about our safety and the many other areas that he was forever reminding her about in his letters. But I was right, and she knew it. Our father spoke to us in English as much as possible, and he corrected my pronunciation constantly—not "jes" but "y-es." Y-es, sir. How could she send me to school to learn Spanish when we would be returning to Paterson in just a few months?

But, of course, what I feared was not language, but loss of freedom. At school there would be no playing, no stories, only lessons. It would not matter if I did not understand a word, and I would not be allowed to make up my own definitions. I would have to learn silence. I would have to keep my wild imagination in check. Feeling locked into my stiffly starched uniform, I only sensed all this. I guess most children can intuit their loss of childhood's freedom on that first day of school. It is separation anxiety, too, but mother is just the guardian of the "playground" of our early childhood.

The sight of my cousins in similar straits comforted me. We were marched down the hill of our barrio where Mamá's robin-egg-blue house stood at the top. I must have glanced back at it with yearning. Mamá's house—a place built for children—where anything that could be broken had already been broken by my grandmother's early batch of offspring (they ranged in age from my mother's oldest sisters to my uncle who was six months older than I was). Her house had long since been made childproof. It had been a perfect summer place. And now it was September—the cruelest month for a child.

La Mrs., as all the teachers were called, waited for her class of first-graders at the door of the yellow-and-green classroom. She too wore a uniform: it was a blue skirt and a white blouse. This teacher wore black high heels with her "standard issue." I remember this detail because when we were all seated in rows, she called on one little girl and pointed to the back of the room where there were shelves. She told the girl to bring her a shoebox from the bottom shelf. Then, when the box had been placed in her hands, she did something unusual. She had the little girl kneel at her feet and take the pointy high heels off her feet and replace them with a pair of satin slippers from the shoe box. She told the group that every one of us would have a chance to do this if we behaved in her class. Though confused about the prize, I soon felt caught up in the competition to bring *La Mrs.* her slippers in the morning. Children fought over the privilege.

Our first lesson was English. In Puerto Rico, every child has to take twelve years of English to graduate from school. It is the law. In my parents' school days, all subjects were taught in English. The U.S. Department of Education had specified that as a U.S. territory, the Island had to be "Americanized," and to accomplish this task, it was necessary for the Spanish language to be replaced in one generation through the teaching of English in all schools. My father began his school day by saluting the flag of the United States and singing "America" and "The Star-Spangled Banner" by rote, without understanding a word of what he was saying. The logic behind this system was that, though the children did not understand the English words, they would remember the rhythms. Even the games the teacher's manuals required them to play became absurd adaptations. "Here We Go Round the Mulberry Bush" became "Here We Go Round the Mango Tree." I have heard about the confusion caused by the use of a primer in which the sounds of animals were featured. The children were forced to accept that a rooster says *cockadoodledoo*, when they knew perfectly well from hearing their own roosters each morning that in Puerto Rico a rooster says *cocorocó*. Even the vocabulary of their pets was changed; there are still family stories circulating about the bewilderment of a first-grader coming home to try to teach his dog to speak in English. The policy of assimilation by immersion failed on the Island. Teachers adhered to it on paper, substituting their own materials for the texts, but no one took their English home. In due time, the program was minimized to the one class in English per day that I encountered when I took my seat in *La Mrs.*'s first-grade class.

Catching us all by surprise, she stood very straight and tall in front of us and began to sing in English:

Pollito   Chicken
Gallina   Hen
Lápiz   Pencil
Y Pluma   Pen

"Repeat after me, children: Pollito—Chicken," she commanded in her heavily accented English that only I understood, being the only child in the room who had ever been exposed to the language. But I too remained silent. No use making waves, or showing off. Patiently *La Mrs.* sang her song and gestured for us to join in. At some point it must have dawned on the class that this silly routine was likely to go on all day if we did not "repeat after her." It was not her fault that she had to follow the rule in her teacher's manual stating that she must teach English *in* English, and that she must not translate, but merely repeat her lesson in English until the children "begin to respond" more or less "unconsciously." This was one of the vestiges of the regimen followed by her predecessors in the last generation. To this day I can recite "Pollito—Chicken" mindlessly, never once pausing to visualize chicks, hens, pencils, or pens.

I soon found myself crowned "teacher's pet" without much effort on my part. I was a privileged child in her eyes simply because I lived in "Nueva York," and because my father was in the navy. His name was an old one in our pueblo, associated with once-upon-a-time landed people and long-gone money. Status is judged by unique standards in a culture where, by definition, everyone is a second-class citizen. Remembrance of past glory is as good as titles and money. Old families living in decrepit old houses rank over factory workers living in modern comfort in cement boxes—all the same. The professions raise a person out of the dreaded "sameness" into a niche of status, so that teachers, nurses, and everyone who went to school for a job were given the honorifics of *El Míster* or *La Mrs.* by the common folks, people who were likely to be making more money in American factories than the poorly paid educators and government workers.

My first impressions of the hierarchy began with my teacher's shoe-changing ceremony and the exaggerated respect she received from our parents. *La Mrs.* was always right, and adults scrambled to meet her requirements. She wanted all our school books covered in the brown paper now used for paper bags (used at that time by the grocer to wrap meats and other foods). That first week of school the grocer was swamped with requests for paper, which he gave away to the women. That week and the next, he wrapped produce in newspapers. All school projects became family projects. It was considered disrespectful at Mamá's house to do homework in privacy. Between the hours when we came home from school and dinner time, the table was shared by all of us working together with the women hovering in the background. The teachers communicated directly with the mothers, and it was a matriarchy of far-reaching power and influence.

There was a black boy in my first-grade classroom who was also the teacher's pet but for a different reason than I: I did not have to do anything to win her favor; he would do anything to win a smile. He was as black as the cauldron that Mamá used for cooking stew, and his hair was curled into tight little balls on his head—*pasitas*, like little raisins glued to his skull, my mother had said. There had been some talk at Mamá's house about this boy; Lorenzo was his name. I later gathered that he was the grandson of my father's nanny. Lorenzo lived with

Teresa, his grandmother, having been left in her care when his mother took off for "Los Nueva Yores" shortly after his birth. And they were poor. Everyone could see that his pants were too big for him—hand-me-downs—and his shoe soles were as thin as paper. Lorenzo seemed unmindful of the giggles he caused when he jumped up to erase the board for *La Mrs.* and his baggy pants rode down to his thin hips as he strained up to get every stray mark. He seemed to relish playing the little clown when she asked him to come to the front of the room and sing his phonetic version of "obootifool, forpashioskeeis" leading the class in our incomprehensible tribute to the American flag. He was a bright, loving child, with a talent for song and mimicry that everyone commented on. He should have been chosen to host the PTA show that year instead of me.

At recess one day, I came back to the empty classroom to get something. My cup? My nickel for a drink from the kiosk man? I don't remember. But I remember the conversation my teacher was having with another teacher. I remember because it concerned me, and because I memorized it so that I could ask my mother to explain what it meant.

"He is a funny *negrito*, and, like a parrot, he can repeat anything you teach him. But his Mamá must not have the money to buy him a suit."

"I kept Rafaelito's First Communion suit; I bet Lorenzo could fit in it. It's white with a bow-tie," the other teacher said.

"But, Marisa," laughed my teacher, "in that suit, Lorenzo would look like a fly drowned in a glass of milk."

Both women laughed. They had not seen me crouched at the back of the room, digging into my schoolbag. My name came up then.

"What about the Ortiz girl? They have money."

"I'll talk to her mother today. The superintendent, *El Americano* from San Juan, is coming down for the show. How about if we have her say her lines in both Spanish and English?"

The conversation ends there for me. My mother took me to *Mayagüez* and bought me a frilly pink dress and two crinoline petticoats to wear underneath so that I looked like a pink-and-white parachute with toothpick legs sticking out. I learned my lines, "Padres, maestros, Mr. Leonard, bienvenidos/Parents, teachers, Mr. Leonard, welcome . . ." My first public appearance. I took no pleasure in it. The words were formal and empty. I had simply memorized them. My dress pinched me at the neck and arms, and made me itch all over.

I had asked my mother what it meant to be a "mosca en un vaso de leche," a fly in a glass of milk. She had laughed at the image, explaining that it meant being "different," but that it wasn't something I needed to worry about.

¿LA VERDAD?

Notes on the Writing of *Silent Dancing*, a Partial Remembrance of a Puerto Rican Childhood (A Memoir in Prose and Poetry)

> Many bright colors; many distinct sounds; some human beings, caricatures; comic; several violent moments of being, always including a circle of the scene which they cut out: and all surrounded by a vast space—that is a rough visual description of childhood. This is how I shape it . . .
>
> —Virginia Woolf, "A Sketch of the Past"

I began to work on *Silent Dancing* soon after my first novel, *The Line of the Sun*, was published in 1989. I was not sure what to call what I was shaping into a book. At the time, the somewhat awkward term, creative nonfiction, had not yet been popularized to describe the strange morphing of fictional technique and nonfiction writing. At one point, I mentioned to a friend that I was working on a memoir; in a dubious tone, she said to me: "Why don't you wait till you are famous to write a memoir?" I realized that memoir was not the right label for what I wanted to accomplish in these narratives, as it has come to be attached to celebrity or notoriety, neither of which I possess in enough quantity to justify a book about my exploits. I wrote the preface to *Silent Dancing* in an attempt to give shape to my vision. I turned to Virginia Woolf and to my grandmother for guidance, the strongest voices I had known in my formative years. Everyone is afraid of Virginia Woolf and I never knew anyone who would tangle with my *abuela*, especially after she had made one of her pontifical declarations. I chose my allies carefully.

At that time I had no models for the book I had envisioned, which was a blending of poetry and prose. In the essays I hoped to dramatize key events I had witnessed or participated in through the use of fictional techniques. I was not interested in telling my life's story, which was, still is, I hope, very much in progress. I wanted my *moments of being* to be created out of the melding of experiences that I had first filtered through my early poems. It was my aim to have these narratives joined at the hip to the poems, sometimes, but not always, directly addressing one another. It was my intention that the poems amplify meaning by refraction, not as a handy mirror, there merely to serve the essays.

I hoped the book could be experienced personally, entered into as one does a novel, expecting to live an alternate life. I wanted the stories to have the direct psychic impact on the reader that conventional autobiography and nonfiction seemed to lack, since their aim was often telling a life, not sharing it. I knew that the events of my life, although not extraordinary, might seem foreign and my characters unfamiliar to some readers, yet I hoped that they, the readers, would be willing to suspend disbelief, would want to do so, because the story itself was interesting, perhaps even relevant to some aspect of their lives, and not necessarily because they wanted or needed to know about Judith Ortiz Cofer's life. I trusted the poems to establish an emotional link between reader and text, a common ground. The role of the poet is to locate within the language of the raw human experience what Czeslaw Milosz called "the only homeland."

Poems are always true. You can feel their truth; it resonates within you like the sound of pure crystal. And when you hear good poems, the question, *did this really happen?*, which we often hear from inexperienced readers, is of no consequence because it does not matter. The truth of poetry is like quantum physics. One should accept it even if one does not quite grasp it. *Es la pura verdad.*

"Look into Thy Heart and Write."
—*Sir Philip Sidney*

Nag. Nag. Nag. I believe Sir Philip may have been admonishing himself when he spoke these words. As a writer I am a self-nag. The questions I have, that I need answered, are nagging questions that try to be answered in poems, stories, essays, and novels. In writing *Silent Dancing*, one of the questions I asked myself was: how does nonfiction arrive at the truth that lies beyond the fact? What proportion of facts is necessary to make a story a work of creative nonfiction as opposed to fictionalized autobiography? Is Tim O'Brien's novel in stories, *The Things They Carried*, less true than his memoir *If I Die in a Combat Zone*? Which book teaches you the truth of the Viet Nam experience and its effects on a generation of young men, such as the author himself—who in a story calls the narrator Tim O'Brien? Is it simply a matter of sticking to the facts? In my work of fiction, *The Line of the Sun*, I drew heavily on autobiographical material, yet gave myself complete license to explore potential and alternate lives for my characters that were often based on real living people. Of course I had the usual disclaimer in the front of the book—any similarity between the characters and events in this novel is purely coincidental, etc. . . .

Here is another disclaimer. And this is a fact. In writing fiction, I feel free to invent the emotional landscape of my characters in order to advance the plot; I will do almost anything to advance the plot—but I am a scrupulous researcher of historical facts and events. I *try* to be accurate in my reporting of things that actually happened and in descriptions of places that exist in the real world, although names and other less important details may be changed to protect both the innocent and the guilty. Factual accuracy is an important part of the contract my books offer to my readers. It does not mean I do not make mistakes. But they are honest mistakes. Accuracy in reporting confirmable information is a rule I follow in all my writing. The truth of art is different from the fact of history. Both may claim to be *la verdad*, but to appropriate or revise factual truth, unless you have established the appropriate contract with your reader, is a sort of moving violation. Excluded from this injunction are, of course, science fiction, fantasy, speculative writing—these genres operate under a separate set of assumptions which are normally a given between reader and text.

Guns, La Familia, Lies, and Memory

I once read about a criminal law professor who asked a class to write down their accounts of an incident they had just witnessed in his classroom in which a student had drawn a gun on a classmate during an argument. This classical experiment first took place in 1901. It has been reenacted thousands of times over the past century with astonishingly similar results. No one remembers the truth with perfect accuracy. Yet we often expect eyewitness accounts to serve as the basis for our judgments in events including daily occurrences—car wrecks, minor and major accidents, and personal confrontations—and, of course, in court proceedings leading to legal and criminal indictments.

In writing my novel, I used objective and subjective sources to give my scenes credibility. I researched the geography, weather, and history of my locations. I called my mother and other relatives in New Jersey and Puerto Rico. Then I chose the most interesting versions of family stories and fictionalized them. But in writing *Silent Dancing*, I wanted to stay within view of the actual events; after all, it was to be based on my life. In gathering factual background information for the essays, I found my facts in books and documents as usual. The credibility problem, I soon discovered, began with the accounts my personal informants were giving me: *Abuela, Abuelo, Mami, Tío, Tía*—my relatives were approximately as reliable in their descriptions of events we had all shared as had been the eyewitnesses in the classic experiment of the gun-shot. If I asked them to tell the story in a group, the dominant talkers usually took charge of the "facts," constantly correcting the speaker; others might be nodding in polite agreement, or the Doubting Thomases would be shielding their contemptuous gazes from the nosy one (*yo*) who had come into their midst to challenge them about the past. When I interviewed them individually, the stories varied dramatically, even wildly, one from the other.

Are my relatives liars? Are they more inventive than other people's relatives? Were they revising the past for my benefit? I do not think so. I have read various studies on the nature of memory, and I am convinced that the past is something most of us revise automatically, and without malice or evil intent or even any conscious awareness of doing so. We are constantly changing our personal narrative so that it matches our idea of who we are and in what role we see ourselves—but our version of *la pura verdad* is, of course, not necessarily what others may have experienced, even if they were participants in our moment of being. And so, in retrospect, we are never in quite the same place as others; even when we are physically together, our minds are processing the same information through our own very private filters. Our memories are shaped individually and independently. The angle, the focus, the lighting, make all the difference in how the memory will be preserved and our individual perception is what makes us completely unique, at least to ourselves. Our story must be original, and we will make sure that it is, by revising it as we live and learn.

Once I understood that memory is relative, and that my relatives were practicing their particular theory of relativity, I made my decision to go with Virginia Woolf's definition of what constitutes the truth in writing from memory—personal impressions, the tracks you follow back to your moments of being. I chose to write *Silent Dancing* out of my deepest emotional connections to my unique version of past events. This is where the poems became even more crucial to the undertaking.

What Took Me to La Verdad

The poems in *Silent Dancing* were written years before the essays and were my first attempts at investigating the truth of my life as a witness to it; I wanted to understand the dichotomy at the center of my particular human experience and perhaps along the way learn how it affected those of us caught up in it. And more than that, I wanted to make art out of my discoveries, which means that I had to find the universal in the particular: how could I make my individual life experience as a Puerto Rican girl growing up on the island and on the mainland part of a homeland I could share through language? My humble discovery: that we are all strangers in a strange land at some point in our lives—at some time in our lives we have all felt alienated, confused, unable to make ourselves understood. In my essay, "The Looking-Glass Shame," I propose that we all go through our foreigner phase; at least in adolescence, we become the minority. If we have common ground, then my work is more than a sociological introduction into the secret lives of Puerto Ricans. It is a story of transformation through language. Anyway, that is how *I* shape it.

CHAPTER 2

In the Midst of the Puerto Rican Barrio

"A Facsimile of the Island"

Were they less Puerto Rican, those two people who yearned for their island all their lives, and who taught me to love it and respect it?

—*Judith Ortiz Cofer qtd. in Ocasio, "The Infinite Variety of the Puerto Rican Reality" 736*

In 2013, while speaking to Don Noble, host of Alabama's Public Television interview series "*Bookmark*," Judith Ortiz Cofer recalled her rather unique childhood and early teenage years in Paterson, New Jersey. Although her young parents had agreed that her father joining the armed forces facilitated their departure for the United States, they certainly had different approaches in their children's acculturation. Ortiz Cofer remembered that it had been her mother's decision to make Paterson their home, even though her father had been stationed in Brooklyn Yard in New York City. Her father had an older brother already living in Paterson, where a Puerto Rican community had started to flourish. Her mother yearned not only for the companionship of close family members but, as Ortiz Cofer stressed to Noble, aspired to live in "a facsimile of the island in the midst of the Puerto Rican barrio." It was, in short, a place where her mother "was very happy living with the music blaring and the smell of rice and beans." Indeed, Paterson was, as Ortiz Cofer remembered, "a smorgasbord of an ethnic population. There were Jews, Italians, Irish, Puerto Ricans, and some people from South America and Cuba, but mainly Puerto Ricans in the core of the city" (Ocasio, "Words" 27).

In her father's agreement, though, he could have been attempting to protect his young family from the openly racist propaganda that had proliferated in New York City since 1947, as newspapers often warned their readers about "the dangers of a postwar 'Puerto Rican influx'" (Lorrin 141). The number of Puerto Ricans settling in urban areas in New Jersey had already increased as New York City became less of an attractive settlement option.

Her father was, however, "the ambitious immigrant," who demanded "his children learn to be Americans and to speak in English as much as possible" (qtd. in Noble). It had been his decision to transfer his children from Public School Number 11 to St. Joseph Catholic School, composed mainly of Irish and Italian students, and to move his family out of the barrio to a quieter Jewish neighborhood where he rented an apartment above a Jewish deli. A studious man, it was also his demand that his children take their school textbooks every time they traveled to Hormigueros during his long deployments.

The contrast in rather dissimilar living arrangements was at the root of a strongly felt perception of her life experiences as a migrant child, which Ortiz Cofer defined as a sense of "dislocation": "It was a very lonely situation but a couple of things happened. I read to fend off loneliness. I learned to think of myself not as the pretty girl but the smart girl. I accumulated the sense that I could observe people and learned. I think that this dislocation of my life provided me with the tools to become a writer" (qtd. in Noble). Ortiz Cofer often underscored that feeling of dislocation as a common one in migrant children: "As a child going back and forth to Puerto Rico, I became very observant; I guess children who are lonely because they are dislocated and relocated geographically and emotionally become observers of life" (qtd. in Ocasio, "Puerto Rican Literature" 45).

After World War II, Puerto Rican workers arrived in the United States in large numbers, partially promoted by the Puerto Rican government, which actively sought out "the incorporation of Puerto Rican migrants in the United States during 1940s and 1950s, the period displaying the largest migration wave in the twentieth century" (Meléndez 3). Governmental efforts included the instauration of a Migration Division, which opened an office in New York City in 1947 that aimed "to manage the expectations, rights and needs of migrants who considered themselves citizens of two nations" (Lauria Santiago).

In the case of the Ortiz family, two factors facilitated their move with "greater participation by Puerto Ricans in the armed forces; pent-up travel demand; surplus aircraft and pilots, resulting in cheaper and more accessible air travel" (Rodríguez 7). Ortiz Cofer often underscored the military's influence on her father's departure from the Island and his generation's forced embrace of a different kind of life in the United States: "My father came from a family that all found an escape through the military. He was much more, as you can tell from my books, adjusted to the fact that history had forced him out of the island. He was not going to stay there and be a laborer; he was going to move to the United States and accept the consequences" (qtd. in Ocasio, Interview 8). There was, however, a price to pay: "He was very intelligent and military life stifled him. And yet he looked around him and saw his friends who were factory workers and others imprisoned by the economy and their own lack of skills, so he stayed in the Navy and became more and more withdrawn. I can only imagine his loneliness on a ship full of people who did not speak his native language, far away from his family" (qtd. in Kallet 71).

Puerto Ricans traveling to the United States in the mid-1950s were targeted for specific sites in the country, including New York City, New Jersey, Connecticut, and Chicago (Rodríguez 3). As Ortiz Cofer poignantly illustrates in her memoir *The Cruel Country*, readily available air connections and cheap PanAm flights afforded her mother yet another peculiar living arrangement: "When I was between the ages of two and fifteen, my family shuttled back and forth between Paterson, New Jersey, and Puerto Rico. Our annual migration followed the patterns of my father's tours of duty with the navy. When he reported for overseas duty at Brooklyn Yard, we boarded the airbus for San Juan, where relatives would be waiting at the airport to drive us to our pueblo of Hormigueros, all the way across the island" (30). Her reference to an "airbus" stresses the ease of air traveling from San Juan to key U.S. cities in the Northeast, which gave way to the first airborne migration to the United States following World War II (Whalen 25; Rodríguez 7).

Furthermore, Ortiz Cofer often underscored the effects of yet another phenomenon in Puerto Rican migrant history. An "airbus" commute with "access to low-cost air travel [that] created a transnational bridge" (Acosta Belén and Santiago 87) brought to the United States an extraordinary number of Puerto Ricans. Commonly referred to as "commuter nation" (Acosta Belén, "*Adiós*" 2), Ortiz Cofer described to Noble her unusual situation in rather simple terms: "My father would go for three to four months at a time to deliver cargo in Europe with his ship in the Seventh Fleet. My mother did not want to stay in Paterson when she had the opportunity to go back to her very crowded family home on the island. Every six months my father would pack off to go to Europe and my mother would joyfully yank us out of the school and take us back to her mother's house, which often had like thirteen grandchildren in it because all of her daughters would come home. We had these rowdy Spanish language few months and then came back to our lonely apartment above the Jewish deli." The arrangement was rather disruptive, as she illustrated in reference to the first two times she came back to Paterson: "The first time I was two, but then my father left on an extended tour with the Navy, and we went back to Puerto Rico. We spent a couple of years in Paterson and then I attended first and second grade in Puerto Rico. The first time that I came back to Paterson to enter the world of school I was already in the third grade. By that time Spanish had become my first language again and there was the culture shock of going into the classroom" (Kallet 69).

A modern airport located in Carolina, a rising metropolitan city on the outskirts of San Juan, was inaugurated in 1955 and facilitated an active gateway between Puerto Rico and the United States. The Ortizes were among the pioneering Puerto Ricans to settle in New Jersey. In 1954, "approximately 26,000 Puerto Ricans resided in the state 'on a yearly basis' [. . .] in addition to 8,000 'seasonal' farm workers brought in that year for the harvest season" (Jiménez de Wagenheim 107). As late as 1971, according to a report by ASPIRA, a community-based association seeking to provide educational resources to the Puerto Rican and Latinx communities, Newark, New Jersey, was functioning as a "bridge" between Puerto Rico and northeastern U.S. cities due to convenient and affordable air travel: "A minimum of four daily flights land there [Newark airport] from Puerto Rico; the number is increased on weekends and other peak-travel seasons. Three and a half hours cushion the cultural shock. Five dollars down will get almost anyone an airplane ticket either way. The total cost in the 'cucaracha' or 'quiquiriqui' is $57.00 one way. [The midnight and early morning weekday flights called so by Puerto Ricans because of the early hour of the flight and the modest means of the people who predominately [sic] use these flights.] According to airline officials the traffic is heavy. Puerto Ricans constitute approximately 78% of the total number of passengers traveling to and from San Juan" (Hidalgo 11).

Those earliest Puerto Ricans who settled in urban areas in New Jersey faced tremendous hardships. A report drafted in 1955 estimated that around two thousand Puerto Ricans were living in Paterson (Jones 9). It was not an easy transition: "The Puerto Rican urban worker is handicapped in obtaining work by reason of language, prejudice towards newcomers, failure to understand his cultural background, as well as skin color in many instances" (35). They also experienced rather horrendous living conditions, including illegal "overcrowding of rooms and apartments" (24).

For monolingual children, such as Ortiz Cofer, there was not much time for a cultural adjustment. They were thrown into the role of "child interpreter"; in the words of Ortiz Cofer, she became her mother's "personal translator," who, in the absence of her husband, completely deferred to Ortiz Cofer for official communication with monolingual English speakers: "I thought of my role as her personal translator as another immigrant chore, child labor that set me apart from other kids, who were lucky enough to live exclusively in English" (*Cruel Country* 17). Indeed, even in the early 1970s, Puerto Rican children still continued to serve the roles of linguistic and cultural interpreters for their elders, an imposed responsibility that went against traditional Puerto Rican family roles: "Many adults are dependent on their children to act as spokesmen when English becomes the necessary tool of communication. The dependence on the young creates a cultural conflict and a reversal of accepted roles of adults and children. The familiar Puerto Rican saying 'Los niños hablan cuando las gallinas mean' [Children should remain silent] is violated when officials such as teachers, case workers, etc., use children as the medium of communicating with their parents" (Hidalgo 33).

Ortiz Cofer, as a child interpreter, experienced the direct consequences of such a role: "The situation is more destructive when these officials censor and criticize the parents via child translation. Children soon learn that control of English also gives them power" (Hidalgo 33). She became obsessed with the power of the word. Furthermore, in *The Cruel Country* she emphasized that her early skills as an interpreter defined her future career as a type of cultural informant: "Knowledge, facts, books, mastery of words—these have always been my weapons and my tools, from my role as child interpreter in an immigrant family to my career as a teacher and writer" (17). This deeply felt role as an insightful cultural interpreter, which Ortiz Cofer often related to her ontological condition of being "de afuera," a direct reference to her upbringing as an outsider to both the United States and to the island of Puerto Rico, directly determines the ideological parameters of her literary production.

This chapter highlights Ortiz Cofer's narrative pieces centering around her experience of displacement from her native Hormigueros to Paterson, where she arrived in 1955 as a monolingual child. Like many other families, the Ortizes found themselves overwhelmingly unprepared for city life and, in particular, often struggled with the social and economic limitations imposed on them as inhabitants of El Barrio. Nonetheless, Puerto Ricans achieved "the creation of a new breed of American identities on the mainland; for it is along with the Chicano presence in the United States that this migration provided the impetus for a Latino identity" (Soto-Crespo xi–xii). In "Silent Dancing," Ortiz Cofer celebrates that urban Boricua culture through the documentation of iconic spatial markers such as "el bildin," where family and social traditions are maintained, creating "a facsimile of the Island." These tenement apartments were also symptomatic of the urban changes rapidly taking place in Paterson: "Puerto Ricans are living in the slum sections of town, the boarding house districts, or the dilapidated houses in good sections of town and the oldest sections of the community" (Jones 22).

Boricua urban barrios in Paterson, New Jersey, remained a trademark of a narrative project that sought to document the peculiarities of the Puerto Rican migrant experience. Throughout her literary career, Ortiz Cofer developed bold characters illustrative of a tightly knit socioeconomic island culture that had readapted to the physical and social circumstances of urban neighborhoods in Paterson. As Ortiz Cofer documented, the Puerto Rican barrio and Paterson at large had begun to struggle with social changes propelled in part by events surrounding the civil rights movement. "El bildin" was also a space of social contestation. The short story "Nada," which received the O. Henry Award in 1994, explores the impact of the military on the Boricua youth through the narration of events that led to a grieving mother's suicide on hearing about her son's death during the Vietnam War.

El Barrio is nonetheless a place for the celebration of transplanted Puerto Rican traditions. For instance, la bódega, the small corner store that sells typical produce, such as vegetable roots and imported products from the Island, becomes an important social site that connects the newly arrived with an established Boricua community. In the long story "Corazón's Café," readers follow Corazón and Manuel's love story, which begins in rural Puerto Rico, highlighting the origin of many Puerto Rican migrants, who as Jíbaros, or peasants, were proud cultural repositories of a rich countryside way of living. Their journey ends at El Barrio across the Hudson River, where they establish a successful bódega for Boricua residents hungry for food that, if only for a while, could quench their nostalgia for absent family and friends. A mysterious Latin American–born character, Inocencia, cleverly placed in the plotline as a representative of the multiethnicities at the heart of an urban Latinx community, makes this story particularly exciting.

Puerto Ricans encountered racism both as monolingual individuals and as persons of color. Children were not exempted from hurtful microaggressions, particularly in public settings, such as their schools. Two narrative pieces, "American History" and "My Rosetta," exemplify ways in which Puerto Rican children often dealt with rampant xenophobia from their school mentors. "American History" is a fictional story that takes place on a seemingly normal school day that is suddenly interrupted by the somber news of President John F. Kennedy's assassination. Elena, an inhabitant of El Building, recounts a number of altercations with fellow Black students that culminate in the racist comments of a teacher, who interprets the behavior of the students as insensible in the context of the news. Yet that is not the only "American history" lesson learned that day. Later Elena suffers open discrimination when a White woman denies her entrance into her home, located at the margins of El Barrio, where Elena was hoping to meet the woman's son for a study session.

Devoted teachers appear often in Ortiz Cofer's stories as individuals who aid Boricua children in the process of individuation as Latinx youth. "My Rosetta" is highly reflective of her upbringing as a Roman Catholic, perhaps an autobiographical snapshot of her experiences as a student at St. Joseph Catholic School, where she was a minority among a predominantly Irish and Italian student body. This is the story of a fourteen-year-old girl, who, because she attends public school, is enrolled in her neighborhood church for after-school confirmation lessons. Her instructor, Sister Rosetta, who had been rumored to have been "arrested for taking part in a civil rights demonstration," became her most unusual mentor. The lessons learned from a rebellious sixties nun who had managed to rally fellow nuns to force the local bishop to modernize their heavy habits, read more like a syllabus for the liberated youth of the mid-1960s: the music of Indian composer Ravi Shankar and other non-mainstream folk music, Eastern philosophy, and world literature "in the guise of teaching Catholic doctrine." Above all, the Boricua youth learned that her rebelliousness was indeed a fighting spirit, *la lucha*, as Puerto Ricans often refer to their struggle to survive in the "alien culture of the American city." In the end, she too would join that lucha but not "before I could understand who I was in my more complex double world of school and home." That fight will continue to be drawn out thematically in the narrative pieces that explore her dual cultural background as a Georgia Rican and Latina writer.

SILENT DANCING

We have a home movie of this party. Several times my mother and I have watched it together, and I have asked questions about the silent revelers coming in and out of focus. It is grainy and of short duration, but it's a great visual aid to my memory of life at that time. And it is in color—the only complete scene in color I can recall from those years.

We lived in Puerto Rico until my brother was born in 1954. Soon after, because of economic pressures on our growing family, my father joined the United States Navy. He was assigned to duty on a ship in Brooklyn Yard—a place of cement and steel that was to be his home base in the States until his retirement more than twenty years later. He left the Island first, alone, going to New York City and tracking down his uncle who lived with his family across the Hudson River in Paterson, New Jersey. There my father found a tiny apartment in a huge tenement that had once housed Jewish families but was just being taken over and transformed by Puerto Ricans, overflowing from New York City. In 1955 he sent for us. My mother was only twenty years old, I was not quite three, and my brother was a toddler when we arrived at *El Building*, as the place had been christened by its newest residents.

My memories of life in Paterson during those first few years are all in shades of gray. Maybe I was too young to absorb vivid colors and details, or to discriminate between the slate blue of the winter sky and the darker hues of the snow-bearing clouds, but that single color washes over the whole period. The building we lived in was gray, as were the streets, filled with slush the first few months of my life there. The coat my father had bought for me was similar in color and too big; it sat heavily on my thin frame.

I do remember the way the heater pipes banged and rattled, startling all of us out of sleep until we got so used to the sound that we automatically shut it out or raised our voices above the racket. The hiss from the valve punctuated my sleep (which has always been fitful) like a nonhuman presence in the room—a dragon sleeping at the entrance of my childhood. But the pipes were also a connection to all the other lives being lived around us. Having come from a house designed for a single family back in Puerto Rico—my mother's extended-family home—it was curious to know that strangers lived under our floor and above our heads, and that the heater pipe went through everyone's apartments. (My first spanking in Paterson came as a result of playing tunes on the pipes in my room to see if there would be an answer.) My mother was as new to this concept of beehive life as I was, but she had been given strict orders by my father to keep the doors locked, the noise down, ourselves to ourselves.

It seems that Father had learned some painful lessons about prejudice while searching for an apartment in Paterson. Not until years later did I hear how much resistance he had encountered with landlords who were panicking at the influx of Latinos into a neighborhood that had been Jewish for a couple of generations. It made no difference that it was the American phenomenon of ethnic turnover which was changing the urban core of Paterson, and that the human flood could not be held back with an accusing finger.

"You Cuban?" one man had asked my father, pointing at his name tag on the Navy uniform—even though my father had the fair skin and light-brown hair of his northern Spanish background, and the name Ortiz is as common in Puerto Rico as Johnson is in the U.S.

"No," my father had answered, looking past the finger into his adversary's angry eyes. "I'm Puerto Rican."

"Same shit." And the door closed. My father could have passed as European, but we couldn't. My brother and I both have our mother's black hair and olive skin, and so we lived in El Building and visited our great-uncle and his fair children on the next block. It was their private joke that they were the German branch of the family. Not many years later that area too would be mainly Puerto Rican. It was as if the heart of the city map were being gradually colored brown—*café con leche brown*. Our color.

The movie opens with a sweep of the living room. It is "typical" immigrant Puerto Rican decor for the time: the sofa and chairs are square and hard-looking, upholstered in bright colors (blue and yellow in this instance), and covered with the transparent plastic that furniture salesmen then were so adept at convincing women to buy. The linoleum on the floor is light blue; if it had been subjected to spike heels (as it was in most places), there were dime-sized indentations all over it that cannot be seen in this movie. The room is full of people dressed up: dark suits for the men, red dresses for the women. When I have asked my mother why most of the women are in red that night, she has shrugged, "I don't remember. Just a coincidence." She doesn't have my obsession for assigning symbolism to everything.

The three women in red sitting on the couch are my mother, my eighteen-year-old cousin, and her brother's girlfriend. The novia is just up from the Island, which is apparent in her body language. She sits up formally, her dress pulled over her knees. She is a pretty girl, but her posture makes her look insecure, lost in her full-skirted dress, which she has carefully tucked around her to make room for my gorgeous cousin, her future sister-in-law. My cousin has grown up in Paterson and is in her last year of high school. She doesn't have a trace of what Puerto Ricans call "la mancha" (literally, the stain: the mark of the new immigrant—something about the posture, the voice, or the humble demeanor that makes it obvious to everyone the person has just arrived on the mainland). My cousin is wearing a tight, sequined, cocktail dress. Her brown hair has been lightened with peroxide around the bangs, and she is holding a cigarette expertly between her fingers, bringing it up to her mouth in a sensuous arc of her arm as she talks animatedly. My mother, who has come up to sit between the two women, both only a few years younger than herself, is somewhere between the poles they represent in our culture.

It became my father's obsession to get out of the barrio, and thus we were never permitted to form bonds with the place or with the people who lived there. Yet El Building was a comfort to my mother, who never got over yearning for *la isla*. She felt surrounded by her language: the walls were thin, and voices speaking and arguing in Spanish could be heard all day. *Salsas* blasted out of radios, turned on early in the morning and left on for company. Women seemed to cook rice and beans perpetually—the strong aroma of boiling red kidney beans permeated the hallways.

Though Father preferred that we do our grocery shopping at the supermarket when he came home on weekend leaves, my mother insisted that she could cook only with products whose labels she could read. Consequently, during the week I accompanied her and my little brother to *La Bodega*—a hole-in-the-wall grocery store across the street from El Building. There we squeezed down three narrow aisles jammed with various products. Goya and Libby's—those were the trademarks that were trusted by her *mamá*, so my mother bought many cans of Goya beans, soups, and condiments, as well as little cans of Libby's fruit juices for us. And she also bought Colgate toothpaste and Palmolive soap. (The final *e* is pronounced in both these products in Spanish, so for many years I believed that they were manufactured on the Island. I remember my surprise at first hearing a commercial on television in which Colgate rhymed with "ate.") We always lingered at La Bodega, for it was there that Mother breathed best, taking in the familiar aromas of the foods she knew from Mamá's kitchen. It was also there that she got to speak to the other women of El Building without violating outright Father's dictates against fraternizing with our neighbors.

But he did his best to make our "assimilation" painless. I can still see him carrying a real Christmas tree up several flights of stairs to our apartment, leaving a trail of aromatic pine. He carried it formally, as if it were a flag in a parade. We were the only ones in El Building that I knew of who got presents on both Christmas Day and *Día de Reyes*, the day when the Three Kings brought gifts to Christ and to Hispanic children.

Our supreme luxury in El Building was having our own television set. It must have been a result of Father's guilty feelings over the isolation he had imposed on us, but we were among the first in the barrio to have one. My brother quickly became an avid watcher of *Captain Kangaroo* and *Jungle Jim*. I loved all the family series, and by the time I started first grade in school, I could have drawn a map of Middle America as exemplified by the lives of characters in *Father Knows Best*, *The Donna Reed Show*, *Leave It to Beaver*, *My Three Sons*, and (my favorite) *Bachelor Father*, where John Forsythe treated his adopted teenage daughter like a princess because he was rich and had a Chinese houseboy to do everything for him. Compared to our neighbors in El Building, *we* were rich. *My* father's Navy check provided us with financial security and a standard of life that the factory workers envied. The only thing his money could not buy us was a place to live away from the barrio—his greatest wish, Mother's greatest fear.

In the home movie the men are shown next, sitting around a card table set up in one corner of the living room, playing dominoes. The clack of the ivory pieces was a familiar sound. I heard it in many houses on the Island and in many apartments in Paterson. In Leave It to Beaver, *the Cleavers played bridge in every other episode; in my childhood, the men started every social occasion with a hotly debated round of dominoes: the women would sit around and watch, but they never participated in the games.*

Here and there you can see a small child. Children were always brought to parties and, whenever they got sleepy, were put to bed in the host's bedroom. Babysitting was a concept unrecognized by the Puerto Rican women I knew: a responsible mother did not leave her children with any stranger. And in a culture where children are not considered intrusive, there was no need to leave the children at home. We went where our mother went.

Of my preschool years I have only impressions: the sharp bite of the wind in December as we walked with our parents towards the brightly lit stores downtown; how I felt like a stuffed doll in my heavy coat, boots, and mittens; how good it was to walk into the five-and-dime and sit at the counter drinking hot chocolate.

On Saturdays our whole family would walk downtown to shop at the big department stores on Broadway. Mother bought all our clothes at Penney's and Sears, and she liked to buy her dresses at the women's specialty shops like Lerner's and Diana's. At some point we'd go into Woolworth's and sit at the soda fountain to eat.

We never ran into other Latinos at these stores or when eating out, and it became clear to me only years later that the women from El Building shopped mainly at other places—stores owned by other Puerto Ricans, or by Jewish merchants who had philosophically accepted our presence in the city and decided to make us their good customers, if not real neighbors and friends. These establishments were located not downtown but in the blocks around our street, and they were referred to generically as *La Tienda*, *El Bazar*, *La Bodega*, *La Botánica*. Everyone knew what was meant. These were the stores where your face did not turn a clerk to stone, where your money was as green as anyone else's.

One New Year's Eve we were dressed up like child models in the Sears catalogue—my brother in a miniature man's suit and bow tie, and I in black patent-leather shoes and a frilly dress with several layers of crinoline underneath. My mother wore a bright-red dress that night, I remember, and spike heels; her long black hair hung to her waist. Father, who usually wore his Navy uniform during his short visits home, had put on a dark civilian suit for the occasion: we had been invited to his uncle's house for a big celebration. Everyone was excited because my mother's brother Hernán—a bachelor who could indulge himself with luxuries—had bought a home movie camera, which he would be trying out that night.

Even the home movie cannot fill in the sensory details such a gathering left imprinted in a child's brain. The thick sweetness of women's perfumes mixing with the ever-present smells of food cooking in the kitchen: meat and plantain *pasteles*, as well as the ubiquitous rice dish made special with pigeon peas—*gandules*—and seasoned with precious *sofrito* sent up from the Island by somebody's mother or smuggled in by a recent traveler. *Sofrito* was one of the items that women hoarded, since it was hardly ever in stock at La Bodega. It was the flavor of Puerto Rico.

The men drank Palo Viejo rum, and some of the younger ones got weepy. The first time I saw a grown man cry was at a New Year's Eve party. He had been reminded of his mother by the smells in the kitchen. But what I remember most were the boiled *pasteles*—plantain or yucca rectangles stuffed with corned beef or other meats, olives, and many other savory ingredients, all wrapped in banana leaves. Everybody had to fish one out with a fork. There was always a "trick" pastel—one without stuffing—and whoever got that one was the "New Year's Fool."

There was also the music. Long-playing albums were treated like precious china in these homes. Mexican recordings were popular, but the songs that brought tears to my mother's eyes were sung by the melancholy Daniel Santos, whose life as a drug addict was the stuff of legend. Felipe Rodríguez was a particular favorite of couples. He sang about faithless women and brokenhearted men. There is a snatch of one lyric that has stuck in my mind like a needle on a worn groove: "*De piedra ha de ser mi cama, de piedra la cabecera . . . la mujer que a mí me quiera . . . ha de quererme de veras. Ay, Ay, corazón, ¿por qué no amas . . . ?*"

I must have heard it a thousand times since the idea of a bed made of stone, and its connection to love, first troubled me with its disturbing images.

The five-minute home movie ends with people dancing in a circle. The creative filmmaker must have asked them to do that so that all of them could file past him. It is both comical and sad to watch silent dancing. Since there is no justification for the absurd movements that music provides for some of us, people appear frantic, their faces embarrassingly intense. It's as if you were watching sex. Yet for years, I've had dreams in the form of this home movie. In a recurring scene, familiar faces push themselves forward into my mind's eye, plastering their features into distorted close-ups. And I'm asking them: "Who is *she*? Who is the old woman I don't recognize? Is she an aunt? Somebody's wife? Tell me who these people are."

"No, see the beauty mark on her cheek as big as a hill on the lunar landscape of her face—well, that runs in the family. The women on your father's side of the family wrinkle early; it's the price they pay for that fair skin. The young girl with the green stain on her wedding dress is *La Novia*—just up from the Island. See, she lowers her eyes when she approaches the camera, as she's supposed to. Decent girls never look you directly in the face. *Humilde,* humble, a girl should express humility in all her actions. She will make a good wife for your cousin. He should consider himself lucky to have met her only weeks after she arrived here. If he marries her quickly, she will make him a good Puerto Rican-style wife; but if he waits too long, she will be corrupted by the city—just like your cousin there."

"She means me. I do what I want. This is not some primitive island I live on. Do they expect me to wear a black mantilla on my head and go to mass every day? Not me. I'm an American woman, and I will do as I please. I can type faster than anyone in my senior class at Central High, and I'm going to be a secretary to a lawyer when I graduate. I can pass for an American girl anywhere—I've tried it—at least for Italian, anyway. I never speak Spanish in public. I hate these parties, but I wanted the dress. I look better than any of these *humildes* here. *My* life is going to be different. I have an American boyfriend. He is older and has a car. My parents don't know it, but I sneak out of the house late at night sometimes to be with him. If I marry him, even my name will be American. I hate rice and beans. It's what makes these women fat."

"Your *prima* is pregnant by that man she's been sneaking around with. Would I lie to you? I'm your great-uncle's common-law wife—the one he abandoned on the Island to marry your cousin's mother. I was not invited to this party, but I came anyway. I came to tell you that story about your cousin that you've always wanted to hear. Remember that comment your mother made to a neighbor that has always haunted you? The only thing you heard was your cousin's name, and then you saw your mother pick up your doll from the couch and say: 'It was as big as this doll when they flushed it down the toilet.' This image has bothered you for years, hasn't it? You had nightmares about babies being flushed down the toilet, and you wondered why anyone would do such a horrible thing. You didn't dare ask your mother about it. She would only tell you that you had not heard her right and yell at you for listening to adult conversations. But later, when you were old enough to know about abortions, you suspected. I am here to tell you that you were right. Your cousin was growing an *Americanito* in her belly when this movie was made. Soon after she put something long and pointy into her pretty self, thinking maybe she could get rid of the problem before breakfast and still make it to her first class at the high school. Well, *Niña*, her screams could be heard downtown. Your aunt, her Mamá, who had been a midwife on the Island, managed to pull the little thing out. Yes, they probably flushed it down the toilet, what else could they do with it—give it a Christian burial in a little white casket with blue bows and ribbons? Nobody wanted that baby—least of all the father, a teacher at her school with a house in West Paterson that he was filling with real children, and a wife who was a natural blond.

"Girl, the scandal sent your uncle back to the bottle. And guess where your cousin ended up? Irony of ironies. She was sent to a village in Puerto Rico to live with a relative on her mother's side: a place so far away from civilization that you have to ride a mule to reach it. A real change in scenery. She found a man there. Women like that cannot live without male company. But believe me, the men in Puerto Rico know how to put a saddle on a woman like her. *La Gringa*, they call her . . . ha, ha, ha. *La Gringa* is what she always wanted to be . . ."

The old woman's mouth becomes a cavernous black hole I fall into. And as I fall, I can feel the reverberations of her laughter. I hear the echoes of her last mocking words: *La Gringa, La Gringa!* And the conga line keeps moving silently past me. There is no music in my dream for the dancers.

When Odysseus visits Hades to see the spirit of his mother, he makes an offering of sacrificial blood, but since all the souls crave an audience with the living, he has to listen to many of them before he can ask questions. I, too, have to hear the dead and the forgotten speak in my dream. Those who are still part of my life remain silent, going around and around in their dance. The others keep pressing their faces forward to say things about the past.

My father's uncle is last in line. He is dying of alcoholism, shrunken and shriveled like a monkey, his face a mass of wrinkles and broken arteries. As he comes closer I realize that in his features I can see my whole family. If you were to stretch that rubbery flesh, you could find my father's face, and deep within *that* face—mine. I don't want to look into those eyes ringed in purple. In a few years he will retreat into silence, and take a long, long time to die. *Move back, Tío,* I tell him. *I don't want to hear what you have to say. Give the dancers room to move. Soon it will be midnight. Who is the New Year's Fool this time?*

NADA

Almost as soon as Doña Ernestina got the telegram about her son's having been killed in Vietnam, she started giving her possessions away. At first we didn't realize what she was doing. By the time we did, it was too late.

The army people had comforted Doña Ernestina with the news that her son's "remains" would have to be "collected and shipped" back to New Jersey at some later date, since other "personnel" had also been lost on the same day. In other words, she would have to wait until Tony's body could be processed.

Processed. Doña Ernestina spoke that word like a curse when she told us. We were all down in El Basement—that's what we called the cellar of our apartment building: no windows for light, boilers making such a racket that you could scream and almost no one would hear you. Some of us had started meeting here on Saturday mornings—as much to talk as to wash our clothes and over the years it became a sort of women's club where we could catch up on a week's worth of gossip. That Saturday, however, I had dreaded going down the cement steps. All of us had just heard the news about Tony the night before.

I should have known the minute I saw her, holding court in her widow's costume, that something had cracked inside Doña Ernestina. She was in full luto—black from head to toe, including a mantilla. In contrast, Lydia and Isabelita were both in rollers and bathrobes: our customary uniform for these Saturday morning gatherings—maybe our way of saying "No Men Allowed." As I approached them, Lydia stared at me with a scared-rabbit look in her eyes.

Doña Ernestina simply waited for me to join the other two leaning against the machines before she continued explaining what had happened when the news of Tony had arrived at her door the day before. She spoke calmly, a haughty expression on her face, looking like an offended duchess in her beautiful black dress. She was pale, pale, but she had a wild look in her eyes. The officer had told her that—when the time came—they would bury Tony with "full military honors"; for now they were sending her the medal and a flag. But she had said, "No, gracias," to the funeral, and she sent the flag and medals back marked *Ya no vive aquí.* Does not live here anymore. "Tell the Mr. President of the United States what I say: No, gracias."

Then she waited for our response.

Lydia shook her head, indicating that she was speechless. And Elenita looked pointedly at me, forcing me to be the one to speak the words of sympathy for all of us, to reassure Doña Ernestina that she had done exactly what any of us would have done in her place: yes, we would have all said *No, gracias,* to any president who had actually tried to pay for a son's life with a few trinkets and a folded flag.

Doña Ernestina nodded gravely. Then she picked up the stack of neatly folded men's shirts from the sofa (a discard we had salvaged from the sidewalk) and walked regally out of El Basement.

Lydia, who had gone to high school with Tony, burst into tears as soon as Doña Ernestina was out of sight. Elenita and I sat her down between us on the sofa and held her until she had let most of it out. Lydia is still a young woman who has not yet been visited too often by *la muerte.* Her husband of six months has just gotten his draft notice, and they have been trying for a baby—trying very hard. The walls of El Building are thin enough so that it has become a secret joke (kept only from Lydia and Roberto) that he is far more likely to escape the draft due to acute exhaustion than by becoming a father.

"Doesn't Doña Ernestina *feel anything*?" Lydia asked in between sobs. "Did you see her, dressed up like an actress in a play—and not one tear for her son?"

"We all have different ways of grieving," I said, though I couldn't help thinking that there *was* a strangeness to Doña Ernestina and that Lydia was right when she said that the woman seemed to be acting out a part. "I think we should wait and see what she is going to do."

"Maybe," said Elenita. "Did you get a visit from *el padre* yesterday?"

We nodded, not surprised to learn that all of us had gotten personal calls from Padre Álvaro, our painfully shy priest, after Doña Ernestina had frightened him away. Apparently, el padre had come to her apartment immediately after hearing about Tony, expecting to comfort the woman as he had when Don Antonio died suddenly a year ago. Her grief then had been understandable in its immensity, for she had been burying not only her husband but also the dream shared by many of the barrio women her age—that of returning with her man to the Island after retirement, of buying *a casita* in the old pueblo, and of being buried on native ground alongside *la familia*. People *my* age—those of us born or raised here—have had our mothers drill this fantasy into our brains all of our lives. So, when Don Antonio dropped his head on the domino table, scattering the ivory pieces of the best game of the year, and when he was laid out in his best black suit at Ramírez's Funeral Home, all of us knew how to talk to the grieving widow.

That was the last time we saw both her men. Tony was there, too—home on a two-day pass from basic training—and he cried like a little boy over his father's handsome face, calling him Papi, Papi. Doña Ernestina had had a full mother's duty then, taking care of the hysterical boy. It was a normal chain of grief, the strongest taking care of the weakest. We buried Don Antonio at Garden State Memorial Park, where there are probably more Puerto Ricans than on the Island. Padre Álvaro said his sermon in a soft, trembling voice that was barely audible over the cries of the boy being supported on one side by his mother, impressive in her quiet strength and dignity, and on the other by Cheo, owner of the bodega where Don Antonio had played dominoes with other barrio men of his age for over twenty years.

Just about everyone from El Building had attended that funeral, and it had been done right. Doña Ernestina had sent her son off to fight for America and then had started collecting her widow's pension. Some of us asked Doña Iris (who knew how to read cards) about Doña Ernestina's future, and Doña Iris had said: "A long journey within a year"—which fit with what we had thought would happen next: Doña Ernestina would move back to the Island and wait with her relatives for Tony to come home from the war. Some older women actually went home when they started collecting social security or pensions, but that was rare. Usually, it seemed to me, somebody had to die before the island dream would come true for women like Doña Ernestina. As for my friends and I, we talked about "vacations" in the Caribbean. But we knew that if life was hard for us in this barrio, it would be worse in a pueblo where no one knew us (and had maybe only heard of our parents before they came to Los Estados Unidos de América, where most of us had been brought as children).

When Padre Álvaro had knocked softly on my door, I had yanked it open, thinking it was that ex-husband of mine asking for a second chance again. (That's just the way Miguel knocks when he's sorry for leaving me—about once a week—when he wants a loan.) So, I was wearing my go-to-hell face when I threw open the door, and the poor priest nearly jumped out of his skin. I saw him take a couple of deep breaths before he asked me in his slow way—he tries to hide his stutter by dragging out his words—if I knew whether or not Doña Ernestina was ill. After I said, "No, not that I know," Padre Álvaro just stood there, looking pitiful, until I asked him if he cared to come in. I had been sleeping on the sofa and watching TV all afternoon, and I really didn't want him to see the mess, but I had nothing to fear. The poor man actually took one step back at my invitation. No, he was in a hurry, he had a few other parishioners to visit, etc. These were difficult times, he said, so-so-so many young people lost to drugs or dying in the wa-wa-war. I asked him if he thought Doña Ernestina was sick, but he just shook his head. The man looked like an orphan at my door with those sad, brown eyes. He was actually appealing in a homely way: that long nose nearly touched the tip of his chin when he smiled, and his big crooked teeth broke my heart.

"She does not want to speak to me," Padre Álvaro said as he caressed a large silver crucifix that hung on a thick chain around his neck. He seemed to be dragged down by its weight, stoop-shouldered and skinny as he was.

I felt a strong impulse to feed him some of my chicken soup, still warm on the stove from my supper. Contrary to what Lydia says about me behind my back, I like living by myself. And I could not have been happier to have that mama's boy Miguel back where he belonged—with his mother, who thought that he was still her baby.

But this scraggly thing at my door needed home cooking and maybe even something more than a hot meal to bring a little spark into his life. (I mentally asked God to forgive me for having thoughts like these about one of his priests. *Ay bendito*, but they too are made of flesh and blood.)

"Maybe she just needs a little more time, Padre," I said in as comforting a voice as I could manage. Unlike the other women in El Building, I am not convinced that priests are truly necessary—or even much help—in times of crisis.

"Sí, Hija, perhaps you're right," he muttered sadly—calling me "daughter" even though I'm pretty sure I'm five or six years older. (Padre Álvaro seems so "untouched" that it's hard to tell his age. I mean, when you live, it shows. He looks hungry for love, starving himself by choice.) I promised him that I would look in on Doña Ernestina. Without another word, he made the sign of the cross in the air between us and turned away. As I heard his slow steps descending the creaky stairs, I asked myself: what do priests dream about?

When el padre's name came up again during that Saturday meeting in El Basement, I asked my friends what they thought a priest dreamed about. It was a fertile subject, so much so that we spent the rest of our laundry time coming up with scenarios. Before the last dryer stopped, we all agreed that we could not receive communion the next day at mass unless we went to confession that afternoon and told another priest, not Álvaro, about our "unclean thoughts."

As for Doña Ernestina's situation, we agreed that we should be there for her if she called, but the decent thing to do, we decided, was give her a little more time alone. Lydia kept repeating, in that childish way of hers, "Something is wrong with the woman," but she didn't volunteer to go see what it was that was making Doña Ernestina act so strangely. Instead, she complained that she and Roberto had heard pots and pans banging and things being moved around for hours in 4-D last night—they had hardly been able to sleep. Isabelita winked at me behind Lydia's back. Lydia and Roberto still had not caught on: if they could hear what was going on in 4-D, the rest of us could also get an earful of what went on in 4-A. They were just kids who thought they had invented sex: I tell you, a telenovela could be made from the stories in El Building.

On Sunday Doña Ernestina was not at the Spanish mass and I avoided Padre Álvaro so he would not ask me about her. But I was worried. Doña Ernestina was a church cucaracha—a devout Catholic who, like many of us, did not always do what the priests and the Pope ordered but who knew where God lived. Only a serious illness or tragedy could keep her from attending mass, so afterward I went straight to her apartment and knocked on her door. There was no answer, although I had heard scraping and dragging noises, like furniture being moved around. At least she was on her feet and active. Maybe housework was what she needed to snap out of her shock. I decided to try again the next day.

As I went by Lydia's apartment, the young woman opened her door—I knew she had been watching me through the peephole—to tell me about more noises from across the hall during the night. Lydia was in her baby-doll pajamas. Although she stuck only her nose out, I could see Roberto in his jockey underwear doing something in the kitchen. I couldn't help thinking about Miguel and me when we had first gotten together. We were an explosive combination. After a night of passionate lovemaking, I would walk around thinking: Do not light cigarettes around me. No open flames. Highly combustible materials being transported. But when his mamá showed up at our door, the man of fire turned into a heap of ashes at her feet.

"Let's wait and see what happens," I told Lydia again.

We did not have to wait for long. On Monday Doña Ernestina called to invite us to a wake for Tony, a *velorio*, in her apartment. The word spread fast. Everyone wanted to do something for her. Cheo donated fresh chickens and island produce of all kinds. Several of us got together and made arroz con pollo, also flan for dessert. And Doña Iris made two dozen *pasteles* and wrapped the meat pies in banana leaves that she had been saving in her freezer for her famous Christmas parties. We women carried in our steaming plates, while the men brought in their bottles of Palo Viejo rum for themselves and candy-sweet Manischewitz wine for us. We came ready to spend the night saying our rosaries and praying for Tony's soul.

Doña Ernestina met us at the door and led us into her living room, where the lights were off. A photograph of Tony and one of her deceased husbands, Don Antonio, were sitting on top of a table, surrounded by at least a dozen candles. It was a spooky sight that caused several of the older women to cross themselves. Doña Ernestina had arranged folding chairs in front of this table and told us to sit down. She did not ask us to take our food and drinks to the kitchen. She just looked at each of us individually, as if she were taking attendance in a class, and then said: "I have asked you here to say good-bye to my husband Antonio and my son Tony. You have been my friends and neighbors for twenty years, but they were my life. Now that they are gone, I have nada. Nada. Nada."

I tell you, that word is like a drain that sucks everything down. Hearing her say *nada* over and over made me feel as if I were being yanked into a dark pit. I could feel the others getting nervous around me too, but here was a woman deep into her pain: we had to give her a little space. She looked around the room, then walked out without saying another word.

As we sat there in silence, stealing looks at each other, we began to hear the sounds of things being moved around in other rooms. One of the older women took charge then, and soon the drinks were poured, the food served, all this while the strange sounds kept coming from different rooms in the apartment. Nobody said much, except once when we heard something like a dish fall and break. Doña Iris pointed her index finger at her ear and made a couple of circles and out of nervousness, I guess, some of us giggled like schoolchildren.

It was a long while before Doña Ernestina came back out to us. By then we were gathering our dishes and purses, having come to the conclusion that it was time to leave. Holding two huge Sears shopping bags, one in each hand, Doña Ernestina took her place at the front door as if she were a society hostess in a receiving line. Some of us women hung back to see what was going on. But Tito, the building's super, had had enough and tried to get past her. She took his hand, putting in it a small ceramic poodle with a gold chain around its neck. Tito gave the poodle a funny look, then glanced at Doña Ernestina as though he were scared and hurried away with the dog in his hand.

We were let out of her place one by one but not until she had forced one of her possessions on each of us. She grabbed without looking from her bags. Out came her prized *miniaturas*, knickknacks that take a woman a lifetime to collect. Out came ceramic and porcelain items of all kinds, including vases and ashtrays; out came kitchen utensils, dishes, forks, knives, spoons; out came old calendars and every small item that she had touched or been touched by in the last twenty years. Out came a bronzed baby shoe and I got that.

As we left the apartment, Doña Iris said "Psst" to some of us, so we followed her down the hallway. "Doña Ernestina's faculties are temporarily out of order," she said very seriously. "It is due to the shock of her son's death."

We all said "Sí" and nodded our heads.

"But what can we do?" Lydia said, her voice cracking a little. "What should I do with this?" She was holding one of Tony's baseball trophies in her hand: 1968 Most Valuable Player, for the Pocos Locos, our barrio's team.

Doña Iris said, "Let us keep her things safe for her until she recovers her senses.

And let her mourn in peace. These things take time. If she needs us, she will call us." Doña Iris shrugged her shoulders. "Así es la vida, hijas: that's the way life is."

As I passed Tito on the stairs, he shook his head while looking up at Doña Ernestina's door: "I say she needs a shrink. I think somebody should call the social worker." He did not look at me when he mumbled these things. By "somebody" he meant one of us women. He didn't want trouble in his building, and he expected one of us to get rid of the problems. I just ignored him.

In my bed I prayed to the Holy Mother that she would find peace for Doña Ernestina's troubled spirit, but things got worse. All that week Lydia saw strange things happening through the peephole on her door. Every time people came to Doña Ernestina's apartment—to deliver flowers, or telegrams from the Island, or anything—the woman would force something on them. She pleaded with them to take this or that; if they hesitated, she commanded them with those tragic eyes to accept a token of her life.

And they did, walking out of our apartment building, carrying cushions, lamps, doilies, clothing, shoes, umbrellas, wastebaskets, schoolbooks, and notebooks: things of value and things of no worth at all to anyone but the person who had owned them. Eventually winos and street people got the news of the great giveaway in 4-D, and soon there was a line down the stairs and out the door. Nobody went home empty-handed; it was like a soup kitchen. Lydia was afraid to step out of her place because of all the dangerous-looking characters hanging out on that floor. And the smell! Entering our building was like coming into a cheap bar and public urinal combined.

Isabelita, living alone with her two little children and fearing for their safety, was the one who finally called a meeting of the residents. Only the women attended, since the men were truly afraid of Doña Ernestina. It isn't unusual for men to be frightened when they see a woman go crazy. If they are not the cause of her madness, then they act as if they don't understand it and usually leave us alone to deal with our "woman's problems." This is just as well.

Maybe I *am* just bitter because of Miguel—I know what is said behind my back. But this is a fact: when a woman is in trouble, a man calls in her mamá, her sisters, or her friends, and then he makes himself scarce until it's all over. This happens again and again. At how many bedsides of women have I sat? How many times have I made the doctor's appointment, taken care of the children, and fed the husbands of my friends in the barrio? It is not that the men can't do these things; it's just that they know how much women help each other. Maybe the men even suspect that we know one another better than they know their own wives. As I said, it is just as well that they stay out of our way when there is trouble. It makes things simpler for us.

At the meeting, Isabelita said right away that we should go up to 4-D and try to reason with *la pobre* Doña Ernestina. Maybe we could get her to give us a relative's address in Puerto Rico—the woman obviously needed to be taken care of. What she was doing was putting us all in a very difficult situation. There were no dissenters this time. We voted to go as a group to talk to Doña Ernestina the next morning.

But that night we were all awakened by crashing noises on the street. In the light of the full moon, I could see that the air was raining household goods: kitchen chairs, stools, a small TV, a nightstand, pieces of a bed frame. Everything was splintering as it landed on the pavement. People were running for cover and yelling up at our building. The problem, I knew instantly, was in apartment 4-D.

Putting on my bathrobe and slippers, I stepped out into the hallway. Lydia and Roberto were rushing down the stairs, but on the flight above my landing, I caught up with Doña Iris and Isabelita, heading toward 4-D. Out of breath, we stood in the fourth-floor hallway, listening to police sirens approaching our building in front. We could hear the slamming of car doors and yelling in both Spanish and English. Then we tried the door to 4-D. It was unlocked.

We came into a room virtually empty. Even the pictures had been taken down from the walls; all that was left were the nail holes and the lighter places on the paint where the framed photographs had been for years. We took a few seconds to spot Doña Ernestina: she was curled up in the farthest corner of the living room, naked.

"Como salió a este mundo," said Doña Iris, crossing herself.

Just as she had come into the world. Wearing nothing. Nothing around her except a clean, empty room. Nada. She had left nothing behind—except the bottles of pills, the ones the doctors give to ease the pain, to numb you, to make you feel nothing when someone dies.

The bottles were empty too, and the policemen took them. But we didn't let them take Doña Ernestina until we each had brought up some of our own best clothes and dressed her like the decent woman that she was. *La decencia.* Nothing can ever change that—not even la muerte. This is the way life is. *Así es la vida.*

CORAZÓN'S CAFÉ

I

Corazón knew that she should go back to the apartment now. It was after closing time, and soon the street would be deserted. But she felt less alone here in the café, among the shelves that she and Manuel had stocked together, than she did in their apartment. It had been their home among the barrio neighbors who had also been their customers for ten years. Although she had often talked of moving to a house in the suburbs, especially after their store had started paying for itself, she knew that Manuel loved El Building for the same reasons that others claimed to hate it. It had vida. It was filled with the life energies of generations of other Island people; the stairs sagged from the weight of their burdens, and the walls had absorbed the smells of their food. El Building had become their country now. But Corazón did not know if she could call it home now that Manuel was gone.

Corazón was sitting behind the counter as if expecting a rush of customers at that hour. But what came to her were memories. From where she sat she could read the labels of cans that reminded her of Manuel's special way of doing things.

Habichuelas rojas, the cans of red kidney beans they stacked in a little pyramid. There were little sacks next to it holding the long grain rice that Puerto Ricans like to eat. The only logic that Manuel followed in stocking his shelves was based on his idea of what most people wanted to see in a barrio store: foods that go together arranged in interesting ways in one area: rice and beans, with plantains nearby, as well as cans of sliced breadfruit, pumpkin, and other side dishes to inspire more creative meals. The whole store was arranged in possible meal combinations. And there was the "international" section where imported goods for the other Latino customers were displayed by nationality. Exotic canned products from Brazil, "Cuban" fruit drinks now bottled in Miami, black frijoles from Mexico, and assorted candies from several South American countries with curious names like Suspiros and Merengues.

Leaning over, she could smell the fresh coffee they kept in a can on the counter to serve free to customers. The aroma took her back to the time she had met Manuel.

II

It had been a hot afternoon on the Island. He came out to wait on her from where he had been grinding coffee beans behind the counter of el mercado

González when she had walked in, her face streaked with tears after a confrontation with her father. She had been sent to buy a bottle of Palo Viejo rum.

Manuel had put the bottle in a brown sack, never taking his eyes away from her face. He had touched her hand with his fingers as he handed it to her. Later, she had smelled the fresh coffee on her skin. She had avoided washing that hand all day because by bringing it to her nose, she could recall the pleasure of his touch.

And his face was beautiful. She had always thought that it was not right to say that of a man, but as a plain woman who always noticed beauty in others, she considered herself a fair judge of *la belleza*. And Manuel had a face as lovely as Jesus in those paintings where he is offering you His Sacred Heart. Manuel had a little beard then too (which he had grown to look older than his eighteen years when he had asked for the job at the store). But the beard only framed and softened his features. His eyes were almond-shaped with long eyelashes that made shadows on his cheeks when he looked down to figure an account for a customer. His lips were an invitation for a kiss: full and sensuous.

The most attractive thing about Manuel to Corazón was the fact that Manuel seemed to be unaware of his good looks. He worked twelve-hour days at the mercado, then he went home to help his widowed mother take care of the house and the little plot of land where she grew a few vegetables. They subsisted on Manuel's small salary and on the money his mother made by cooking for other people's parties. That is how Manuel had learned to cook, by helping his mother in the kitchen.

Corazón's situation was the reverse. Her mother had died in childbirth, leaving her to her older sister's care. Consuelo had been little more than a child herself when she had to take over the house. Their father was a heavy drinker, becoming more reclusive and bitter as he got older. He provided for his daughters, bringing in money from his job as foreman at the factory, but he seemed indifferent to their emotional needs. Anger and violence were always a possibility when he was home. "Go get me a pint of Palo Viejo" was his usual greeting to Corazón in the evening. By the time she was eighteen, the task had become an unbearable humiliation. But if it wasn't Corazón, it would have to be her sister, Consuelo, who was older and secretly engaged to a man who had warned her (or so Consuelo had told Corazón) that if her old man forced her to go buy rum, he would come over and beat him senseless. They did not want more violence at home, did they? And besides, at twenty-five years of age, Consuelo believed this was her last chance at marriage. Consuelo had promised Corazón that she would wait until Corazón had finished high school, then she would marry and leave town.

Meeting Manuel gave Corazón hope and a plan for the future. She had loved him immediately. But he was so timid that she found herself directing the courtship. She started by going on any pretext to the mercado, where she practiced seducing him with her eyes. She gave him looks she had learned from the Mexican movies at the cinema. But he simply looked embarrassed and lowered his eyes in confusion. Since Corazón was well aware of the fact that she was not beautiful, at first she thought he was rejecting her in his own gentle way. But the attraction was real. She could detect the electrically charged space between them when he faced her across the counter. He was just too shy to speak. Finally, Corazón decided to take action. One day she slipped him a note with the money as she paid for the groceries. It simply said, *Manuel, meet me behind the mercado at nine tonight.* Then she left quickly before he could say no. It was a daring plan. She had to get Consuelo to help her carry it out.

After dinner their father usually sat alone in his room listening to the radio. Consuelo and Corazón were supposed to wash the dishes, make the beds, and occupy themselves with sewing, reading, or some other "quiet" activity until he declared that it was time for bed at around ten. He never came into their room, though, and it was possible for one of them to sneak out of the house through the window, which led directly to a thickly overgrown backyard. The banana trees, the huge breadfruit tree, and the assorted plants that their mother had once cultivated but were now like a forest provided great cover. From years of playing in that wilderness as children, they both knew their way to the road by moonlight. So far, it had been Consuelo who sneaked out to meet her man. This night, it would be Corazón. Consuelo expressed concern about her sister's decision, but she also told the radiant girl that love had made her almost beautiful that night. Corazón smiled ironically at the "almost beautiful" but felt too excited to allow her sister's words to hurt her as they usually did. Consuelo offered to brush Corazón's glossy black hair. It was the one thing Corazón was proud of—she had beautiful hair like their mother's. She examined her face carefully in the mirror. She did not think herself vain, but for Manuel, she wished she were prettier. Corazón's face was the result of the history of Puerto Rico. Her high cheekbones and oval eyes came from her father's Taino Indian and African ancestry. From her mother's forebears in Spain Corazón had received the long, thin nose, curly black hair, and lightened complexion that made her skin neither copper nor tan but somewhere in between. Corazón wished she were thinner; her large bosom made her look heavier than she was. She wished she looked more like her mother, who, like Consuelo, had been a tiny delicate-featured woman with porcelain skin. She knew this from the wedding picture her father had on his dresser. She had seen him stare at it for hours while he drank and listened to the old songs on his radio.

Corazón let herself out of the window with her sister's help.

"Remember, I will be expecting you in two hours," Consuelo had whispered to her. "And please, Corazón, don't . . ." She had started to lecture her about not doing anything foolish, anything she might regret, but Corazón had already turned away from her older sister and was plunging into the garden's shadows.

Manuel was waiting for her on the back steps of the store. Her own daring had made her feel reckless, and she leaned down and kissed his mouth. It tasted like a sweet, moist fruit straight from the tree of summer. He pulled her down on the cool cement steps next to him.

"Corazón," he spoke her name for the first time, "what shall we do?" She knew immediately what she would say, and it would always be that way. Manuel would ask her to make the important decisions, and she always would.

"Marry me," she said.

"I have to take care of my mother. She is not well, and she's only got me."

"We will take care of her together, Manuel." Corazón felt like someone who dives from a sinking ship into the ocean. She would do anything to be with this man. She felt a sense of destiny, *el destino*, a powerful force taking over her life.

That night they began to make plans. Corazón would finish her schooling that year, then they would announce their engagement. She found it easy to take the lead with Manuel. She placed her eager mouth on his, and he responded with a tenderness and passion she could control by merely wishing it. He seemed to gauge her needs and give her exact quantities of passion—no more, no less. He smiled and nodded as she began to make plans for their future, even that first night when they knew not much more about each other than what their bodies told them—that they wanted to be together more than they wanted anything else.

Manuel walked Corazón home, as far as the large tree at the edge of the overgrown garden. They held each other for a long time, then said a quiet good night with promises of another meeting in a few nights. Corazón climbed through the window into the room, where she found Consuelo sobbing on her bed.

"What is it, Consuelo, what is wrong?" Corazón stroked her sister's hair. She feared something awful had happened in her house, since Consuelo was crying so hard that her whole body trembled in Corazón's arms. After a few minutes, Consuelo sat up in bed and laid her head on her sister's lap, letting Corazón wipe the tears from her face with her skirt.

"It's father. He found my letters to Gustavo and he is furious. Oh, Corazón. He called me out to the living room, and I had a terrible time explaining why you had not come out with me. I told him you were feverish and had taken medicine. But he was too angry to care about you. He wants Gustavo to come over tomorrow. I'm so afraid."

"How did he find the letters, Consuelo?" Corazón knew that their father avoided their private rooms, as he did most places and people that reminded him of his wife. He would not even allow flowers in the house, because she had always had things blossoming and growing in her home. His grief had turned him inside out, and he wore all his bitterness on the surface of his skin. He had withdrawn into his room with his bottle and treated his daughters like bad memories, avoiding looking at their faces, which were composites of his and his dead wife's, yet jealously guarding them.

"I had put them in my missal. I guess I left it out on the table by mistake. He must have seen the papers sticking out."

Corazón gently lifted her sister's face and looked deeply into her eyes. Rising from the bed, she walked to the dresser. She was quick to figure out that Consuelo had wanted the old man to find the letters. It was like her sister to manipulate events to suit her needs. Though Corazón loved Consuelo very much, she had sometimes felt hurt and offended by her sister's somewhat devious ways of getting what she wanted. It was as if, in having to accept the responsibilities of a widower's home and a young sister to take care of, Consuelo had decided she could never trust anyone to treat her fairly, so she kept secrets and maneuvered people. Now she was hurrying up her future before Corazón could get too much of a head start. Corazón knew what would happen in the next few days. A wedding date would be set for Consuelo and Gustavo to marry and thus save their father's dignity.

"Consuelo, I thought you were going to wait for me to finish school before you married Gustavo." Corazón's tone let her sister know what she suspected. Consuelo rose abruptly from the bed, wiping the last of her tears from her face.

"If you are old enough to be with a man, my dear little sister, you are old enough to take care of yourself."

That was the moment in the lives of the two sisters when Corazón began to understand that in matters of love for men, family loyalty takes second place. Consuelo's maternal concern for Corazón evaporated when she felt an encroachment on her right as the eldest to marry first. She had come to this conclusion while she waited for her younger sister to return from meeting her man.

The wedding was planned rapidly. It was to be a simple ceremony at home, since Don Emilio, their father, would not agree to attend a church wedding. The witness was their aunt, who brought flowers for the bride in spite of her brother's ban and cooked a meal for the groom's parents. The couple would stay with his family at first, then leave for New Jersey, where Gustavo had been offered a job as a mechanic by his godfather, who owned a garage. Consuelo was a beautiful bride, painful to her father's eyes, since she resembled his wife so much. Right after the priest said his final blessing, Don Emilio retired to his room and closed the door on the party. Corazón helped her sister change clothes for the one-night honeymoon in the nearest city of Ponce. Though there had been tension between them in the past weeks, she was grateful to her sister for all her years of devoted care. She stood behind Consuelo, who was sitting at her dresser, and helped her remove the little crown of fresh flowers, *azucenas*, white lilies from her hair.

"Be happy," she had said, and she had meant it.

But Corazón's life in her father's house without her sister for company became a daily torment. Right after work, the old man would lock himself in his room to drink, and he did not emerge until morning. He did not speak to Corazón except to order her to do something around the house or to send her to the store for his main needs in those dark days: cigarettes and rum. Feeling desperately alone, one night Corazón looked outside her window and decided to go toward the one point of light in the distance—Manuel's house.

She found her way there in almost total darkness. Manuel's mother's house stood alone outside of town, and the streetlights gave way to a dirt road long before their few acres of land began. Corazón stumbled and cut herself on sharp rocks, and once coming upon a creek, she fell into the shallow water before finding the stepping-stones by moonlight. When she arrived, she was hurt, bleeding, and soaked to the skin through her thin dress. The house loomed above her on stilts.

Corazón sat on the ground where she could see Manuel moving behind the translucent curtains like a figure in a dream. She was exhausted, and he seemed beyond her reach. She allowed herself to cry a little, as she watched him turn off the light and come to the window to close the shutters against the mosquitoes as he prepared for bed. Corazón ran to the house and stood under his startled eyes.

"Corazón!" He could not believe what he was seeing. But she just reached her arms up to him, and by leaning his body halfway out of the window, he reached her and pulled her into his room. Without speaking they came together in the dim room that smelled of the warm milk sweetened with cinnamon he drank each evening, of soap and man's cologne. He unbuttoned her dress and dried her with his soft cotton shirt, and he kneeled on the floor and removed her sandals. Then he lifted her up in his arms like a child and took her to his bed, where she shivered until he enfolded her body with his own.

He kept repeating her name, "Corazón, Corazón," as if he were talking to himself, warning himself to be gentle with her. He kissed her mouth until she trusted herself enough to kiss him back, and only when she let her body respond to his hands did he push himself gently into her. He was patient as she experienced first pain, then pleasure so intense that she laughed aloud in surprise. He said, "Hush, mi Corazón, Mamá's in there." He pointed toward the wall. Corazón felt afraid that his mother had heard them. But their desire was stronger than caution and they made love again, quietly, falling asleep exhausted when it was almost light outside.

Sleeping in Manuel's arms had come as naturally as breathing to Corazón. The first morning in his mother's house, however, began with her awakening alone in his room. She heard a woman's soft voice on the other side of the thin wall and Manuel's deeper voice responding. But she could not make out the words. She considered jumping out of the window and running back to her home. Perhaps she could sneak back into her room before her father noticed her absence.

As she hurriedly dressed in clothes that smelled of the muddy water with which they were splattered, Manuel walked in with a woman's bright yellow dress on his arm. He handed it to her. Smiling, he said: "My mother thinks it will fit you."

Corazón had never met anyone like Doña Serena. She was so thin that the veins on her arms could be seen through her skin like lines on a map. She wore her gray hair pulled back tightly in a bun. There was no trace of makeup on her face, which was vaguely reminiscent of Manuel's—in the darkness of the pupils and the high forehead. But she looked wispy and fragile—almost otherworldly.

Manuel had told Corazón that his mother was not well, yet both of them worked constantly. That first morning when Corazón had shyly walked out of Manuel's room wearing the yellow dress that was too tight on her, she had been greeted by Doña Serena at a table set for three. Without comment Doña Serena had motioned Corazón over to her and had kissed the fearful girl on the cheek. Over a delicious breakfast of homemade bread and guava jelly, mother and son had discussed their plans for the day, including the wedding. Early that morning Doña Serena had arranged for the priest to marry them that same day in a simple ceremony in her living room. On her way to talk to the priest, she had stopped by Corazón's father's house. Don Emilio had refused to talk to her, saying only that he did not want to hear anything that had to do with Consuelo or Corazón anymore. Doña Serena had packed a few things in a bag for the girl. The wedding would take place after Manuel got home from the bodega and before they cooked the three dozen pasteles that a new customer had ordered. Corazón had looked in amazement at the older woman, who spoke these things in a calm voice. She felt a sense of peace, sitting in that sunny kitchen with these two people she would now call her family. After his mother went into the kitchen, Manuel asked Corazón if she agreed to Doña Serena's plans. Corazón assured him that she had never been happier about anything in her life. It was as if she had a mother again to take care of her.

And though there was little money, the three of them could have lived happily enough except for two awful things that followed one another in rapid succession. During the first year of their marriage, Doña Serena had begun experiencing excruciating pains in her chest. At first she did not want to go to the doctor, but Corazón finally persuaded her by telling her that she too had reason to have an examination.

The older woman had become her confidante in the last six months. Though she spoke very little herself, she listened attentively for hours to Corazón's story of her own mother's early death and the bitterness of life with an alcoholic father. The two women worked together all day. In the morning they tended the little garden. In the afternoons they prepared giant pots of ingredients for the meat pies to be delivered to people's houses by Manuel when he came home. The late evenings belonged to the couple as Doña Serena watched her telenovelas, the soap operas that she loved, on a little television set in her room. The noise made by the TV gave the lovers enough freedom to enjoy each other in their room next to hers.

They made love with the window thrown wide open to the smells of the Island, all concentrated on Doña Serena's property—her little garden of herbs with the pungent oregano overwhelming all the other aromatic plants, the cayenne peppers, the cilantro, the tasty Puerto Rican coriander, the *pimientos y ajíes* that went into her condiments and permeated even the naked wood of the house with the smell of food cooked in her kitchen every day. The breeze blew through the trees that surrounded and protected the little plot of cultivated ground, and it too added a special fragrance from the papaya with its pendulous fruit hanging delicately from its slender branches, and the banana trees that, even when not laden with stalks of the fat little *guineitos niños* that are melt-in-the-mouth sweet when fried, still bore the leaves that the expert cook knows should be used to wrap food that is boiled—to add the final touch of taste and also to make food a gift to be unwrapped in celebration. Manuel whispered these things to her as they lay in each other's arms at night. She laughed gently at his love of cooking and his amazing knowledge of plants and food; not long before, she had believed these interests were strictly feminine, but his hands caressing her body were also a revelation of what a real man could be. He was a passionate lover but patient, teaching her how to attain the most pleasure from her body. Her body. It was suddenly a marvelous thing, her body; a source of pleasure to a beautiful man, and now she was carrying his child. After lovemaking she placed his hand on her abdomen. Half asleep, he said: "You are enjoying my cooking, Corazón," and, chuckling, "there is more woman here than I married."

Corazón smiled in the dark, her face buried in his neck. She was savoring the moment, postponing telling him until after she went with Doña Serena to her doctor the next day. There had been happiness followed by concern on the older woman's face as she had examined Corazón's belly. Doña Serena had been a midwife for many years, though she had given up the practice some time ago when her strength had started to fail her.

"What is it, what is the matter?" Corazón had perceived Doña Serena's anxiety as her hands traced the tight roundness of her womb.

"It may be nothing, Hija, just an old woman's apprehensions about her first grandchild, but I want you to promise me something."

"What, Doña Serena?" Corazón felt a cold shiver run down her spine, a sense that something was wrong.

"That you will not tell Manuel about your pregnancy yet. Tomorrow I will take you to my doctor for tests." She had taken Corazón's hand in hers. "It is best to make certain in these matters, querida, men do not like to be disappointed about babies."

"I will wait until tomorrow to tell Manuel," Corazón had promised, something like fear settling in her chest so that she had trouble breathing.

And as the afternoon passed in its slow way, as it does in the country when the days are hot and humid, Corazón forgot about her anxiety and talked to her mother-in-law about the future—a topic that Doña Serena never contributed much to, knowing that it was not for her, instead listening attentively, closely, trying to picture what she would not be around to see. Mainly they talked about Manuel, who was at the center of their lives then. He wanted to open his own store. He was dissatisfied with the strictly mercenary way that his boss ran the mercado, caring only for the profits. Manuel wanted, even back then, to offer people more than a place to buy their groceries; he wanted to create the ideal food store where he would teach his customers how to select each fruit and vegetable and how to cook them too. Doña Serena and Corazón smiled as they discussed Manuel's missionary commitment to his dream of a store. They also worried together about his health. Though it seldom happened, sometimes Manuel experienced shortness of breath and dizzy spells that drove him into a darkened room where he would lie on the floor until he regained control of his breathing. He made excuses for not seeing a doctor, but the women plotted about how to get him there. In her usual reticent way, Doña Serena did not say much, but Corazón intuited that the mother feared that whatever made her chest hurt as if a jagged blade was being thrust through her ribs could also be part of Manuel's problem. All that she put aside, though, after Corazón announced her pregnancy and especially after Doña Serena's expert midwife's hands had discovered a more imminent tragedy taking shape within Corazón's body.

The doctor confirmed it. The pregnancy would not come to full term. Neither would any other. Corazón's womb was incapable of sustaining a baby; it would not stretch to accommodate a living fetus even for the minimum time needed. She would never bear a live child. The doctor recommended an immediate abortion and hysterectomy. Corazón collapsed in Doña Serena's arms. And when Manuel came into her room at the hospital before she was taken to the operating room, she pretended to be asleep. She could not look at him.

He was more loving and tender with her after that. Once he said to her that she was all he wanted, that he was happier than he had ever been. But seeing that Corazón's grief was too overwhelming for words of consolation, he never mentioned their lost child again.

Doña Serena died in her bed. The doctor expressed surprise that she had not cried out. An artery had burst. The pain must have been so unbearable that she had lost consciousness, or else she had chosen to keep it to herself. Corazón secretly believed that Doña Serena had always borne more than anyone knew. She was the kind of woman who is called a *sufrida*—one who accepts pain *and* sacrifice as her lot and her privilege. While Manuel wept over his saintly mother, Corazón felt cheated. She was angry that another chance at a mother's love and companionship had been taken away from her and, most unfair of all, that she herself could never have a child to make her life complete. She looked at Manuel kneeling by the coffin, his shoulders shaking with sobs, and for the first time, she saw that she would now have to be strong for both of them. She would have to take him by the hand and lead him where he wanted to go in life. In her anger, Corazón also felt strength filling her with determination. He wanted a store of his own, but he had no idea how to get it. She would now have a lot of time on her hands. She would start planning a future for them. What else was there for her to do?

"Manuel." She offered him her hand. "It is time to go home now." And he got on his feet and followed her into their future.

III

Corazón wished she could move everything out of the store that night. She did not think she could stay in this place without Manuel. When Tito, the super, Doña Iris, Elenita from El Building, Joe Mendez, the lawyer, and old Don Cándido came by for their cup of coffee and their groceries, they would find the place as empty as the day she and Manuel had stepped in and Manuel had turned and hugged her. It had been just what he wanted: a blank canvas on which to create his dream of a store where both the body and the spirit could be nourished. Had that been ten years ago already?

It was nearly midnight. Corazón sat on her high stool behind the counter with only the security lights on. She allowed the tears to come. She felt so alone without the man she had loved and worked with for one brief decade. She should have made Manuel take better care of himself. After Doña Serena's funeral, she had made Manuel go to the doctor for a complete physical examination. Her worst fears had been confirmed. Like his mother, he suffered from a congenital heart defect: one of the valves was too small, it constricted the flow of blood during times of anxiety or stress. Surgery was advised but at very high risk. And of course, being young and full of energy at that time, Manuel had chosen to wait; there was always a reason: money, the right time—after they had saved enough to come to America, after they bought the store. It was as if he didn't want to know that his heart was failing him. Then two days ago, the sudden, swift coronary after unloading a truck with Inocencia. Corazón had watched the two men working like brothers, in silent camaraderie, as they always did, in perfect unison—Inocencia inside the truck, handing down boxes to Manuel, who stacked them in the back room of the store. Corazón had noticed the paleness of Manuel's skin and the heavy perspiration, though it was a cold day. But she had been busy waiting on customers in front. When she heard the truck drive away with Inocencia at the wheel—on its way back to Miami to pick up fresh produce from the Island—Corazón had gone to find Manuel and insist that he take a break. But he had already collapsed, as quietly as had his mother all those years before. Corazón knew CPR and worked feverishly to bring him back, shouting all the while for an ambulance. There was one customer in the store—the old man, who spoke no English but who managed to dial the number written on the bulletin board behind the counter. The ambulance arrived and took her and Manuel to an emergency room, where he was declared dead on arrival.

Inocencia would have to be told about Manuel's death. She had to be there when he arrived in the morning. More than anything else, except perhaps the wake scheduled at the Ramírez funeral home for the next day and following that, the funeral—where Corazón expected most of the population of the barrio to show up, and to have to stand up to all the condolences by people who loved Manuel—she hated to have to break the news to Inocencia.

She remembered the day the Peruvian Indian had first appeared at the store. They had been doing all the work themselves then, from stocking to waiting on customers ten hours a day, and Manuel was driving to the docks of New York and occasionally to Miami for the fresh Island products he insisted on having. They could not afford to hire help yet, with the store just barely breaking even as they established themselves in the barrio. People here were slow to trust newcomers and loyal to the old bodega, Cheo's place, which was really more a domino hall and package shop. The ice had been broken when Manuel and Cheo became friends and encouraged each other's customers to patronize both places. That was one of Manuel's gifts, in Corazón's eyes—he had the magic touch when it came to people. One morning Manuel drove up to the front of the store in the rental truck he had used to pick up stock in the city. As usual, Corazón got ready to help him unload. As she watched Manuel stack the cartons in the back, she noticed a man squatting in front of the front door, basically blocking her way. She observed him for a minute, trying to determine whether he looked suspicious and she should call the Paterson police. He looked like a statue carved in bronze, totally immobile, unblinking. He was wearing a heavy wool poncho that covered most of his compact body. His face was purely Indian: the sculpted cheekbones, long nose, and onyx eyes of the Inca. His age could have been anywhere from twenty to fifty. There were no lines to indicate the passing of time on this man's face. He watched Manuel as intently as Corazón watched *him*. Then, with a slow and fluid motion, he rose from his squatting position and approached the back of the truck. Although Corazón was ready to take action should he make any threatening move, the man simply stood there until Manuel raised his eyes and acknowledged him with a puzzled nod. He had not been aware of his presence; that was obvious to Corazón. Since Manuel was holding up an obviously heavy box of canned goods, the man extended his arms toward Manuel, Manuel passed the carton down, and the action was repeated again and again until the truck was unloaded. It was like a choreographed dance. Corazón did not see either man's lips move. No words had been exchanged between them. But by the time she unlocked the front door to let them in, Corazón knew they had an employee.

After the shelves had been stocked, the men went in the back to crush the cartons, and although Corazón strained to hear, all she could make out was an occasional chuckle from Manuel and murmurs that were impossible to decipher. When they finally emerged, the man had removed his poncho, and Corazón noticed how thin, almost emaciated he was, but strong-looking like a runner. The tendons in his arms were like brown cords. He was as small as a twelve-year-old boy, but he had the look of a man who had endured much.

"This is Inocencia Belaval, Corazón. He is from Peru."

Corazón almost extended her hand to the silent Inocencia, but he was looking down at the floor and not at her during the introduction. It was a gesture of respect, not humility. Corazón observed the almost imperceptible bow of the head, and how Inocencia looked directly into her husband's eyes after Manuel had spoken her name. It was all stated in silence: Inocencia acknowledged her as his boss's wife, but he worked for Manuel only. Corazón understood this and was a little irritated by it. The store belonged as much to her as to Manuel. In fact, she kept the books, paid the bills, and made all the decisions except those in the only area that really interested Manuel—the ordering of stock and its display in the store. But as the weeks passed and she saw how important Inocencia's quiet companionship was to Manuel, she began to feel differently about him. It was not a competition for Manuel's attention; Corazón noticed how inconspicuous Inocencia made himself when she was around. He was always busy in the back, organizing, sweeping, counting, and emerging only when she got busy with customers. Then he would simply do what needed to be done, from bagging to carrying groceries for old people or pregnant women across the street to El Building, where most of their customers lived. Corazón became curious as to what he did when he was not working, and she asked Manuel where Inocencia lived and whether he had a family. Manuel said that all he knew was that Inocencia had a room in a boarding house and that he had a wife and children in a mountain village in Peru. Apparently, Inocencia had walked and hitched rides from Peru to Mexico, lived there for a while and then crossed over to the United States. He had made his way to New York by bus, then to Paterson after he found out that there were better job opportunities here. Manuel also admitted that Inocencia was not a United States citizen.

"But that could get us in trouble with the law, Manuel." Corazón had really felt frightened about having an illegal alien working for them. But Manuel had smiled mysteriously and opened his ledger, where he had a stack of documents with the United States Customs and Immigration seal on them.

"I have contacted an attorney, Corazón. The process has been started to make Inocencia a citizen. It will take some time, but we can do it."

"We can do it?" Corazón had felt offended that Manuel had done this without consulting her—the first time in their married lives that he had failed to confide in her. But she managed to keep her anger in check when she realized that Manuel wanted to do this for his friend without her help.

The men's friendship had grown and deepened. Corazón was aware of it and knew that perhaps Manuel was filling a need that she had not been able to fulfill in their lives: a son.

IV

The two years after Doña Serena's death had been years of hard work and sacrifice for Corazón and Manuel. Heartbroken, Manuel poured all his energies into the catering business which Corazón now directed from Doña Serena's house. Their goal was to save enough money to move to the States and open a store.

Reluctantly, Corazón had contacted her sister, Consuelo, now living with her husband in Paterson and expecting a child. It was Consuelo, lonely for her sister, who encouraged them to make the move. She would find them an apartment in the building where she lived. Corazón made herself believe that leaving the Island and starting a new life in America would help her get over the tragedy of being childless. At the end of two years, they had sold the little plot of land and house Doña Serena had left them and taken the airplane from San Juan to New York.

Corazón had not let her fear of the future show as they landed at La Guardia Airport nor as they rode in Gustavo's car through the labyrinthine city and across the gray Hudson River toward another maze of buildings which would be their new home. She and Manuel held hands in the back seat. At least they had each other.

Manuel had taken to barrio life quickly; she saw how the crowded apartment building everyone called El Building suited him. Each person he met was a future customer of his dream store. He became popular with the women because he spent time talking about food with them. The men liked him because he brought with him the dreams they had all had once and forgotten: to start a business in America, to prosper.

Corazón went with him to look for locations and soon they found the place they wanted. It had once been an Italian deli, and Manuel claimed that he could still smell in the wood the spices that had been sold there. It had "corazón y alma," he claimed, making a pun with her name, "heart and soul." So they had rented the place and Manuel had hired an unemployed artist from the Island to paint the sign on their window. He had not allowed Corazón to come to the place that day. He had wanted to surprise her. That night he took her to see the huge letters blocked in brilliant red: CORAZÓN'S CAFÉ. Under it there was a plump heart with the inscription "M ama C" in the middle. Manuel loves Corazón. She had cried. Manuel had his dream and she had him. What more could she ask for? She knew the answer to her own question. A child, a child. But she buried it deep in her heart that night as she stood in front of Corazón's Café. She was lucky enough.

Slowly the store had become part of the barrio. Manuel, Inocencia, and she worked as a team. There were good years and bad, but she had settled into a role that she had not foreseen. Some of the residents of El Building saw her as a confidante. It must have been the way she appeared, sitting behind the counter: a plump mother to everyone. She had gained weight—which Manuel said he liked: "The more of Corazón there is, the more of Corazón I love," he was fond of saying. A childless woman who knew how to keep secrets, she was unusual in the barrio where women married young, had more children than they could afford, and passed the time gossiping at each other's kitchen tables. Not everyone was like that, of course. Some of the young women graduated from high school and got good jobs and good places to live in the suburbs. She saw the changes that came over them. They were slim, spoke only English even when addressed in Spanish, and came to her store to buy Puerto Rican products only during holidays. The Island to them was an exotic place where their parents had been born long ago. Corazón listened to their mothers' laments about their hijas and *el olvido*. It was not hard for the young people to forget the barrio. Life there was hard. But, as Manuel liked to say, at least there was life in the barrio. To him the suburbs were a fancy prison where you went to retire from life. And so Corazón also learned to stop wanting her own house. After all, there was only the two of them. They didn't need much room. And besides, they spent ten to twelve hours a day in the store, going home only to sleep.

And her life had meaning—all the people who depended on her and Manuel to provide them with a taste of home. There was not a birth, funeral, or holiday celebrated in the barrio that they were not a part of: Manuel was never happier than when he was planning the food to celebrate life and never more beautiful in Corazón's eyes than when he comforted the grieving widow or orphan with food prepared with all the care and love he had to give. And she made it possible by doing all the work needed to make his labor of love easy for him. She learned to speak good English in order to deal with suppliers and creditors. She took accounting courses at night school and kept books. She paid bills and made telephone calls. They were a good team, she and Manuel.

But she had again been betrayed by El Destino. Fate had tricked her once more and taken away her man, her partner, her anchor in life. Corazón heard the clock's hands move—it was that quiet in the store. It was midnight.

V

She must have fallen asleep sometime during the night, her head cradled on her arms on the counter. When Corazón opened her eyes it was to find Inocencia outside the door, standing like a statue. She had no idea how long he had been there, but obviously he had seen her through the glass and not come in while she was asleep, although he had a key. She glanced at the wall clock as she hurried to open the front door. It was 5:45. They usually opened at six in order to serve coffee and pastries to those heading for work. Corazón mentally prepared for the day as she always had, even though she was also making plans to tell Inocencia that she was going to close Corazón's Café. She would ask Cheo to give the man a job. She was certain he would hire Inocencia. It had been a standard joke between Manuel and Cheo that Inocencia was the kind of worker you had to keep a secret or someone would steal him away. But it had been loyalty, not just the modest salary they were able to pay him, that had kept him at the café for eight years. Inocencia was now a United States citizen and had brought his wife and two teenage children to Paterson. Corazón had been surprised that he was old enough to have grown children. And she had developed a good relationship with his family too, although they, like Inocencia, kept very much to themselves. Manuel had been beside himself with joy when the official citizenship papers had come through. And it had been the one and only time when Corazón had heard Inocencia laugh aloud. She opened the door and helped Inocencia bring in the boxes of frozen pasteles, the banana leaves in iced containers for the women who preferred to make their own, and all the other holiday food that had to be driven from Miami up to Paterson for Thanksgiving and Christmas. She waited until the truck was empty and Inocencia was taking his usual break, sitting on a crate, smoking a cigar he had bought from a Cuban tobacconist: his only indulgence. Corazón then came into the storeroom.

In Spanish she said: "Inocencia, I have something important to tell you." He looked not at her but at the smoke rising in a spiral from the cigar in his hand.

"Manuel is dead. Está muerto." The words were so powerful on her tongue that Corazón broke down in sobs. She covered her face, knowing that this would embarrass the shy and reserved Inocencia. But she felt a warm hand on her shoulder and uncovered her face. He had come closer and was standing in front of her, looking straight into her eyes. He too had tears streaming down his cheeks.

"Ya lo sé," he said. He knew it already. Before she could ask him how he knew, a loud knock came at the door. Without thinking, Corazón rushed to the front. It was six in the morning. Old Doña Iris, wrapped in a black shawl, was peering in the store through the glass. When Corazón unlocked the door, she saw that a small crowd had gathered in front. Doña Iris walked imperiously in as she always did but came directly toward Corazón, who had not yet assumed her place on the high stool behind the counter. The old woman hugged Corazón tightly, planted a loud kiss on her cheek, then demanded in her loud voice:

"Did my banana leaves come in? How am I going to make pasteles in time for Thanksgiving without the leaves?" And she headed for the freezer in the back of the store. The others came in more quietly, but each one of them stopped to embrace her. Her sister, Consuelo, and her niece, Cory, who was also Corazón's goddaughter, took their place next to her as her family while she received condolences from her neighbors and customers. Inocencia came out to help her make coffee and serve *pastelillos*, and Corazón listened to them talk about her Manuel. Even when everyone had left for their daily occupations, and Inocencia was in the back organizing and sweeping as he did every day, Corazón felt Manuel's presence in the store. Would the loneliness come back after he was laid to rest far away from the barrio? Could she bear to keep doing alone the things they had done together all these years? And there was still the empty apartment she would return to that night. Corazón allowed these questions to come and go as she waited on her customers that day. And when Roberto rushed in to say that Lydia had given birth to a little boy that morning and that she wanted more than anything else for Corazón to come see them at St. Joseph's Hospital and to bring her something sweet to eat, what could she do? She promised the excited young man that she would be there that afternoon. And when Don Cándido came in, looking as old as Methuselah but still willing to proclaim his views on the world to anyone who would listen, she listened. He had lost two sons to ideology in Cuba. One fighting for Fidel and the other one, a poet the government did not approve of, languishing in a prison. Don Cándido had made up his mind not to die before his son was freed. He kept himself alive by writing letters to judges, politicians, and the president and by talking and talking and talking. Corazón's Café was his forum and his refuge.

"*Libertad!*" Don Cándido waved a rolled-up newspaper at her as he headed for the coffee pot. And Corazón sat down to listen. He would drink several cups of espresso, talk about politics, read her a poem his son had written years ago before his imprisonment, and then leave—recharged—to visit his few surviving old friends, to talk away death for one more day.

The day passed quicker than she had expected, since each customer demanded her attention in a complete way. That afternoon she left the store in Inocencia's hands and took the bus to St. Joseph's Hospital. Lydia, whose mother had passed away from cancer, was waiting for her with the tiny bundle in her arms. She asked Corazón to hold him.

The baby had the face of a wise old man and a shock of black hair at the very top of his head. Corazón pronounced him beautiful. Roberto burst into the room with a bunch of flowers in his hands. He shouted from the door: "Is Manuel awake?"

Hearing her husband's name said with so much joy stunned Corazón. Lydia hurried to explain.

"I was just about to tell you, Corazón. We have decided to name our son Manuel."

"Manuel," Corazón said, and the tiny boy in her arms opened his eyes and began to cry for his mother.

That night Corazón and Inocencia closed Corazón's Café together and walked to El Building—he had accompanied her there without asking. He stood silently while she searched her purse for her apartment key. Knowing him as she did, Corazón knew he was waiting for her to say something.

"I will meet you at 5:30 tomorrow, Inocencia. We have a lot to do before the funeral." She had had to pause after the awful word, but Inocencia continued to listen as if he knew that her sentence was not finished—"and a lot to do before Thanksgiving and Christmas."

"Buenas noches, Doña Corazón." Inocencia had never spoken her name directly to her; he had always called Manuel *Don* Manuel, although they were more like brothers than boss and employee.

"Buenas noches, *Don* Inocencia," Corazón replied and saw the brief smile pass over Inocencia's serious face before he nodded and disappeared around the corner. Corazón then entered El Building. At the bottom of the staircase, she took a deep breath, remembering Manuel's claim, that, simply from the lingering smells, he could tell her what each family in each apartment had had for dinner that evening and whether they had bought the condiments at Corazón's Café. Corazón inhaled deeply the aromas of her country and started the climb up to her home.

AMERICAN HISTORY

I once read in a *Ripley's Believe It or Not* column that Paterson, New Jersey, is the place where the Straight and Narrow (streets) intersect. The Puerto Rican tenement known as El Building was one block up from Straight. It was, in fact, the corner of Straight and Market; not "at" the corner, but *the* corner. At almost any hour of the day, El Building was like a monstrous jukebox, blasting out *salsas* from open windows as the residents, mostly new immigrants just up from the island, tried to drown out whatever they were currently enduring with loud music. But the day President Kennedy was shot, there was a profound silence in El Building, even the abusive tongues of viragoes, the cursing of the unemployed, and the screeching of small children had been somehow muted. President Kennedy was a saint to these people. In fact, soon his photograph would be hung alongside the Sacred Heart and over the Spiritist altars that many women kept in their apartments. He would become part of the hierarchy of martyrs they prayed to for favors that only one who had died for a cause would understand.

On the day that President Kennedy was shot, my ninth-grade class had been out in the fenced playground of Public School Number 13. We had been given "free" exercise time and had been ordered by our P.E. teacher, Mr. DePalma, to "keep moving." That meant that the girls should jump rope and the boys toss basketballs through a hoop at the far end of the yard. He in the meantime would "keep an eye" on us from just inside the building.

It was a cold gray day in Paterson. The kind that warns of early snow. I was miserable, since I had forgotten my gloves and my knuckles were turning red and raw from the jump rope. I was also taking a lot of abuse from the black girls for not turning the rope hard and fast enough for them.

"Hey, Skinny Bones, pump it, girl. Ain't you got no energy today?" Gail, the biggest of the black girls who had the other end of the rope yelled, "Didn't you eat your rice and beans and pork chops for breakfast today?"

The other girls picked up the "pork chop" and made it into a refrain: "pork chop, pork chop, did you eat your pork chop?" They entered the double ropes in pairs and exited without tripping or missing a beat. I felt a burning on my cheeks, and then my glasses fogged up so that I could not manage to coordinate the jump rope with Gail. The chill was doing to me what it always did, entering my bones, making me cry, humiliating me. I hated the city, especially in winter. I hated Public School Number 13. I hated my skinny flat-chested body, and I envied the black girls who could jump rope so fast that their legs became a blur. They always seemed to be warm while I froze.

There was only one source of beauty and light for me that school year. The only thing I had anticipated at the start of the semester. That was seeing Eugene. In August, Eugene and his family had moved into the only house on the block that had a yard and trees. I could see his place from my window in El Building. In fact, if I sat on the fire escape I was literally suspended above Eugene's backyard. It was my favorite spot to read my library books in the summer. Until that August the house had been occupied by an old Jewish couple. Over the years I had become part of their family, without their knowing it, of course. I had a view of their kitchen and their backyard, and though I could not hear what they said, I knew when they were arguing, when one of them was sick, and many other things. I knew all this by watching them at mealtimes. I could see their kitchen table, the sink and the stove. During good times, he sat at the table and read his newspapers while she fixed the meals. If they argued, he would leave and the old woman would sit and stare at nothing for a long time. When one of them was sick, the other would come and get things from the kitchen and carry them out on a tray. The old man had died in June. The last week of school I had not seen him at the table at all. Then one day I saw that there was a crowd in the kitchen. The old woman had finally emerged from the house on the arm of a stocky middle-aged woman whom I had seen there a few times before, maybe her daughter. Then a man had carried out suitcases. The house had stood empty for weeks. I had had to resist the temptation to climb down into the yard and water the flowers the old lady had taken such good care of.

By the time Eugene's family moved in, the yard was a tangled mass of weeds. The father had spent several days mowing, and when he finished, I didn't see the red, yellow, and purple clusters that meant flowers to me from where I sat. I didn't see this family sit down at the kitchen table together. It was just the mother, a red-headed tall woman who wore a white uniform—a nurse's, I guessed it was; the father was gone before I got up in the morning and was never there at dinner time. I only saw him on weekends when they sometimes sat on lawn chairs under the oak tree, each hidden behind a section of the newspaper; and there was Eugene. He was tall and blond, and he wore glasses. I liked him right away because he sat at the kitchen table and read books for hours. That summer, before we had even spoken one word to each other, I kept him company on my fire escape.

Once school started, I looked for him in all my classes, but P.S. 13 was a huge, overpopulated place and it took me days and many discrete questions to discover that Eugene was in honors classes for all his subjects; classes that were not open to me because English was not my first language, though I was a straight A student. After much maneuvering I managed "to run into him" in the hallway where his locker was—on the other side of the building from mine—and in study hall at the library, where he first seemed to notice me but did not speak; and finally, on the way home after school one day when I decided to approach him directly, though my stomach was doing somersaults.

I was ready for rejection, snobbery, the worst. But when I came up to him, practically panting in my nervousness, and blurted out: "You're Eugene. Right?" He smiled, pushed his glasses up on his nose, and nodded. I saw then that he was blushing deeply. Eugene liked me, but he was shy. I did most of the talking that day. He nodded and smiled a lot. In the weeks that followed, we walked home together. He would linger at the corner of El Building for a few minutes then walk down to his two-story house. It was not until Eugene moved into that house that I noticed that El Building blocked most of the sun and that the only spot that got a little sunlight during the day was the tiny square of earth the old woman had planted with flowers.

I did not tell Eugene that I could see inside his kitchen from my bedroom. I felt dishonest, but I liked my secret sharing of his evenings, especially now that I knew what he was reading, since we chose our books together at the school library.

One day my mother came into my room as I was sitting on the windowsill staring out. In her abrupt way she said: "Elena, you are acting 'moony.'" *Enamorada* was what she really said—that is, like a girl stupidly infatuated. Since I had turned fourteen and started menstruating my mother had been more vigilant than ever. She acted as if I was going to go crazy or explode or something if she didn't watch me and nag me all the time about being a señorita now. She kept talking about virtue, morality, and other subjects that did not interest me in the least. My mother was unhappy in Paterson, but my father had a good job at the blue jeans factory in Passaic, and soon, he kept assuring us, we would be moving to our own house there. Every Sunday we drove out to the suburbs of Paterson, Clifton, and Passaic, out to where people mowed grass on Sundays in the summer and where children made snowmen in the winter from pure white snow, not like the gray slush of Paterson, which seemed to fall from the sky in that hue. I had learned to listen to my parents' dreams, which were spoken in Spanish, as fairy tales, like the stories about life in the island paradise of Puerto Rico before I was born. I had been to the Island once as a little girl, to grandmother's funeral, and all I remembered was wailing women in black, my mother becoming hysterical and being given a pill that made her sleep two days, and me feeling lost in a crowd of strangers all claiming to be my aunts, uncles, and cousins. I had actually been glad to return to the city. We had not been back there since then, though my parents talked constantly about buying a house on the beach someday, retiring on the island—that was a common topic among the residents of El Building. As for me, I was going to go to college and become a teacher.

But after meeting Eugene I began to think of the present more than of the future. What I wanted now was to enter that house I had watched for so many years. I wanted to see the other rooms where the old people had lived and where the boy I liked spent his time. Most of all, I wanted to sit at the kitchen table with Eugene like two adults, like the old man and his wife had done, maybe drink some coffee and talk about books. I had started reading *Gone with the Wind*. I was enthralled by it, with the daring and the passion of the beautiful girl living in a mansion, and with her devoted parents and the slaves who did everything for them. I didn't believe such a world had ever really existed, and I wanted to ask Eugene some questions, since he and his parents, he had told me, had come up from Georgia, the same place where the novel was set. His father worked for a company that had transferred him to Paterson. His mother was very unhappy, Eugene said, in his beautiful voice that rose and fell over words in a strange, lilting way. The kids at school called him the Hick and made fun of the way he talked. I knew I was his only friend so far, and I liked that, though I felt sad for him sometimes. Skinny Bones and the Hick was what they called us at school when we were seen together.

The day Mr. DePalma came out into the cold and asked us to line up in front of him was the day that President Kennedy was shot. Mr. DePalma, a short, muscular man with slicked-down black hair, was the science teacher, P.E. coach, and disciplinarian at P.S. 13. He was the teacher to whose homeroom you got assigned if you were a troublemaker, and the man called out to break up playground fights, and to escort violently angry teenagers to the office. And Mr. DePalma was the man who called your parents in for "a conference."

That day, he stood in front of two rows of mostly black and Puerto Rican kids, brittle from their efforts to "keep moving" on a November day that was turning bitter cold. Mr. DePalma, to our complete shock, was crying. Not just silent adult tears, but really sobbing. There were a few titters from the back of the line where I stood, shivering.

"Listen," Mr. DePalma raised his arms over his head as if he were about to conduct an orchestra. His voice broke, and he covered his face with his hands. His barrel chest was heaving. Someone giggled behind me.

"Listen," he repeated, "something awful has happened." A strange gurgling came from his throat, and he turned around and spit on the cement behind him.

"Gross," someone said, and there was a lot of laughter.

"The president is dead, you idiots. I should have known that wouldn't mean anything to a bunch of losers like you kids. Go home." He was shrieking now. No one moved for a minute or two, but then a big girl let out a "yeah!" and ran to get her books piled up with the others against the brick wall of the school building. The others followed in a mad scramble to get to their things before somebody caught on. It was still an hour to the dismissal bell.

A little scared, I headed for El Building. There was an eerie feeling on the streets. I looked into Mario's drugstore, a favorite hangout for the high school crowd, but there were only a couple of old Jewish men at the soda bar, talking with the short order cook in tones that sounded almost angry, but they were keeping their voices low. Even the traffic on one of the busiest intersections in Paterson—Straight Street and Park Avenue—seemed to be moving slower. There were no horns blasting that day. At El Building, the usual little group of unemployed men were not hanging out on the front stoop, making it difficult for women to enter the front door. No music spilled out from open doors in the hallway. When I walked into our apartment, I found my mother sitting in front of the grainy picture of the television set.

She looked up at me with a tear-streaked face and just said: "Dios mío," turning back to the set as if it were pulling at her eyes. I went into my room.

Though I wanted to feel the right thing about President Kennedy's death, I could not fight the feeling of elation that stirred in my chest. Today was the day I was to visit Eugene in his house. He had asked me to come over after school to study for an American history test with him. We had also planned to walk to the public library together. I looked down into his yard. The oak tree was bare of leaves, and the ground looked gray with ice. The light through the large kitchen window of his house told me that El Building blocked the sun to such an extent that they had to turn lights on in the middle of the day. I felt ashamed about it. But the white kitchen table with the lamp hanging just above it looked cozy and inviting. I would soon sit there, across from Eugene, and I would tell him about my perch just above his house. Maybe I would.

In the next thirty minutes I changed clothes, put on a little pink lipstick, and got my books together. Then I went in to tell my mother that I was going to a friend's house to study. I did not expect her reaction.

"You are going out today?" The way she said "today" sounded as if a storm warning had been issued. It was said in utter disbelief. Before I could answer, she came toward me and held my elbows as I clutched my books.

"Hija, the president has been killed. We must show respect. He was a great man. Come to church with me tonight."

She tried to embrace me, but my books were in the way. My first impulse was to comfort her, she seemed so distraught, but I had to meet Eugene in fifteen minutes.

"I have a test to study for, Mamá. I will be home by eight."

"You are forgetting who you are, Niña. I have seen you staring down at that boy's house. You are heading for humiliation and pain." My mother said this in Spanish and in a resigned tone that surprised me, as if she had no intention of stopping me from "heading for humiliation and pain." I started for the door. She sat in front of the TV, holding a white handkerchief to her face.

I walked out to the street and around the chain-link fence that separated El Building from Eugene's house. The yard was neatly edged around the little walk that led to the door. It always amazed me how Paterson, the inner core of the city, had no apparent logic to its architecture. Small, neat, single residences like this one could be found right next to huge, dilapidated apartment buildings like El Building. My guess was that the little houses had been there first, then the immigrants had come in droves, and the monstrosities had been raised for them—the Italians, the Irish, the Jews, and now us, the Puerto Ricans, and the blacks. The door was painted a deep green: *verde*, the color of hope. I had heard my mother say it: *Verde Esperanza*.

I knocked softly. A few suspenseful moments later the door opened just a crack. The red, swollen face of a woman appeared. She had a halo of red hair floating over a delicate ivory face—the face of a doll—with freckles on the nose. Her smudged eye makeup made her look unreal to me, like a mannequin seen through a warped store window.

"What do you want?" Her voice was tiny and sweet-sounding, like a little girl's, but her tone was not friendly.

"I'm Eugene's friend. He asked me over. To study." I thrust out my books, a silly gesture that embarrassed me almost immediately.

"You live there?" She pointed up to El Building, which looked particularly ugly, like a gray prison with its many dirty windows and rusty fire escapes. The woman had stepped halfway out, and I could see that she wore a white nurse's uniform with "St. Joseph's Hospital" on the name tag.

"Yes. I do."

She looked intently at me for a couple of heartbeats, then said as if to herself, "I don't know how you people do it." Then directly to me: "Listen. Honey. Eugene doesn't want to study with you. He is a smart boy. Doesn't need help. You understand me. I am truly sorry if he told you that you could come over. He cannot study with you. It's nothing personal. You understand? We won't be in this place much longer, no need for him to get close to people, it'll just make it harder for him later. Run back home now."

I couldn't move. I just stood there in shock at hearing these things said to me in such a honey-drenched voice. I had never heard an accent like hers except for Eugene's softer version. It was as if she were singing me a little song.

"What's wrong? Didn't you hear what I said?" She seemed very angry, and I finally snapped out of my trance, I turned away from the green door and heard her close it gently.

Our apartment was empty when I got home. My mother was in someone else's kitchen, seeking the solace she needed. Father would come in from his late shift at midnight. I would hear them talking softly in the kitchen for hours that night. They would not discuss their dreams for the future, or life in Puerto Rico, as they often did; that night they would talk sadly about the young widow and her two children, as if they were family. For the next few days, we would observe *luto* in our apartment; that is, we would practice restraint and silence—no loud music or laughter. Some of the women of El Building would wear black for weeks.

That night, I lay in my bed, trying to feel the right thing for our dead president. But the tears that came up from a deep source inside me were strictly for me. When my mother came to the door, I pretended to be sleeping. Sometime during the night, I saw from my bed the streetlight come on. It had a pink halo around it. I went to my window and pressed my face to the cool glass. Looking up at the light I could see the white snow falling like a lace veil over its face. I did not look down to see it turning gray as it touched the ground below.

MY ROSETTA

Sister Rosetta came into my life in 1966, at exactly the right moment. I was fourteen, beginning to stretch my bones after the long sleep of childhood, and the whole nation seemed to be waking up along with me. Each day the transistor radio I took everywhere informed me that the streets were alive with rebellion. Rock and roll filled the airwaves with the throbbing sounds like those the heart makes when you are young and still listening to it—sounds that made me want to dance, yell, break out of my parents' cocoon of an apartment, to sprout wings and fly away from my predictable life and (what I feared most) a predictable future as a good Catholic barrio woman. Instead, I was signed up for classes leading to my confirmation in the Catholic church, spiritual preparation for the bishop's symbolic slap in the face: turn the other cheek, girl, you are now one of us humble followers of Christ. But my teacher in the ways of Christian humility, Sister Rosetta, was anything but the docile bride of Jesus I had expected.

She was not an attractive woman. Her face, although bright with wit, belonged on an Irish guy with a tough job, perhaps a construction foreman or a cop. If a nun's coif had not framed those features—the slightly bulbous nose, plump red-veined cheeks and close-set eyes—this could have been the face of a heavy drinker or a laborer. She walked without grace but with a self-assured step we could hear approaching on the hardwood floors of the church basement where our lessons were held after school on cold winter afternoons in Paterson, New Jersey. Her rosary swinging from side to side on her habit's skirts, she strode in and slammed on the desk top whatever she was carrying that day. Then she'd lift herself onto the desk and face us, hands on hips as if to say, *What a shit job this is.*

And it was. Common knowledge had it that Sister Rosetta was assigned all the routine work of the convent by the Mother Superior to keep her busy and out of trouble. There was a rumor among us public school kids that Sister Rosetta had been arrested for taking part in a civil rights demonstration. And that she had been sent to our mainly Puerto Rican parish so that Father Jones, our saintly missionary pastor, could keep her under his wing. We found it funny to think of the shy, skinny man standing up to Sister Rosetta.

"OK, my little dumplings," Sister Rosetta would greet us, squinting like a coach about to motivate her team. "Today we are going to get in touch with our souls through music. Now listen carefully. You've never heard anything like this." Out of curiosity at first, then in near rapture, that day I listened to the exotic music of Ravi Shankar emerge from the old turntable Sister Rosetta had dragged in. The celestial notes of his sitar enveloped me in a gauzy veil of sound, stirring me in a new way. Sister had tacked the album cover on the cork board, and as I looked deeply into Shankar's onyx eyes he seemed to look back: in his gaze there were answers to questions I was almost ready to ask.

She must have noticed my enchantment, because Sister Rosetta handed me that record album as I was walking out of her overheated classroom. All she said was, "Bring it back without a scratch." Much to my mother's annoyance, I played Shankar's music every day after school in my room while I did my homework. She called it *los gatos peleando*, the cat-fight album; but to me the high, lingering notes were an alarm clock bringing me out of myself, out of ignorance and into the realm of the senses. For my thirteenth birthday I had received my own turntable and a Felipe Rodríguez album of Puerto Rican boleros, the romantic ballads my parents danced to at parties. I played the record occasionally for their sake, but Rodríguez's deep-throated laments about lost loves and weak women in tears did not appeal much to me. I liked the leaping, acrobatic images that Shankar's music induced, replacing my childhood dreams of flight.

In the guise of teaching Catholic doctrine, Sister Rosetta managed to introduce each of her classes to an eclectic curriculum that included folk music, Eastern philosophy, classical music, dance and yoga, world literary masterpieces, and popular culture. I watched in awe as this stocky, plain woman transformed herself into the most attractive person I knew whenever she talked with passionate eloquence about things all the other adults either ignored or disdained.

One day I was reading a book I had picked up in a restaurant booth. It was well worn, the front cover torn off as if someone had intended to hide his choice of reading material, and I had slipped it into my coat pocket before my parents noticed. "Lust" appearing several times on the back cover blurbs had enticed me to read the first chapter. Then the story had caught me in its sensational web: sex and sin described in clinical detail, right there in sentences and paragraphs just like the ones in my schoolbooks; characters who used drugs for fun; women who gained power through seduction.

This was a whole world I had only glimpsed in previews for movies I would not see when my father would take my mother and me to the theater that showed Spanish language films during the slow time on Sunday afternoons. I looked forward to these little forbidden clips that even in their brevity were more revealing than the Mexican or Argentinian films we watched, films with their predictable Cinderella themes of poor but talented (and, most important of all, *virtuous*) young women rescued from poverty, or from the danger of falling into a life of sin, by rich handsome men—after, of course, having surmounted many obstacles to their love. The characters were almost always great dancers and singers, and a mariachi band usually popped out from behind props to serenade the lovers at the appropriate moment. My parents held hands during the double feature, rapt in their escape into the fantasy. *May as well take what you can get*, I'd remind myself as I ate my popcorn, all the while making up in my head my own versions of the movies I did not get to see.

The book I had in my hands that day in Sister Rosetta's classroom, where I had arrived early to do my secret reading in solitude, had taken me into a dark, fascinating realm. Here were forbidden acts described in ordinary prose, no sermonizing about hells with boiling rivers of blood awaiting the sinners to be found in between the lies. Here was sanitized debauchery. Here was a world where drugs, sex, and fashion were all expensive pastimes. I knew about drug addiction from the news and neighborhood gossip, but the people shown there were either poor and dirty or exotic: hippies, gypsies, ghetto dwellers, and runaways, the lost people of our barrio who were the *drogadictos* our parents warned us about often. But in this book, drug use was exciting and glamorous. The women's clothes were described in the same intensely detailed manner as the rush they got from the pills and the diverse sex.

Transported out of my body by the text, I did not hear Sister Rosetta come in. She plucked the book out of my hands and, to my dismay, began reading aloud. In her no-nonsense voice, with that New Jersey accent, the drug-and-seduction scene sounded preposterous.

When Sister Rosetta slammed the book down on my desk, I kept my eyes lowered in shame. After a few moments, however, I was tricked by her silence into looking up, expecting an explosion of angry words. Instead, I saw Sister Rosetta trying hard not to laugh aloud.

"Girlie," she said, still chuckling as she went over and closed the door, it was still ten minutes until class time, "why are you reading this trash?" She didn't wait for an answer. "Because it's there. Right? And as far as trash goes, this is pretty interesting." She let out her characteristic loud whistle to indicate that she was impressed. "Tell me, does reading this make you feel good or does it just tickle your fancy?"

Although baffled by her question, I was grateful that she had not reprimanded me, and I tried to think of an answer. I did feel excited about the things described in the book, of course, but I couldn't confess these feelings to Sister Rosetta or to anyone for that matter. I hadn't gone to confession for weeks because I could not bring myself to tell the priest about my dirty thoughts. Every day I risked dying without the sacraments, my soul blackened by mortal sin.

"I enjoy reading this book, Sister."

"I can see why. You want to know things your parents or I will not teach you, and this book tells you about them—in glorious detail!" She laughed again. Then she sat on her desk and looked closely at me. "Honey, I can tell you have a hungry mind. Don't feed it junk. You wanna read about sex? It's mankind's favorite subject, from the Bible to Fanny Hill. People just can't stop writing about it. Next time you come, I'll have a few good books with plenty of sex in them for you. But these books weren't written by some glamour puss for the money. They're art."

My face was burning. I couldn't believe that a nun, even the radical Sister Rosetta, was talking about sex so openly and offering to bring me books on the subject. For a minute I thought she was testing me, waiting for me to apologize and do penance. But students were now milling outside the door, and Sister Rosetta just said, "I'll keep this," dropping the book deep into one of her habit's bottomless pockets.

The next week she handed me a paper sack containing *Women in Love*, *Madame Bovary*, and *Wuthering Heights*. They were public library copies; she had actually checked out two books that I thought might be included in the Church's list of banned writings! All she said was, "Make sure you put them in the drop box by the due date."

Of course, I went home and lost myself in them. D. H. Lawrence appealed to me most, with his reckless immersion into language. Flaubert was too careful and precise for my taste. (I did not yet suspect that I had begun to read a page for the effect the words had on me rather than just for the juicy parts.) But it was the storm surging within Heathcliff that transported my imagination to places I wasn't yet quite able to identify.

Sister Rosetta continued to feed me books, neither asking me what I wanted nor quizzing me on their considerable effects. Under her tutelage, I read Hawthorne, Poe, *The Odyssey*, the stories of Katherine Anne Porter, Dante, the Romantic poets, even James Joyce (whose *Ulysses* was totally impenetrable, so I gave up on it). And always there was D. H. Lawrence, my dark, mysterious man, and the Brontës who, like me, lived on the small planet of circumstance, spoke to me about boundaries and how a smart woman might take flight through art. All the words I did not yet possess were my source of secret torment and joy. Sister Rosetta's was a reading list without apparent order, but it all came together inside me. My vocabulary expanded, my English improved, my restlessness doubled.

From these books I learned about desire and passion, but also how to think about strong emotions. In grammar school I had once read a story about a boy who wanted muscles. An old man promises to teach him how to build his body in exchange for the boy's help with chores and errands. Day after day the boy chops wood, rakes the yard, paints the place, and does endless physical tasks for his mentor. Finally, many weeks later, the boy approaches the old man about keeping his end of the bargain. "It is time," the boy tells him. "I have done everything you have asked me to do: now teach me how to build muscles." Instead of answering, the old man leads the boy to a mirror. "Flex your arm," he says. And to the boy's amazement there are muscles in his arms.

I too was getting stronger without knowing it. I had begun to develop the inner eye that I needed to really see my life in the barrio and to look beyond it toward what I wanted from life. Why did the women around me complain about their lives of solitude and servitude but not take action? The only answer I got: *Así es la vida, Niña*. That's the way it is, our lives, your life, *la vida*. But why wouldn't I go into church with my head uncovered as men did? Why did I have to advertise my sexual status by the color of the *mantilla* I was told to wear: white for señoritas and black for married women? That seemed a silly custom to me. Did God really care about such minutiae, or was this simply another male prerogative, to be able to identify which women were still available and which were already someone else's property? When I asked, however, I was told that my question was *impertinente*, and that I was a *malcriada*, an ill-mannered child and an embarrassment to my parents. This was a word always spoken in a sort of angry hiss during family arguments, a word that implied I was risking more than I could fathom.

But there were too many illogical rules, especially for girls and women, that were simply followed by mothers and taught to daughters: do not interrupt or join men's conversations; serve men first at meals; and, more infuriating to me than anything else, I was told that all boys (including my brother) needed to be outside more and more as they got older in order to "experience" the world. Girls, however, needed to stay home more each year because the world became more dangerous for a female as she matured.

As the walls of our apartment were closing in on me, I became determined to break out from what I saw as a suffocating cycle of acceptance and adherence to tradition. In my adolescent anger I failed to see that my dark fantasy of flight from everything my Puerto Rican family and neighbors stood for was in large part a normal stage of rebellion in the special setting of the barrio. There was so much there that I already loved: the sense of security that it gave my parents, the familiarity that was an oasis from *la lucha* whenever they came back from the alien culture of the American city to this Spanish-speaking island where favors were the currency most valued and the rules of the game were familiar. You do for me, I do for you; mi *casa es su casa*, and remember *Compadre/Comadre*, when we are away from our *patria*, we are all *compañeros*, *¿Verdad?* But even then I perceived that there was a suspension of disbelief involved. To play out the barrio-as-island fantasy, everyone had to agree not to question the rules.

My rebellion began at this delicate juncture: I wanted, needed to learn how to see things for what they were before I could understand who I was in my more complex double world of school and home. The image I had in mind for myself was split: aligned with Joan Baez when I was feeling lyrical, but fiercely with Angela Davis when I seethed with the self-righteous fury of my struggle for autonomy. I wanted to break free, but first I had to have the right tools and a map for my great escape. Rosetta showed me how to get my hands on them.

A week before the bishop was due at our church to say confirmation mass, Sister Rosetta burst into our classroom with the layers of her skirts held high by huge safety pins, her muscular calves in the thick white cotton stockings displayed before our startled eyes. She had always worn the sleeves of the voluminous habit rolled back to her elbows, but this new alteration to the traditional medieval costume of the Sisters of Charity made her an outrageous sight to behold. I had never seen a nun's ankles, much less her legs. Without referring to her curious appearance, she taught the lesson for the day—a strange one if we were being programmed for humility. She talked about Christ's "righteous anger" at the money changers in the temple, how He had rebelled against an evil practice although it had been accepted in His time as tradition. As I took in Sister's every word, adding new ones to my vocabulary of rebellion, I felt my own chest filling up with the breath of Joan of Arc leading her soldiers to a holy battle. Rebellion.

"What is tradition?" she challenged, facing us in her military at-ease stance—eyes narrowed to slits.

After a long silence, I raised my hand: "Tradition is something that has always been done," I said.

"Like what? Gimme an example." With eyebrows raised nearly to her headgear, Sister Rosetta challenged me to state my position, to take a stand.

"Like wearing only certain types of clothes?" I cautiously ventured.

She smiled ironically at me, the eyebrows moving toward each other. "That is almost correct. Tradition is doing something because it has always been done. Sometimes this is good. It preserves culture, gives us tried-and-true ways to do things. But is it always good to do something in a particular way only because it has always been done that way?" She didn't wait for an answer this time: "No! Slavery was around for centuries; should we have kept that system? The guillotine is a quaint tradition. How about child labor?"

She rose to her full power as an orator that day. We looked at each other in amazement as Sister Rosetta listed horrors that at one time or another had been defended as tradition. Prejudice, cruelty to others, wars started with "traditional" enemies—it was a revelation to me to think from this new perspective, the beginning of hope for an argument against my parents' ways. Sister Rosetta's verbal rampage sparked the thought in my mind that it was possible to break free from a cycle. I began to understand that special power of words, the excitement that an image can generate.

Out of breath and her face flushed a bright red, Sister Rosetta concluded the day's class with a reading from Thoreau's "Civil Disobedience." Emboldened, I raised my hand again: "Is the idea of tradition sometimes used as an excuse for not changing things that need to be changed?" Her face relaxed, not quite into a smile but something better. What I had said was not yet my own thought. I had a good memory for quotes even then—a skill I later found useful for making impassioned speeches to my baffled relatives and as the lone Latina English student at college trying to impress her teachers. But leaders like to be quoted, and Sister Rosetta "noticed" me as a separate being in her captive motley crew of an audience.

Sister Rosetta's speech to us had been a rehearsal for a campaign she planned to initiate during the bishop's visit to our parish. Apparently, she had been in correspondence with other progressive nuns around the country. They had started a petition to modify the nun's traditional vestments so as to bring the Sisters of Charity into the twentieth century by liberating their limbs from the primitive shackles of cloth and heavy crosses, even as regular women were freeing their bodies from the modern harnesses of bras and girdles (at least the ones under the dreaded age of thirty that Abbie Hoffman warned us would be the end of innocence). I was behind Sister Rosetta one hundred percent. On our last day of class she brought in a box of "Hello My Name Is" stickers on which was printed, VOTE BLUE! in bold marker script. She asked us to wear them on our choir robes the day of confirmation. As it turned out, only a few of us did, since most of the other kids in my class thought that Sister Rosetta had gone too far this time and that the bishop's visit was the wrong time for politics.

On confirmation day I wore my VOTE BLUE! sticker proudly over my heart, pinned to my red and white choir robe. Did I imagine this, or did the bishop's hard eyes fall on the message right before he gave me my ceremonial slap? My cheek was still stinging when my mother came up to kiss me. Tears were in her eyes and also in mine, but for different reasons. Sister Rosetta's campaign was ultimately successful, since reform was in the air then, "the times they were a-changing" even in the Church. The caravan of cars she led to wherever nuns go to vote came back blowing horns in victory, and though many of the older sisters chose to keep their dangerous bulky habits, the younger ones, the strong new Sisters of Charity, walked with new freedom in reasonably lightweight, slate-blue outfits that did not come in the one-size-fits-all pattern of the old days.

That was doubtless a memorable triumph for Sister Rosetta. Though she may never know it, I regard myself as another of her triumphs. What *I* remember about the year I spent under this remarkable woman's tutelage are her teaching me to see with my whole self, not just with my eyes. Thanks to her, I learned that the power of knowledge lies in seeking the answer to the question I can always ask of the past, the present, and the future: *why?* Even now I can recall that summer, call up almost any memory in living color and in stereophonic sound, thanks to Sister Rosetta's training of my mind and her education of my senses. Her awareness-raising seminars were ridiculed by other nuns and laughed at by her more conservative students, but they gave me my first essential tool as a writer: the ability to absorb sensory detail from the pungent aroma of *la vida*, the siren call of religion, the aftertaste of victory. I learned to re-experience it all at will in my mind and later on the page. Those months were the beginning of my long affair with the word, or should I say my lifetime commitment to it? The seductive power of language was introduced into my life when I needed it the most by the most unlikely and remarkable of my mentors, my radical sister, my Rosetta.

CHAPTER 3

Boricua Women and Latinas

Facing Gendered Categorization and Stereotypes

> Art elevates our world beyond our daily struggle for survival. It gives us la lucha; that is the real fight for meaning and purpose. Without stories we will be empty shells performing necessary tasks without the satisfaction of knowing why. We are our stories and by reading them, writing them or sharing them we form our place like an island rising from the seafloor that we can call common ground. These islands start in the abstractions of what we share, not in the particulars. We are not the same in our choices of where we live, what we eat, how we present ourselves to the world, but we are one in our human experiences of birth and death, and out of this shared consciousness of experiences rises our common ground.
>
> —*Judith Ortiz Cofer, The West Carolina University Writers' Festival (2016)*

Judith Ortiz Cofer proudly billed herself as a Puerto Rican born on the island and raised in New Jersey and Augusta, Georgia, who in her last stage of production wrote from a bicultural perspective as a "Georgia Rican." Her ideological approach to literature highlighted the Puerto Rican struggle, which she often referred to as *la lucha*, a common term used in Puerto Rico that underscores the fights against adversities inherent in daily living. Although Ortiz Cofer's la lucha referred to the physical struggles of Boricuas to establish themselves within mainstream cultures, this popular term also had a strong activist connotation as used among Boricua political groups. Student-based groups, such as the Young Lords, had used direct references to armed fighting as their call to action. Their movement, which began in 1969, has been described as a direct attempt to aid Boricua communities in New York City and Chicago in dealing with their daily struggles in severely underserved barrios: "Many of the original Young Lords had been involved in the student and anti-war movements and wanted to apply the skills gained in that work to creating a community-based revolutionary organization" ("Palante!").

Like the earliest Latino and Latina writers, Ortiz Cofer was a pioneer spokesperson on behalf of her own ethnic communities while also functioning as an agent of social change. Nonetheless, as Blas Falconer and Lorraine M. López have underscored, readers must avoid a monolithic approach to reading Latinx literature, particularly by "resisting reductive, essentialist cultural narratives": "All Latinos share some Latin American heritage. Apart from this, there is no essential or singular trait of Latino identity" (1). For Ortiz Cofer, that Latina identity was heavily rooted in her experiences as a Boricua child and a young person growing up in New Jersey and Georgia.

In the introduction to *Lessons from a Writer's Life* (2011), a collection of short articles intended as a primer for young readers, Ortiz Cofer introduces the thematic parameters of her literary production as such: "I drew from my experiences as a child growing up in my native Puerto Rico, and later in New Jersey and Georgia, to create a structure for the pieces in this book. Together they tell the story of my self-invention as an American writer and teacher" (viii). Nonetheless, a notable undercurrent is Ortiz Cofer's positioning of herself as a devoted learner, stemming from her inherent condition as a newly arrived individual always in search of knowledge about her new surroundings. In "A Life Boat," she describes her initial childhood experiences as an immigrant: "Like the poet, the immigrant is primarily a metaphor maker, a translator of experience. Struggling between languages, I learned this skill early: how to answer the question ¿Cómo se dice? by making a comparison, by trying to access the unfamiliar road by following the familiar *camino* first" (22). She found her way in a different cultural milieu by "master[ing] a new language," a process not without considerable bumps in the road, so to speak: "These are the moments that are seared into the memory of a child struggling to master a new language: when you fail to know what everyone is supposed to know, and therefore to be 'like everyone else'" (22).

Overcoming a deeply felt sense of social alienation is the subject of "It's Like This," which emphasizes the different ways that she and her mother achieved cultural survival. Her mother chose to return to the island after the death of Ortiz Cofer's father and, without much effort, "reinvented herself as an island Puertorriqueña" (29), a shift that Ortiz Cofer contrasts against her own condition as a predominantly English-speaker: "In writing to and about her I have discovered that we newcomers to America are morphers rather than assimilationists, at least those of us who cannot or will not melt into the American pot. We shift our shapes, learn new vocabularies, and move ourselves or our modes to a climate that better suits our skin or personality types. I stayed with English, she returned to Spanish, and we live, with our choice of mother tongue, very different lives" (29).

Indeed, as she highlights in "What I Know," the first lesson she learned as a immigrant child was the power of the English language: "Early in my American life, I discovered the power of language to transform my reality, to shape my future. My reality then was intrinsically connected to Spanish and to my native culture, which was the small but familiar and safe world our parents could offer us within the confines of our home and the boundaries of our barrio" (viii). As a monolingual child, Ortiz Cofer was acutely affected by the frequent trips to Puerto Rico that allowed her family to live for extended periods of time in both Puerto Rico and New Jersey. That type of "back and forth" living pattern was indeed a rather peculiar displacement process that Edna Acosta Belén and Carlos E. Santiago have described in similar terms: "This uninterrupted *ir y venir* (back-and-forth movement) that stateside Puerto Ricans have with their homeland has introduced a new model of im/migrant assimilation and relationship to Anglo-American society that differs from the traditional 'melting pot' ideology" (87). Against the traditional permanent immigration processes, the ease of air travel "fostered a pattern of circular migration unheard of among other groups, who would do everything they could to stay permanently" (Morales 48).

During her early teenage years, Ortiz Cofer continued to experience extreme cultural immersion. In 1969, at the age fifteen, her father moved the family to Augusta, Georgia, where he had relatives in military service at nearby Fort Gordon. In *The Cruel Country*, she fully documented the cultural shock of arriving in Augusta. Her first impression of the iconic sleepy Southern town was not a positive one compared to the home she left behind. She remembers the great visual contrasts between two opposite geographies: "This Georgia landscape—I have described it in my work as 'Martian'—is as different from my native Island as any two places can be" (21).

The move was intended to be a temporary way out of Paterson. In the 1960s, as Ortiz Cofer underscores in *The Cruel Country*, Paterson was "a troubled place, racially torn and being considered as a candidate for urban renewal, if not urban resurrection" (162). The move coincided with her father's retirement from military service due to health conditions, which Ortiz Cofer described many years later as an acute depression that led to his suicide in a car accident. In an unexpected turn of events, the Ortiz family stopped their frequent stays in Puerto Rico. Although the family had a stable home for the first time and were no longer shifting among schools, they were cut off from access to the plentiful Puerto Rican popular culture found in Paterson's barrios.

For Ortiz Cofer, a New Jersey–raised Puerto Rican teenager, moving to the Deep South was certainly, as she described, "a traumatic shift" (*Cruel Country* 31). Though the family was leaving behind "riots and civil unrest" (31), Ortiz Cofer was privy to the racial strife that was also taking place in Augusta amid the civil rights movement. She was, in her own words, "the foreign girl, the dark child with a New Jersey-Puerto Rican accent, starting my sophomore year at the school where the all-white population was about to be forced to accept black as an alternate human color" (32). As it had been her experience in Paterson, she yet again experienced socio-ethnic alienation: "I stood outside both tight circles, feeling invisible" (32).

The impact of her transition to the peculiarities of Georgia's racial and cultural differences is the subject of "Who Is the Alien?" in *Lessons from a Writer's Life*. This is the most complete account of her initial impressions of Augusta, comparing her family's cultural uneasiness as that of "exiles in a foreign country" (14). The move had been particularly difficult for her mother, who felt that "all she knew and loved had been taken away from her: the Spanish-speaking neighbors, the barrio with its familiar business establishments, church services in her own language, and most social activities with other Puerto Rican people—the things that made her life in exile bearable, all gone" (14). Similarly, Ortiz Cofer noted her acute feeling of being "an alien in my new school" while facing a similar battle that she had experienced in Paterson: "It was a turbulent time of race tensions, and I entered a world as strange to me as some of the planets visited by the Star Trek crew" (12). Not white or black, her Latina phenotypic characteristics continued to set her apart as an ethnic other: "Everything about me, my black hair, my dark complexion, my New Jersey-accented speech, and my Spanish-speaking parents, set me apart in a culture that was much more homogeneous than the multiethnic barrios I had known in New Jersey" (12). Away from "the diversity of the barrios and multiracial society of New Jersey," Ortiz Cofer was immersed into a highly racialized, biracial society: "In the South there were two colors represented in the population, and the line between them was clearly drawn" (15). Or was it as black and white as it seemingly appeared to be?

Questions about cultural adaptation are at the heart of Ortiz Cofer's late literary production and were often the subject of professional presentations as a Latina writer. In particular, she addressed her concept of "home" at the National Council for Teachers of English (NCTE) annual convention in 2002: "I define homeland as the locale from which my creative energy arises, not necessarily a geographical location, but rather a state of being that confers in me a sense of belonging. Now that I have written a few books, I am discovering a pattern in my work: all of my years in America, I have been weaving my life into the tapestry of American history, I have been blending the language of my origin, my dreams and my imagination, Spanish, to the language of my survival, English, in order to create a new way of being an American" (unpublished speech). That tapestry included her exploration of Southern culture, particularly her experiences as a long-term resident of Georgia. She had in mind a series of projects inspired by Georgia sayings that she found especially colorful. In interviews recorded in 2008 and 2010, she spoke to me about "a book that is tentatively called 'Peach Pit Corazón.' The title came from the fact that I heard a Southern woman say, 'That man of mine has a peach pit heart,' and I said, 'What does that mean?' She said, 'Don't you know, honey, the hardest thing next to a rock is a peach pit?'" (Ocasio, "Interview" 2).

Her last permanent home before her untimely death was in Louisville, at the heart of a rural area she liked to refer to as the piney woods, where her husband built their house on a former family farm: "I recently gave a presentation about making my casa in the piney woods of Georgia. I have been here for over twenty years and only recently has it dawned on me that I am at home, that I don't have to go anywhere. I was always prepared to go somewhere. It has its limit, but now whenever I travel, the place that I yearn to go back to is here. I redefined home as the place where people you love want to be" (unpublished interview with Ocasio).

Ortiz Cofer was often a keynote speaker addressing pressing issues that predominantly affected Latinx communities. In 2003, she appeared at "The Power of Latinos for a Stronger Georgia," a conference organized by University of Georgia's Center for Continuing Education, and as a featured guest on *The Infinite Mind*, hosted by Fred Goodwin, on a special program, "Between Two Worlds: Mental Health Care for Latinos." In 1988, she was highlighted in *Birthwrite: Growing Up Hispanic*, a production of Arizona's KAET, a PBS affiliate.

Ortiz Cofer also brought to the forefront issues related to Latina-identified individuals breaking ground in academic or professional settings. *Woman in Front of the Sun* (1999) explores the often taxing and complex physical and psychological processes undertaken by Latina writers while finding their voice in a mainstream intellectual spaces. She furthered this feminist interest as coeditor of *Sleeping with One Eye Open* (2000), a collection of essays by women writers facing gender-based obstacles that highlights Ortiz Cofer's creative nonfiction essay, "The Woman Who Slept with One Eye Open: Notes on Being a Writer."

This chapter examines Ortiz Cofer's narrative and creative nonfiction essays that explore contested Boricua and Latina and Latinx experiences in the United States. As a committed Latina activist, Ortiz Cofer often handled questions regarding her interest in documenting the sociopolitical backgrounds of her characters: "I am not a political writer in that I never take an issue and write a story about it. The people in my stories deal with political issues but only in accordance with the needs of their personal lives" (qtd. in Gordon 7). The pieces "Las Muchachas," "The Year of Our Revolution," and "American Beauty" are coming-of-age stories. "Las Muchachas" underlines how the young female Boricua protagonists were severely restricted by the socioeconomic background of the barrio. Harsh mother-daughter generational struggles are the subject of "The Year of Our Revolution," a mirror into the effects of the sexual revolution of the nineteen-sixties upon youth Boricuas. The lucha extended outside the boundaries of the barrio; "American Beauty," an unpublished story, poignantly portraits a Latina youth as she valiantly challenges the false accusation by a white clerk of stealing cheap beauty products.

Ortiz Cofer's development as a committed feminist activist and literary critic is the subject matter of the critical articles "In Search of My Mentors' Gardens," "Taking the Macho," and "A Brief Account of the Adventures of My Appropriated Kinsman, Juan Ortiz, Indian Captive, Soldier, and Guide to General Hernando de Soto." She underscores the influence of Southern women writers Flannery O'Connor and Alice Walker on her in "In Search of My Mentors' Gardens," in which she reflects on voices she read while living in the Deep South, feeling "still baffled by the contradictions of the Southern character." On the other hand, "Taking the Macho" and "A Brief Account of the Adventures of My Appropriated Kinsman" are prime examples of Ortiz Cofer's interest in documenting strong historical figures. "Taking the Macho" explores strong Indigenous female characters, such as the Caribbean female chiefs or the legendary Amazons, as proof of a matriarchy that conflicted with the Roman Catholic gender roles imposed by the Spaniards. A similar rereading of historical accounts is found in her appropriation of the storyline of Juan Ortiz, an earlier explorer of the Florida territory who was captured by Indigenous groups in 1528. Ortiz managed to adapt to his new environment, learning Indigenous languages and different cultural traditions. As she states, Juan Ortiz became yet another unusual mentor in navigating cultural differences, while turning him into a founding Latino: "I claim Juan Ortiz as my adopted forebear; part of a series of choices and circumstances that brought the two of us to the American South—creating, through time, a common ground."

Three critical essays, "My Word Hunger," "Out of the Darkness: Writing to Survive La Lucha," and "The Myth of the Latin Woman: I Just Met a Girl Named María," develop theoretical approaches to subject matters often explored in literary formats. "My Word Hunger" details her relationship to the Spanish language, the sentimental language of her childhood and early youth, which continued to exert an enormous influence on her personally and professionally: "Do I speak Spanish? Yes, I speak Spanish. I speak survival Spanish. I speak yearning Spanish, I speak nostalgic Spanish. I dream in Spanish. The dream-Spanish trickles down into my poems, stories, and essays. And en mi vida, el español de mis sueños y mi corazón suffices." The struggle to maintain the Spanish language as the expression of a personal identity is extended to *la lucha* for cultural survival in "Out of the Darkness: Writing to Survive La Lucha." As Ortiz Cofer describes it, *la lucha* is "the gradual wearing down of the immigrant's constantly embattled psyche," which here she illustrates through classical literary references to survival stories and her own life as "an unexceptional story of initiation into a new culture." "Out of the Darkness" is also outstanding for its incorporation of poetry, a genre that was a central component in Ortiz Cofer's overall literary production.

In "The Myth of the Latin Woman," Ortiz Cofer criticizes oversexualized images of Latina women, what she describes as "the Hispanic woman as the 'Hot Tamale' or sexual firebrand," as seen in iconic films like *West Side Story*. This is indeed Ortiz Cofer's most critical and feminist article, written on behalf of "thousands of Latinas without the privilege of education or the entrée into the society that I have. For them life is a struggle against the misconceptions perpetuated by the myth of the Latina as whore, domestic or criminal."

At the time of her death, Ortiz Cofer was working on a book of essays on the theme of "apparitions," which she described to me as such: "I am also working on connecting the apparition of the Virgin in my hometown of Hormigueros, La Monserrate, with the Conyers, Georgia, apparition. I am talking about the different ways that cultures either accept or reject such apparitions ("Latina Writer" 2). Although the collection remained unfinished, one lyrical essay, "The Sign," was published in 2008. It is a powerful proclamation of the intrinsic value of migrant workers and an ode to the Marian tradition of Our Lady of Guadalupe as transplanted in the rural Georgia fields. At the heart of the article is a powerful statement of the migrant workers' important role in Georgia's agriculture.

LAS MUCHACHAS

So, they started calling us by our baby names and trying to make us their *nenas* again, offering to take us shopping and sharing their *Vanidades* magazines. We saw their fear, and we played up to it. "Ramonita, Carmencita, Inesita! ¡Vengan! Let's go downtown and do a little shopping." We saw it for what it was, a trap. They told each other where we were and paid each other *visitas* when we happened to be there. They claimed it was to roll each other's hair in those hideous pink curlers, or to exchange books and magazines in Spanish. But we knew they were spying on us. We didn't fall for it, no señoras. "No tengo ganas," one of us was sure to say, not in the mood for shopping, or "We are working on el homework." We knew our mothers wanted to curb our tastes and desires and we said no, gracias. It was the year of diminutives. Three of us were turning fifteen in the next month and we were ready to bust out of our Catholic school uniforms. Not so much for me, as the school insignia and Sacred Heart patch on my school straps barely stood out. But Ramonita and Carmencita, chests out, proudly displayed their school pride. Our mothers, two primas and a neighbor, all three as close as triplets, saw our wildness and worried. "Pero, hija. You are too young for bras with stuffing." My mother refused to buy me a padded bra, so I stuffed it myself with tissues. I did it right before I stepped out on the street from our front door. I'd once overheard my male cousin tell other boys that he was planning on giving me a box of band aids for my quinceañera. "Save her bra money."

When we knew they were busy reading their Corín Tellado romance novels to each other, and watching their telenovelas, we locked the bedroom door to whoever's apartment it was. Sometimes we turned the radio up loud and we whispered our secret plans. Other times Cousin Brucie played "96 Tears," a good song, over and over—we liked hearing a guy say he cried for a girl—and the stupid "These Boots are Made for Walking," sung in a teeny voice by that girl with Frank Sinatra's face, who could be him in a frilly white mini-dress with knee-high white boots. She couldn't dance, either. She took baby steps as she screeched, "These boots are made for . . ." (baby walking, we also yelled out every time we heard it). "I'm gonna be a professional dancer," Carmen declared, doing a total body spin like she was on ice-skates. "I'm gonna do the hair and makeup for movie stars," Ramona, the Woolworth's makeup queen, exclaimed while wearing a huge hair dryer bonnet attached to the motor by a pipe that sounded like your own private tornado. The whole time her long hair dried in big plastic curlers, she'd be doing our nails, though we'd have to use smelly acetone on them before school Monday. We could get detention for nails in any other color but virginal transparent pink, so why paint them at all? The smell of the nail polish remover would fill the apartment, making my father say, "You are a walking fire bomb, hija. If anyone lights a match next to you, you'll explode like una bomba atómica." And this made mother pause, if she was in the middle of lighting up a Salem mentholated cigarette (good for sore throats—it was la pura verdad if she heard it on the TV), and give me the cuchillo look—death by eye dagger. I kissed my azabache hanging from my gold chain, a little ball of coral and ebony, right next to my confirmation crucifix, to protect me from the Evil Eye. "Gracias por darme el mal ojo, mami," I'd say disdainfully. My own mother giving me the Evil Eye. "Malcriada y maleducada," she'd shoot back. So, if I was the badly raised, ill-mannered daughter, whose fault was that? Better to let it drop. "Ay, Dios mío."

When we were satisfied with our makeup and outfits, Ramona, Carmen (we did not babify our names once we left our apartments), and I walked to downtown Paterson where we bought our *Cosmopolitan* magazine from a disapproving clerk at the Woolworth, ate our hamburgers at the White Castle and planned our lives. We shared our breakout plans from the barrio—fantasies of being discovered for the talents we knew were our gifts from God. If asked, I talked of being a reporter or a teacher in the City (which always meant New York, just across the Hudson, but a million miles away in our minds). I earned good grades in English mainly because I read everything. But for las muchachas there was no serious talk of college yet. It was hard to imagine. We didn't even know what a college campus looked like. When I did think about going away to college, I daydreamed it was like high school, except with students as older versions of the kids I knew. I'd live in a dorm, my own furniture and my own key to my own room, no nosey parents checking for "funny" cigarettes in socks, or evidence of *la vida loca* in my private possessions.

The best part for me was thinking of owning my days, no more reglas at the house, rules your parents invented on the spot to keep you from making any decisions on your own. No more curfew times, no eating rules, not even the etiquette of Puerto Rican greetings, like if you meet an older relative, or family friend, you have to ask for a blessing, "La bendición." If you didn't, they'd complain to others about your lack of *respeto*, "No me pide la bendición." She doesn't ask for my blessing. Snob. Changa. Americanized. Too good for the barrio. If I went away to college, I could open the door of my own room, and not have to ask for permission; I could eat pizza in the middle of the night; I could take a bath that lasted for hours. At home, I couldn't even take a quick shower without announcing it, since the only toilet in the house was in the same room with the tub. No luxurious long tub baths for me—someone always needed to use the bathroom. Small dreams of privacy were attached to my breakout plan. This was the year of easy dreams, no effort on our parts. We were destined to be rich and famous simply for being us. *El destino*, we believed in it like we believed in the Starship Enterprise. To explore new worlds, to boldly go where no muchacha from the barrio had gone before. Oye, you better believe we were going places.

Weekends you might find us in the parking lot of White Castle, leaning on somebody's car, a new one preferably, shiny and smooth. We'd trace its curves with our hands. We'd seen how boys touched their cars. We were mostly sharp angles and fins jutting out, but the hips were sure to round out like eye-catching hubcaps. One of us always brought a transistor radio. When it played one of the songs that made our bodies twitch, we felt something like desire rising from our toes up to our scalps, we exchanged hot glances full of yearning, and sometimes we danced in front of the customers eating their burgers and ogling us. I could read their lips. At least, I knew how lips moved when someone said "Spanish girls," and I knew how the eyes changed when the looking was in contempt. But sometimes it was something else, something more exciting we wanted to elicit from strangers with our bold moves. We swayed to "Wild Thing," going at it like corkscrews, until it built up to a little bump and grind. We trembled at the thought that someone we knew would see us, but the fear was part of it. We needed to feel it. So, we danced in a parking lot; we laughed at ourselves, wild things that we were; and waited for someone to say, "I think your dancing is fantastic, muchachas. Come on tour with us. You can be a Go-Go girl behind one of the British invasion bands." Oye, hey, it's just a matter of time.

Then it was time to go home, our two hours of freedom up. Our parents sent brothers or other male relatives or, worse, they'd come themselves to drag us home. Outside our building, we'd rub the lipstick and eyeliner off each other's faces with a little spit on our pañuelos, the white linen squares our mothers embroidered for us with our initials, no sharing hankies, and I threw them in the tub when I took baths, to wash off the evidence. Like a good girl, una muchacha decente, I washed my panties, and little bra, and my hankie at bath time every night. I hung them smelling of Palmolive soap on a string or wire my father made into a laundry line from one end of the bathroom to the other. But it was OK, only family saw the pastel with tiny flower print underpants, and the A-cup bras hanging like caught white fish. If company knocked unexpectedly, I rushed to take them down. A woman takes care of her own intimate garments. These secret clothes never took the trip to the Laundromat on Saturdays. A woman's underwear is not for public display. Oh, la vida was full of lurking dangers, and we, las muchachas, could not wait to find it, or for it to find us. A blind desire for experience drove us, and what we couldn't articulate, we mimed through our electric bodies, wild things. Our open palms said give us the world, we are ready, and our feet danced and took us as far as we dared. And we loved our lives, until there was nothing more to love with a passion.

One day, the diminutives were dropped, and we claimed our grown women's names. Eventually we stopped being atrevidas, the wildness seemed to fall off like a baby bird's down, or we shed it, a snake's skin. We did not feel it slip off, but it happened. And in one year, we walked away from each other. We went separately into the fog of adulthood. No longer las muchachas, we were las mujeres now, mature young women. And we learned to fear what we once sought, the dangers, the blinding surprise. We walk with caution now, having learned that la vida is doling out what we wished for, the unknown. Sometimes it's a minefield that bursts into shrapnel, leaving us scarred, and other times, rarer times, the days surprise us like a tossed bouquet, floating right into our hands. It goes on and on, this slow adventure, la vida, just like our mothers' telenovelas, postponing the happy ending, but promising one in every episode.

THE YEAR OF OUR REVOLUTION

Mary Ellen

When my senior year began, I was immersed in politics, passion, and poetry; the three P's. All of them embodied in my boy-poet, Gerald. Gerald introduced me to protest music and the poems of Allen Ginsberg, which had a heady effect on both of us. Gerald also introduced me to my best friend in those days, his sister Gail, who once took off her clothes during a peace rally and was arrested for indecent exposure. It wasn't so much exhibitionism that prompted her to remove her blouse in front of city hall; it was love of life—an exuberance I envied.

At home and at Larry Reyes's restaurant, where my parents worked, time stood still. The Cubans talked of returning to their island and plotted the overthrow of Fidel Castro. They competed with each other in their stories of lost riches, of glamorous lives lived in tropical splendor before *La Revolución*. All of them had apparently been doctors, lawyers, socialites and descendants of Spanish aristocracy. Now, though, they worked alongside the Puerto Ricans in factories and textile mills doing menial jobs. My father served them their drinks at the bar—usually Puerto Rican rum with coke, a combination called Cuba Libre—and listened patiently to their weepy tales of lost glory. There was little else he could do for his Cuban *compañeros*. For our people, however, he could do more: He could spend his own money on them because they were his Island brothers and sisters. People knew how soft he was, and he became our barrio's father confessor and social worker, with Puerto Habana as his dispensary. My mother did what she could to help him in his mission. We stayed poor while Larry Reyes grew rich.

But my world was larger than the barrio. I kept in touch with *my* revolution through the air waves. I took my tiny transistor radio everywhere with me. The New York City DJ, Murray the K, hissed or shouted in my ear. He introduced me to the music of Aretha Franklin, Grace Slick and the Jefferson Airplane, Bob Dylan, Marvin Gaye, Santana, Joan Baez, Jimi Hendrix—the mixed-bag he called *our* rock and roll in an intimate whisper, making it sound as if he were talking about having sex. I remember I had been in the tub listening to his show when I'd first heard the Beatles' *Sgt. Pepper's Lonely Hearts Club Band*. I'd slipped down into the water, up to my ears in ecstasy, wanting to drown in sound. Joplin's wails of pain and pleasure made my extremities tingle. When I saw her picture, I couldn't believe how plain she was. But later I saw her perform on TV and witnessed the miracle that music effected on her. When she was deep into a song, Janis became beautiful. Her voice, hoarse and choked with pain, went right through my skin, and I began to understand the meaning of soul, *el duende*, in American music.

Gerald introduced me to sensuality rather than to sex. He practiced Yoga, transcendental meditation, and the art of massage. He decided that passivity and self-denial were the keys to Nirvana. His thing was for us to sit facing each other in his darkened room while he recited his poems to me. They were mainly chants of words that made his soul vibrate, he explained to me—like the strings of a celestial harp.

"Let's lap the cosmos," he'd whisper hoarsely, his mouth half an inch from mine as we sat on his imitation Persian rug: Our legs wrapped around each other, our arms intertwined, our torsos not touching. This position generated the necessary tension that inspired Gerald's verse.

"Lick the stars, stoke my fire, cross the universe on a white horse, swim the Ganges with me."

The images were enough for me. I could listen to his strings of beautiful nonsense all night. I knew it was a love poem in secret code. When Gerald ran out of poetry, he would chant to me: "Om Ah Hum," the tip of his tongue tickling my ear. "Om Ah Hum."

Then we'd get the perfumed oil out of his bag. He always had his essential supplies with him; you never knew when someone might need the magic touch. I would take off my poncho, unbutton my blouse, which was usually a diaphanous Indian cotton creation with little mirrors sewn into it and other symbolic decorations I had added. Gerald liked to guess what each patch was, each embroidered clue to my soul, by just feeling it in the dark.

"Here's comes the sun," he would say, tracing the design over my left breast, "and here is a daisy," his fingertips following each petal of the flower. Then he'd move his hand towards my nipple under the material: "And here is Mary Ellen, Mary Ellen, Mary Ellen, daughter of sun and moon, child of heaven."

He never saw me undressed, but his fingers knew my body. Gerald's Eastern philosophy and his massages in the dark were the erotic pinnacle for me that year.

There was a darker side to Gerald too, and it finally became clear to me, and to Gail, that he was modeling himself on the self-destructive figures that we injected into our unconscious, taking the words of their songs and the needle-sharp notes of their music directly into our veins. Like Hendrix, like Joplin, like Morrison, Gerald became obsessed with death as the ultimate trip. It frightened me when he first suggested that we try a peyote button. He didn't insist when I refused, but I could tell when he'd been reinforcing his mellow grass highs. No longer gentle in the way he touched me, his nails once cut into my flesh. Another time he almost choked me, his fingers locking around my throat until I pried them loose. Frightened, I left Gerald still sitting in the lotus position, staring straight ahead as if catatonic.

The next day he insisted he did not remember hurting me. I showed him the purple marks on my neck, which I had to carefully conceal at home and at school by wearing a turtleneck sweater. He cried and begged me to forgive him. I saw him a few more times, but he was turning inward for company, turning on more often, dropping out of most of his relationships. Gail and I discussed what was happening to Gerald.

"My brother is *into himself* now," Gail told me in her room, where a life-size poster of Morrison, naked to just below the waist, gazed down at us from the ceiling. She admitted to indulging in "groovy" sexual fantasies involving the sexy lead singer for the Doors; his drug-droopy eyes were a dangerous black pool a girl could drown in, and the inviting parted lips a natural wonder to explore. His tight leather pants did not leave much to the imagination, and that was fine. We both knew what Jim Morrison could offer a girl.

"Touch Me" was playing on Gail's turntable, loudly, for privacy while we talked. Downstairs, her mother was baking an apple-cinnamon pie for Gerald, trying to bring him back from his cosmic travels with the aromas of her kitchen. Gerald's father had scarcely spoken to his son for almost two years, since they had driven together into a gas station and the attendant had innocently called his long-haired, pretty son "Miss." Gerald, Sr. had turned the car around, walked back into the house and announced to his wife that the creature wearing a clown suit and beads was not his son anymore.

There had been scenes, tears and misguided attempts at compromise by the well-meaning mother, all of which were met by her son's passive resistance. Her pleas and threats were sometimes rewarded with a sweet kiss and vacant eyes, a flower from her own garden, or the flashing of a "V" for peace. Gerald's spaciness and her husband's silent hostility had almost defeated her. She had at first turned to Gail for comfort, but instead of her darling little girl, she had found a fledgling women's libber and flower-child. Gail suggested to her mother that she leave her square husband and "turn on to life." According to Gail, her mother had instead joined a Bible study group and a bridge club, where other exiled mothers and wives compared their children's terrorist activities and prayed that this rebellious phase turned national epidemic would pass during their lifetimes.

"What do you mean Gerald's *into himself*," I asked Gail. I was feeling resentful about Gerald's new indifference, which he said was really "peaceful acceptance" on his part. This translated to: If I wanted to see him, fine, I could find him; if I didn't want to see him, fine, he would be doing the same thing anyway: getting stoned, listening to "In-a-Gadda-Da-Vida" with the turntable's arm in the up position so that the record album would play continuously without interruption until Gerald left the room and his patient mother came and turned the thing off. The father had bought earplugs.

"Well, Mary Ellen, what it means to Gerald," Gail said, turning to face me on the narrow single bed where we were both stretched out together, almost falling off the sides, "is that he doesn't care about *this* anymore." Catching me off-guard, she pinched my nipple, giggling uncontrollably while I rubbed it. I fell halfway off the bed still managing to give her the finger in outrage.

"Are you on something, girl?"

"I'm high on life, E-le-ni-ta," she said still laughing, enunciating my Spanish name syllable by syllable.

"I want to know what's up with Gerald. Can you get serious?"

"I can tell you what's *not* up with my brother." She laughed again, pointing to Morrison's crotch above us.

"I'm going," I said, tired of her sexual innuendos.

Gail had joined a women's awareness-raising group her first term at City College, and their "thing" was to treat sex as an open topic, to expand their horizons by trying "everything" sexually, which meant that your friends and neighbors were all fair game as potential partners in your choice of adventures. Until the nipple-tweaking impulse had overtaken Gail, I'd felt that as her brother's girlfriend I had safe passage, or diplomatic sexual immunity, around Gail. Apparently, now that Gerald was "into himself"—no longer interested in exploring the universe in my company—Gail had felt she could cross the line.

"Don't be afraid of me, Mary Ellen," Gail's tone turned serious as she gently placed her hand on my shoulder, pulling me back down next to her on the bed. "At this very moment, maybe because I was thinking of the last time Gerald—you know, gave you a massage, I did feel turned on. But I can be cool about it. We can talk."

"How do you know . . . I mean . . . did Gerald tell you . . ." I was shocked that Gail knew about my sessions with Gerald. I had always told her about the poetry and the massages, but, not the other stuff. In spite of my outward bravura and my rebelliousness against my parents' uptight moral values, I felt a little ashamed of letting Gerald touch me the way he did. Because we did it in total darkness in his room, I stupidly believed that no one else suspected what went on.

"I was there," Gail said in a whisper.

My impulse was to jump off the bed and run home. How could Gerald betray me this way? How could Gail call herself my friend when she was a voyeur, a pervert, spying on her best friend's and her brother's most intimate moments together? I surprised myself by just lying stock-still on the bed next to Gail. *And did you touch me too?* I did not ask aloud.

Next to me, her mouth close to my ear, Gail hummed a song we both knew, but did not move either.

Gerald emerged from his dark cocoon enough times to finish high school, although he tested and stretched the limits of Queen of Heaven High's faculty and administration. He might never have graduated if it had not been for our hippie-nun Sister Mary Joseph's intercession—and the fact that he was brilliant. He read and understood philosophy. High-school subjects were child's play to him, for Gerald could interpret the words of Shakespeare, Milton and Blake as well as those of John, Paul, George and Ringo. He couldn't have cared less about the diploma, but somehow, even in the recesses of his chemically saturated brain, he must have known that it would undo the last connection he had to his family and to the world if he did not finish his senior year. Also, he saw life as a series of events that you either allowed to happen to you or you passively resisted. He allowed his high-school graduation to happen to him, then he celebrated his freedom by blowing his mind with acid at a rock festival. The unforeseen consequence of his orgy was half a year in the nuthouse, paid for by his father's insurance company, followed by the realization that the breakdown had been a gift from the karmic forces of rock-and-roll: He would not be drafted.

Gerald's dropping-out had been gradual, though, and my memories of our senior year are like black and white photographs with a shadowy figure at the edge that no one can quite identify. That was Gerald. Gerald in his ankle-length black trench coat, John Lennon-style eyeglasses and hair down to his shoulders, standing just behind me at the café where we listened to the other young men and women in black recite their angry verses and sing their protest songs. More and more I began to lose interest in the mediocre poetry and the mindless repetition of slogans. My own pupa-stage poems were seeking out the concrete image that would years later give shape, form and meaning to my fragmented world.

My mother never met Gerald or Gail, or many of my friends outside the barrio. But she watched me from her window, and she waited and she knew, maybe through her dreams which she believed in, or by my smell, my music, by my wild look. Or maybe by spying on my sidewalk passions with Gerald. She knew that I was staring down the abyss with my boy-poet. So she gave me a choice one night: free love or her love.

María Elena

My hair started turning gray that year, seeing the turmoil on the streets of America and waiting for my daughter to come home from her rallies, demonstrations and sit-ins. Late into the night, I sat in my rocker by the window, waiting to see the pretty girl with the wild black mane of hair hiding herself inside a huge poncho. I watched her coming down the block, clutching her books and papers, head bowed as if she were burdened with the worries of the whole world. Such a serious child. So intent on righting wrongs that she missed all of the good things that I thought a young girl would want: pretty clothes, fiestas, fun with other teenagers. I knew that she liked boys, although those years I had to look very closely to tell the difference between the sexes. Both wore the ragged blue jeans, painted t-shirts and ridiculous jewelry. They let their hair grow and wore it wild and tangled as moss on a tree. From my window I could not always tell if her occasional companions were girlfriends or *novios*.

There was no doubt, however, the night I saw the obscene kiss in front of our building. By the light of the street lamp, I could clearly see the entire spectacle. Although I did not want her to know that I watched her in such a clandestine manner, I was alarmed one night to see the groping and abandoned caresses. It was *el poeta*, Gerald, she wrapped herself around one night. The boy looked like he needed a good night's sleep, a hot meal and a hair brush. I did not understand what she saw in him. Perhaps her enchantment with words and poetry was embodied in the unkempt boy. I knew I had to say something to her about the display on the street. She walked in preceded by the wave of that patchouli oil that permeated her person and everything she touched in those days. It was a pagan smell, calling up for me images of naked people dancing around a fire. I was sitting in the dark living room, so I startled her when I spoke her name.

"Elenita. Please come here for a minute, *niña*," I said, trying to calm myself before speaking.

"What are you doing up so late, Mother? Hey, have you been spying on me?"

"*I* will ask the questions, Elenita." I reached over and turned on the light. Her hands shot up to cover her face as if she had something to hide. But she regained her rebel pose quickly.

"Have you thought about what people in this barrio will say if they see you being intimate with a man right on the sidewalk?"

"You *were* spying on me!"

She was furious, as I knew she would be, but I was determined to speak my thoughts.

"You are forgetting something, *hija*," I spoke calmly so that she would know that I did not intend to be intimidated by her anger. "You live in my house. And as long as you call this home, you will answer to me and your father for your moral behavior."

"Then maybe it's time that I leave your *home*," she answered sharply. And the way she said *su casa* hurt me. "Perhaps you haven't noticed, stuck as you are behind these four walls, that there's been a sexual revolution going on out in the real world." She continued speaking in the same sarcastic tone. "People don't have to ask their parents or anyone for permission before they make love. It's a personal matter, Mother!"

"I call what you are suggesting immoral behavior, *hija*. If you are saying that for girls to pass their bodies around to many men is not a sin, then you are wrong. The body is a temple."

"My body is *my* temple, and I will conduct services any way I want!"

I saw that I could never hope to win a battle of words with my daughter: They were her domain. Even then she could use language to her advantage like no one else I knew. So I brought out my most dangerous and final weapon. Trembling in fear, I said, "I cannot *live* with you if you have given yourself over to a life of sin. I do not want you to go, but you have become a stranger to me."

She looked at me in horror. I knew I had shocked her because she thought that my devotion to her was greater than my objections to anything she could do. And it was. I was playing this game of chance, risking my whole life and my soul—for I could no more give up my child than I could stop breathing—hoping she would understand the gravity of our moral dilemma.

"You're throwing me out?"

She had sunk to the floor in front of my rocker. Her heap of bright rags spread around her, she seemed to shrink into a little girl again. I held back my need to comfort my child, keeping my hands locked together so as not to reach out to her.

"No, Elenita," I spoke firmly although my throat felt constricted by fear. "I am telling you that if the morals we taught you mean nothing, then we are no longer a family. You must make a choice. If you want to live without rules, then you must make a life away from us. On your own."

She sank back on her knees staring at me in disbelief, as if I had suddenly turned into a monster right there in front of her. She had never known that I too could rebel against injustice.

"You don't understand, Mother. Things have changed in the world. A modern woman makes her own choices . . . She has the freedom to choose."

Now she was going to give me a lecture on free love, but I interrupted her.

"Nothing of value to your life is free, Elenita. *Nada. ¿Entiendes?* Not even love. Especially not love. Look around you. Women have always paid a high price for love. The highest price. I am telling you that if you want to be an adult, you have to learn the first lesson: Love will cost you. It is not free."

She sat there taking in my pronouncements. Not in the usual way that people process things. Not *my* Elenita. She was translating and transforming what I had said inside that unknowable mind of hers. And when I would hear my own words again, coming out of her mouth, they would sound foreign to me.

My plan was to walk out on her for once, leaving her there to think about the choices I had given her. But I could not help myself. As I walked past my *niña* sitting stiffly in her pagan costume, I stroked her hair. She lay her wild head inside the circle of my arms for one brief moment, then rushed to her room to drown out the world with her long-playing albums. I will remember that night as the beginning of the end of the worst year in the history of parents and children: 1968, the year of our revolution.

AMERICAN BEAUTY

The minute I step through the electric eye, the drugstore's alarm goes off and several pairs of eyes fall on me, freezing me inside the cage of their suspicion. I stand on the spiky plastic welcome mat, waiting for someone to release me, to say "Go on," it is all a mistake.

The rotund manager, propelling down the center aisle towards me like a nuclear submarine in his too-tight steel gray suit, his pudgy finger aimed at me, orders me in a loud voice, to come back and empty my purse on the counter. I protest, put my hands up. I have not done anything. But his face, folds of hardened rubbery flesh, mouth curling into a tight smile of scorn, eyes almost slits—tells me: Expect no pity. He informs me he will call security if I do not obey. I turn over my bag on the glass case that displays cheap watches, their plastic faces impassively watching me through safety glass—a jury box of Timex ladies' and mens', alarms ready to go off when I am found guilty, none of them showing the right time.

Without touching any of my things, as if I carried the bubonic plague in my handbag, he inspects its contents, poking around inside with a pen he has pulled out of his pocket, letters scrolled on in gold on its side: *We value our customers*. This is what he finds: half a roll of breath mints (tropical flavors), two lipsticks (Brown Sugar Babe and Hot Spice Girl), hair brush, pink sunglasses with slightly scratched lenses, envelope with a letter I am still writing to my mother, small mirror in the shape of red lips; two five-dollar bills, three quarters, two dimes, one nickel, and seven pennies—money I was going to spend on beauty products. He takes his time, looking up, raised eyebrow, after tapping each item with his pen. I know he is acting for the security camera. Finally, finding nothing that looks like his merchandise, he looks me over, toes-to-head as if I were hiding something in my clothing or maybe hidden deep within my bushy foreign hair. I stand like a statue while he stares. His cheeks begin to quiver a little bit. He seems disappointed, almost on the verge of tears. I turn my five jacket pockets inside out for him; leave their linty insides hanging out. I lean over, grab the hem of my skirt, pretending I am going to lift it up for his inspection. His eyes grow almost round in outrage. He gives me a hateful look, makes a sweeping motion with his plump hand, *Get out of my store*. Case dismissed due to lack of hard evidence; not lack of guilt, his mocking smile tells me. He will get me next time.

He maneuvers his huge body, almost stuck between counter and wall, towards our audience of three customers, his sarcastic smile ugly and mean as the crack on the sidewalk that trips you. *We know she's guilty, right friends?* He nods as he passes the elderly couple, and nods again at the girl with blonde dreadlocks, who have waited, maybe hoping for the entertainment of their day to end with cops and handcuffs. But they act as if they too feel cheated. The girl walks out without buying anything, tossing back those heavy yellow ropes of hair. The old people return to the magazine they had been flipping through. I watch as the king of these thirteen aisles of beauty products, two of cough and cold, and one pain relief, goes back through his secret panel at the rear wall of his store, to his office behind the two-way mirror.

I put everything slowly back in my bag, taking my time sorting the coins and putting them each in a different compartment in my bag. I put my make-up in the middle section, zip it up; slide the sunglasses into the outside pocket so they will not be scratched again. I reapply Brown Sugar Babe using the mirror on the beauty side of the jewelry, electronics, and beauty aids counter. I run the brush through my hair. It gets stuck in a tough curl, and I have to spend a few minutes working it out.

This is what I leave on the glass counter top, above the Timex watches, all telling the wrong time: half a roll of mints (the green one on top broken in three places and a little bit dusty), several strands of coarse black hair I have carefully shaped into a question mark, and a ticket stub from the movie *American Beauty*, which I really didn't like all that much.

IN SEARCH OF MY MENTORS' GARDENS

Alice Walker on Flannery O'Connor:

> As a college student in the sixties I read her books endlessly, scarcely conscious of the difference between her social and economic background and my own, but put them away in anger when I discovered that, while I was reading O'Connor—Southern, Catholic, and white—there were other women writers—some Southern, some religious, all black—I had not been allowed to know. For several years, while I searched for, found, and studied black women writers, I deliberately shut O'Connor out, feeling almost ashamed that she had reached me first. And yes, even when I no longer read her, I missed her, and realized that though the rest of America might not mind, having endured it so long, I would never be satisfied with a segregated literature. I would have to read Zora Hurston and Flannery O'Connor, Nella Larsen and Carson McCullers, Jean Toomer and William Faulkner, before I could feel well read at all.

As a college student in the seventies United States I had a similar realization: I needed to write and I had no models of my own kind. In fact, I only remember one woman's name coming up for serious discussion in my classes and that was Virginia Woolf. Like the girl in my fable, I was smitten with English literature but beginning to suspect that it was going to be an unrequited love. Unlike Alice Walker I had no indication that anyone out there was writing for me. My day of revelation arrived years later when I came across a book of stories written by someone whose gender I couldn't decide by the name alone. Flannery. What kind of person would have a name like that? After reading only one story, "Revelation," I knew what kind of person, *my kind*. I had been living in the Deep South for several years by then, and trying to be politically correct and non-judgmental about the strange idioms and customs of my neighbors. (PC, that odious term, had not come into common usage at the time, so I believed I was trying to be polite to my hosts, a good Catholic girl amidst the passionate Protestants). But frankly, I was still baffled by the contradictions of the Southern character. In my own ethnocentricity as a Catholic Puerto Rican woman living in the Bible Belt I saw myself as part of the good minority group: my kind were generous and unbiased, tolerant and forbearing. Someday I was going to write poems and stories extolling these virtues of my people while exposing the Others for the oppressors they were.

"Revelation." O'Connor's stories left me as awestruck as Mrs. Turpin at the pig parlor. But I had a different vision from that of the nice, white Christian lady who believes she knows exactly where she belongs in God's Great Scheme. In the waiting room of a doctor's office, which O'Connor brilliantly constructs as a microcosm of social classes in the South, Mrs. Turpin is struck by a book called *Human Development*, a missile directed at her by a college student whose ire she seems to have raised merely by being who she is. Mrs. Turpin is wounded spiritually by the girl's action as well as physically. She cannot understand why a nice, clean, hardworking lady like herself should be attacked so viciously by this plain girl who is and acts "ugly." The insult added to the injury is being called "you old warthog from hell." This incident leads Mrs. Turpin on a painful introspective journey into her soul of souls. By following the tortured path of her thinking, we learn that her system of values is based on division and classification. Of course, she sets herself near the top of her Christian scale along with others who have attained the American dream of having a little of everything safely. She places the Black people at the bottom with only the poor white trash in a lower slot. She is later shocked to realize not only that her carefully constructed chain of being is rejected by certain others, including the Black people who work for her and who patronize her on cue, but also, and worse, that she has been judged and found morally lacking by those she considered her inferiors. During her visionary trance at the pig parlor, Mrs. Turpin's existential anguish leads her to a vision of eternal truth where her categories go topsy-turvy. From "Revelation":

> There were whole companies of white-trash, clean for the first time in their lives, and bands of black niggers in white robes, and battalions of freaks and lunatics shouting and clapping and leaping like frogs. And bringing up the end of the procession was a tribe of people whom she recognized at once as chosen who, like herself and Claud, had always had a little of everything and the God-given wit to use it right. She leaned forward to observe them closer. They were marching behind the others with great dignity accountable as they had always been for good order and common sense and respectable behavior. They alone were on key. Yet she could see by their shocked and altered faces that even their virtues were being burned away.

And so in one incomparable paragraph Flannery O'Connor sweeps up and away the social, economic, and racial hierarchies of her South—and although the term would not have been available for her to reject then—replaced political correctness with moral correctness. The levels still exist in the world but can be abolished in the heart and mind.

To O'Connor, a practicing Catholic, revelation was God's grace working through an individual. To me, it is another sort of epiphany. Most of us have a sense of ourselves as capable of moral choice and honesty. It is the same obligation of the artist to her art, to be honest, to share the insight, the vision. My revelation in reading O'Connor's "Revelation" was that I too was included in the motley crew she saw as part of Mrs. Turpin's vision. If I substitute the path leading toward heaven with the road toward inclusion in the only reality I know, that of my life here in this country among a diversity of people, then I too can count myself among the believers, perhaps even the saved.

What Alice Walker discovered, and to her great credit shared with her readers, is that O'Connor's art is encompassing of us all in its harsh and terrible beauty. Mrs. Turpin's revelation brings together all the personae of O'Connor's imagination modeled on the people she knew. Like the tough but fair God she believed in, she is equally brutal in her depiction of their foibles as well as gentle in their moments of grace. By using her equal opportunity pen like a scalpel, which always made its incision shockingly close to the jugular, she gave us an unsentimental view of ourselves, made us think, offended us, and delighted us. In the end, when we have met, hated, recognized, and finally pitied the Mrs. Turpin in ourselves, we are both wounded and healed, made better by having gone under the knife.

Honesty as practiced by the writer is what I learned from O'Connor's art. The stories, poetry and essays of Alice Walker taught me that a writer must never reject true art out of ego or self-righteousness, or for political reasons. Walker read and profited from O'Connor's stories although they were written in the colloquial language of another time using what are now considered politically incorrect epithets. I wonder how the feisty Ms. O'Connor would have reacted to being told she could not use the N-word in her work? Her books have been banned from some school libraries for their "racist" language. Yet this is how Alice Walker, one of the most important writers of our time who also happens to be African American, assesses O'Connor's art (the occasion described in "Beyond the Peacock," an essay from *In Search of Our Mothers' Gardens*, is the end of a visit she and her mother made to Andalusia, the O'Connor farm in Milledgeville):

> We walk about quietly, listening to the soft sweep of the peacocks' tails as they move across the yard. I notice how completely O'Connor, in her fiction, has described just this view of the rounded hills, the tree line, black against the sky, the dirt road that runs from the front yard down to the highway. I remind myself of her courage and of how much—in her art—she has helped me to see. She destroyed the last vestiges of sentimentality in white Southern writing; she caused white women to look ridiculous on pedestals, and she approached her black characters—as a mature artist—with unusual humility and restraint. She also cast spells and worked magic with the written word. The magic, the wit, and the mys-

tery of Flannery O'Connor I know I will always love, I also know the meaning of the expression "Take wits you can use and let the rest rot." If ever there was an expression designed to protect the health of the spirit, this is it.

Years after Flannery O'Connor's stories revealed to me that I wanted to be her kind of writer, at least as honest, I encountered Alice Walker's healthy spirit in action in a story that, along with "Revelation," has taught me the power of truth in writing. This is the way the narrator describes herself in "Everyday Use," a story about intellectual hubris and the need to value art for its function in our daily lives:

> . . . I am a large, big-boned woman with rough, man-working hands. In the winter I wear flannel nightgowns to bed and overalls during the day. I can kill and clean a hog as mercilessly as a man. My fat keeps me hot in zero weather. I can work outside all day, breaking ice to get water for washing; I can eat pork liver cooked over the open fire minutes after it comes steaming from the bog. One winter I knocked a bull calf straight in the brain between the eyes with a sledge hammer and had the meat up to chill before nightfall.

No woman on a pedestal there. No easy sentimentality. Only the plain truth.

"Everyday Use" is about a college educated woman who comes home to her mother's house in rural Georgia to claim a family quilt as well as other heirlooms that she wants to display as artifacts. Walker's incisive depiction of the girl who has adopted all the trappings of the progressive Black intellectual in the 60s (has even changed her traditional family name, Dee, to a preposterous sounding African name, Wangero) and realistic portrayal of the strong Mother and the scarred, timid sister is a lesson in making art that transcends social/political/racial boundaries. The fact that they are Black women is important, race is a crucial element of the story, but the knowledge we gain is more universal; it's at the level of what O'Connor called "the eternal truth." In Walker's story, the main symbol of the misuse of history, culture, and art is the family quilt. The sister, scarred by fire, and the mother understand the true value of the quilt. It was made out of the pieces of real lives by women related to them by blood and tradition, for the everyday use of their loved ones. Walker, like O'Connor, rejects the intellectualization of art, its appropriation by outsiders who may have little or no understanding of its original intended true function: to comfort, to heal, to connect, and to share a vision. The vision belongs to the tribe. And that vision may be given to the least rather than to the great.

In "Everyday Use" the mother makes a decision about the quilt that one daughter covets and the other daughter, Maggie, needs:

> When I looked at her like that something hit me in the top of my head and ran down the soles of my feet. Just like when I'm in church and the spirit of God touches me and I get happy and shout. I did something I never had done before: hugged Maggie to me, then dragged her on into the room, snatched the quilts out of Miss Wangero's hands and dumped them into Maggie's lap. Maggie just sat there on my bed with her mouth open.
>
> The quilt is thus put to its rightful use.

Rightful use is what I look for in my life and in my art. I want my stories, poems, and essays to be put to everyday use. I don't want them to be simply tokens of culture and race, or to become artifacts of my particular time in history. I would like some powerful person to dump my words on someone's lap to be used as needed.

Flannery O'Connor once told about giving some of her stories to a neighbor in Milledgeville: ". . . and when she returned them, she said, 'Well, them stories just gone and shown you how some folks *would* do,' and I thought to myself that that was right; when you write stories, you have to be content to start exactly there—showing how some specific folks *will* do, *will* do in spite of everything."

These two writers, who have revealed so much to me, shared with me a belief that human nature is more complex than black and white; and they wrote about both what they saw reflected in their own mirrors and what they observed happening out their windows. Their hope, and mine as their apprentice, is that the reader might also catch a glimpse of herself when she looks into that glass darkly. We can get her to look by our prompting. Preferably by polite prompting, but sometimes we may have to hit her over the head.

TAKING THE MACHO

There is a legend not recorded in history books that in 1496 when Columbus's ships landed on a tiny Caribbean Island so that his crew could refresh themselves, the men were confronted by a tribe of fierce women. Dressed for battle, wearing the plumage of warriors, they "assumed a menacing attitude" in front of the longboats. Astonished—and perhaps also amused by the sight—the men begged the women to allow them to come ashore to rest and eat.

Fernando Colón, the Admiral's son, tells in his biography of his father that the women ordered the sailors to go away, telling them that if they wanted supplies they could sail on to the north shore of the island where there were men who would help them.

But the sea-weary mariners were through playing games by this time. The women's refusal of hospitality was an insult to their macho. So they opened fire on them with their guns. Then they looted the women's village, destroyed what they found, and took the remaining women warriors captive. The women put up such a fight that the Admiral was moved to note their "strange fury." According to Fernando Colón a woman *cacique*, one of the chiefs of the tribe, almost killed "a courageous Canary islander": "She tried to make him prisoner; she grappled with him, threw him to the ground and would have choked him if the other Christians had not come to his aid."

The Christians were not so much impressed as affronted by the fierceness of these *unnatural* females. The captive women told the Admiral, his son reports, that these women had husbands but did not live with them. *They* would summon the men when they wanted to "lie with them." And these were brief purposeful encounters that were determined by the women. Fernando Colón had very likely read of the mythological Amazons of classical legends, so he did not doubt the existence of these macho women of the conquistadors' tales. He also believed in sea monsters and lost cities of gold.

It is not surprising that his writings have been selectively discounted by historians. No sea serpent, no macho woman.

We do have exhaustive studies of the lives of ordinary women in Spanish colonial times: the pious, submissive white women and the aborigine women beaten by history into silence and obscurity and into passive acceptance of the inevitable. Courage, even macho, were no match for disease, enslavement, rape, and genocide. The lucky ones married white men and became the mothers of a new race that lived according to the rules of the conquerors, once Christianity was established on the island. It only took a couple of generations before the Indian population of my native island of Puerto Rico was decimated to a few hundred native people who managed to escape into the mountains. It was not long before no pure-blood native was to be found anywhere on the island. The women of the Conquistadors were not bred for macho, they were ladies. And the only females who could have laid claim to the term had vanished into legend—or to the mountains to die.

In the dictionary, the noun *macho* is defined as the male of the species. However, it is the modifier that interests me: As in *macho man*—literally translated that means male man—a redundancy, or an indication that the adjective can also be attached to another noun such as macho woman?

What were the Caribbean women warriors defending? It was their territory, that is obvious. But no mention is made of any raids and warfare initiated by these women. They apparently *asked* their men to mate with them, and they donned their warrior plumage when they saw invaders approaching. Since historians have determined for us that this is a legend, I take the liberty of interpreting it from my perspective as a woman fiercely protective of her artistic and personal territory. I believe that this tribe of women had made a choice to take control of their lives, including their reproductive function, which they managed by deciding for themselves when they wanted to "lie with their husbands." I can imagine how horrified Columbus's Christians must have been at the very idea, and why they had to bring out their big guns against these women. When you see an aberration, you cross yourself, commend your soul to God, and shoot it.

The interesting thing is that matriarchy in the Caribbean is a historical fact, a system that had functioned for the native people until the Discovery. There is some evidence of the existence of a very powerful tribal chief, a woman *cacique* named Yuisa whose region was on the banks of what is now called the Río Grande de Loíza. This river was sacred to the Indians of Borikén—the name the Indios gave to the island before the gold-crazy Spaniards renamed it Puerto Rico—because it was where many of the spirits they worshipped lived. Yuisa was said to have the power to invoke the spirit that brought good rain and helped the crops to grow. Her male counterpart was the god of storms called Juracán (or Huracán). His fury was devastation. Although her name lives on as that of a great river, the *cacique* Loíza has faded into legend. It is difficult to prove that she existed at all, although anthropologists have found evidence of a strong matriarchal society that linked the indigenous tribes of the Island. Their religion was based on the earth-mother, with the belief that a balance of the male and female elements was the source of harmony in their world.

Anthropologists have speculated that women also participated in the sacred ball games played in the *bateyes*, or ball courts that have been excavated and reconstructed in this century. Fernández de Oviedo in his *General and Natural History of the Indies*, written in the sixteenth century, claims that the games, which were staged as fertility rites, were "usually played by teams of men, or of women; and sometimes teams of both sexes," and that "On still other occasions women played against men and married women against the unmarried." The object of the games reported by the eyewitness de Oviedo was for both women and men to appeal to the gods by their beauty and power. De Oviedo himself seems to have been impressed by the scene: "It is amazing," he wrote, "to see the speed and agility of both sexes."

It was a wondrous *and* disturbing sight for the macho Conquistadors to see women and men going into battle together and playing *pelota* on the same team! The quintessential male game of baseball is often colloquially referred to as *pelota* on the island today. Women do not play *pelota* (ball). Why? The most memorable answer I ever got from a man was: "Because women do not have *pelotas* (balls)." And laughter.

Perhaps because the only world that the Spaniards who colonized the island of my birth could conceive of was one dominated by *pelotas*-equipped machos, I was born into a culture that determined a woman's value by how well she fitted her predetermined feminine role. I felt its constraints from the start, but especially after I discovered that my artistic drive often clashed with male macho. You cannot be passive and *create*. Even the famous examples of women who stayed home and were artists do not mean that these women were passive. Emily Dickinson's life was in her own words "a loaded gun." The ones who are forced into frustrated silence may end up dashing their brains upon the moors, speculated Virginia Woolf, or simply giving up the Gargantuan struggle and settling for being the Angel in the House. Woolf said she continuously tried to kill this solicitous creature so that she could get on with her life as an artist. We can get us to a nunnery where we might be allowed an ecstatic vision or two on an approved subject. Or we can claim our share of macho and confront the longboats.

Using the word "macho" to modify "woman" may be a call to semantic controversy. Can a woman have "macho"? Does she need it? After all, she can have her choice of many other less loaded epithets that mean courage, that mean essentially the same as this masculine modifier. But not quite the same. According to the books it took "macho" to conquer the new world, the "right stuff"—Anglo for macho—to explore space and travel to the moon. It takes balls to do anything dangerous and new, or so it seems. But we may be able to transform an anatomical fact into a useful metaphor. And maybe we need to liberate the word because unless we can claim "macho," we may be doomed to a degree less of what we need for this dangerous exploration of inner space called artistic creation.

This is "macho": On his transatlantic flight Charles Lindbergh flew a specially designed airplane, the "Spirit of St. Louis," that allowed him no forward visibility (he did not want to be trapped in between cabin and fuselage in an emergency so he had the cockpit built far back in the aircraft). He crossed the ocean with *no forward visibility*. This is the kind of macho that best serves the artist. It involves no call to battle. It is an act of pure courage; an act of daring that straddles the line between heroism and foolish bravado. It is done because it is both necessary and unnecessary. If Lindbergh had not crossed the Atlantic, someone else would have. But he had to do it. It was necessary to *him*.

We all walked into that space shuttle with Christa McAuliffe. But did we become part of the sky with her? It took something greater than courage for both these people to step into the unknown. Success, or in their case survival, was not guaranteed. There are no guarantees. That is the only guarantee in a life dedicated to discovery. Next to death, failure may be one of the things that we fear the most. This morning, every morning, when I sit down to fill a page with my best efforts at making language a viable medium for my being, I walk into the unknown. I do not face death in the way the early explorers, Charles Lindbergh, and Christa McAuliffe did, but I too fly without a map, and I have known paralyzing fear. Writing exposes me to the world, daring it to accept me in spite of the fact that I have an overwhelming need to expose its many foibles and failings. The writer is the matador of the empty ring. We incite the beast to attack us, displaying as much red—the color of macho—as we dare, then we hope we are agile enough to avoid its horns—*Por Dios*—one more time. By the time the spectators arrive at the arena, we have retreated to tend to our wounds. All they see is the fire-breathing animal we say we created. Sometimes the crowd waves white handkerchiefs and the monster lives. Other times they walk away in disgust, seeing nothing more than a tired old cow where we had left—or so we believed—*verdad*—we really did—the minotaur.

The writer sits down before a blank page, the painter faces the empty canvas, the sailor sets out toward the edge of the world, the aviator points his craft in the general direction of another continent, a teacher boards a spaceship, anyone steps out of their safe home into the traffic. Who is the wisest? Who will sleep sound and safe in their own bed tonight? There are no guarantees.

Yet most of us would like to believe that we lead sane lives and that we will not come to harm or evil if we do not go out and seek it. The artist goes out, or rather, she goes *in* and finds what disturbs her and what possesses her, and she wrestles with it. She transforms herself into that macho woman that Columbus's son was astonished by: "she tried to make *him* prisoner" (my emphasis). Fernando Colón, like his father and his men, was offended at this unnatural reversal of macho rules: a woman warrior was to him an oxymoron, a contradiction in terms. Didn't this *India* know that a woman cannot conquer a conquistador? That only men can have macho? No, she had not yet been *civilized*, so she believed that if she needed macho, she could summon it out of herself, and that's why she fought back.

A BRIEF ACCOUNT OF THE ADVENTURES OF MY APPROPRIATED KINSMAN, JUAN ORTIZ, INDIAN CAPTIVE, SOLDIER, AND GUIDE TO GENERAL HERNANDO DE SOTO

In 1527, more than a dozen years before Hernando de Soto set foot in La Florida, a failed *conquistador* named Pánfilo de Narváez, alone with his more famous fellow adventurer, Álvar Núñez Cabeza de Vaca, set out from Sanlúcar de Barrameda, Spain, for La Florida—which then included most of what is now called the American Deep South and had been claimed for Spain earlier in the century by Juan Ponce de León—via La Habana, on the island the native Taíno Indians named Caobana and the Spaniards renamed Cuba, where Narváez and his fellow explorers stopped to reprovision their ships. On the last leg of the journey, soon after that last stop, Narváez's ships were blown off course into the Gulf of Mexico by a storm and, running low on supplies, Narváez sent his fleet, all but his own ship, back to La Habana. He ordered his men to meet him further up the coast when the storm abated.

The first party of sailors to go to the rescue of their captain and his landing party could not find him, so a second was sent one year later. On questioning natives, they learned that Narváez had indeed been seen near the agreed-upon meeting point near present-day Tampa Bay. The fiery Narváez, it was reported, had promptly engaged in hostilities with the equally short-fused local Chief Hirrihigua of the Timucua tribe. The chief had lost his nose to Narváez's spear in the encounter, and since then the captain's fate was unknown.

The chief, an important figure in the accounts of the explorations, is described by the de Soto chronicler Garcilaso de la Vega, also known as "El Inca":

> The cacique, who was in the capital of the province, [was?] irritated against the Spaniards because they had some time previous cut off his nose and caused the dogs to devour his mother . . .

This same noseless and irritable cacique met Narváez's would-be rescuers with his version of the Trojan horse maneuver. Somehow he had in his possession a sheet of paper with writing on it (very likely a note Narváez sent him on their first meeting), which he posted on a stick for the Spaniards to spot as they searched the shoreline for signs of the missing captain. The ruse worked; the note was immediately accepted as having been posted by the missing Narváez.

When a landing party of four men went to inspect the paper, the chief's warriors captured them. El Inca describes the torments to which the men were subjected.

> Hirrihigua guarded with care his prisoners, in order to increase by their death the pleasures of a feast which he was to celebrate, in a few days, according to the custom of the country. When the time of the ceremony arrived, he commanded that the Spaniards, entirely naked, should be produced, and that they should be compelled to run by turns from one extremity of the public place to the other; that at times arrows should be shot at them, in order that their death might be the slower, their pain the more exquisite, and the rejoicing more noted and of a longer duration. They immediately obeyed, and the cacique, who assisted at the spectacle, saw with pleasure three of the Spaniards run from one side to the other, searching in vain to escape death. As for the fourth, who was named Juan Ortiz, as he was but about eighteen years of age and a handsome man, the wife and daughters of the cacique interested themselves in his favor. They said that his age was worthy of pity; that he had not taken part in the perfidy of the people of his nation; and, therefore, not having committed any crime worthy of death, it was only necessary to keep him as a slave. The cacique consented to it; but this favor only served to make Ortiz die a thousand deaths.
>
> Juan Ortiz was the only survivor of the landing party.

Juan Ortiz. I fell prey to the lure of a name. My original intention in doing a bit of historical research on the de Soto trek through Georgia had been to confirm what to me, as a Latina in Georgia, was an interesting fact: that Spanish had been the first European language spoken in my adopted state. But the name, Ortiz, my surname, on the pages of a text written long ago, stopped me in my tracks. This ancient historical record materialized at my feet, overlapping with my own unfolding personal story as an Ortiz marooned in the Deep South: Juan and Judith, finding themselves in Georgia, separated only by the landscape or time. And who was the storyteller bringing us together in this moment and out of time? El Inca, the son of a Spanish conquistador and an Incan woman—another author of mixed heritage, who felt compelled to record his version of history. I was enticed to look further into, to reimagine, the brief but eventful life of Juan Ortiz.

He was "only eighteen years of age and a handsome man." His good looks may have saved Juan, for the daughter of Chief Hirrihigua continued to plead for his life even as the chief focused his vengeful attention on the young Spaniard:

> But their pity was cruel to him, for it served only to augment the barbarity of the cacique, who, enraged that Ortiz could endure so many hardships, ordered, on a day of entertainment, that they should kindle a fire in the middle of the public

> square; that they should put a griddle upon the fire; and that they should put his slave upon it, in order to burn him alive.
>
> This order was promptly executed, and Ortiz remained extended upon this griddle until the ladies, attracted by his cries, ran to his assistance. They besought the cacique not to push his vengeance further; they censured his cruelty, and took off the wretched Ortiz half burned, for the fire had already raised upon his body great blisters, of which some having broken covered him with blood. This drew the compassion of the greater part of the spectators. Afterward these merciful daughters had him carried to their house, where they treated him with herbs of which the Indians made use in their complaints, having neither surgeons nor physicians. Finally, at the end of some days, Ortiz was cured of his wounds, there remaining only the scars.

Apparently Juan Ortiz was not only a fine specimen, he was also wise enough to adapt and assimilate to survive. He learned the native language and made himself useful around the camp.

El Inca tells a story about a task assigned to Juan Ortiz by the chief, who continued to test Ortiz's survival skills in spite of the women's protestations: he commanded Ortiz to guard the tribe's burial grounds from animals that would desecrate the shallow graves, warning that the punishment for failure would be death by fire. And in spite of this horrifying prospect, "This poor Spaniard received with joy this order, in hopes of leading a life a little happier than before." Ortiz was given darts to protect himself and orders to remain vigilant day and night. El Inca writes:

> He then went away into the forest, where he acquitted himself strictly of his commission, and especially at night, as he had then the most to fear. However, it happened that once, when he was oppressed by fatigue and had permitted himself to be overcome by sleep, a lion uncovered a coffin and drew from it an infant, which he carried off. The slave awoke at the falling of the planks, ran, approached the coffin, and, no longer finding the body there, believed that finally it was all over with him. Moved by fear and grief, he went to seek the lion, to die fighting him or to make him leave his prey. He knew that at the break of day the subjects of Hirrihigua would come to visit the coffins, and that, if they did not meet with the infant there, he would be cruelly burnt. So that fear making him run here and there, he found himself in a great road in the midst of the forest, and heard a noise as of a dog gnawing a bone. He listened, and in the belief that it was the lion, he crawled through the bushes, and by the light of the moon he saw it, the beast devouring his prey. He therefore took courage and launched one of his darts at him; and because he did not hear him fly, he believed that he had slain him, and remained until daylight to be certain of it, praying to God, with tears, not to abandon him in his misfortune.

In the morning Juan found the lion slain by his dart, and he dragged it to the village "by one paw" along with the remains in the coffin. How heroic he must have appeared to the women—the handsome Spanish warrior, bearing his trophy of a wild animal (most likely a puma or other American wildcat). Did he kneel at Chief Hirrihigua's feet and ask for mercy as he presented him with this fine gift? Was he praying in Spanish to the Holy Mother? Remembering his family so far away? ¡Ave María! He was young and afraid. He may have wept. Whatever he did, it stirred the emotions of the entire tribe, who welcomed him as a hero, and the women of the chief's household pounced on this opportunity to intercede for their hero:

> The cacique was entreated by his daughters to make use of so courageous a slave, and to suppress his resentment on account of so brave a deed.

And, for a while, if reluctantly, the chief treated his slave less cruelly. But Ortiz's reprieve did not last long, for apparently the mere sight of the boy infuriated Hirrihigua, reminding him of the humiliations and personal injury he had suffered at the hands of his enemies. The once-handsome chief's disfigured face must have been a constant torment. Finally, Hirrihigua told his wife and daughters that he intended to have Juan Ortiz burned at the next tribal feast. They knew the chief felt dishonored and that his need for revenge had by now become the driving force of his life—or so I imagine, as I feel myself pulled even deeper into the past between the lines of El Inca's story. This time the passionate Chief Hirrihigua would keep his word.

For unrecorded reasons, perhaps because a different kind of passion for Ortiz had developed in her heart, the chief's eldest daughter risked her life by warning Juan Ortiz of her father's plan. Upon hearing the terrible news, the young man is said to have "appeared half-dead" with fear. At this point, this princess of the Hirrihigua tribe must have decided it was up to her to take action, so she concocted a rescue plot containing all the basic elements of a classic love story. Among her loyal subjects, she found a guide to lead Ortiz to refuge in the village of Chief Mococo, her intended future husband. Ortiz was instructed to beg for shelter and protection from a man who "esteemed her, and even wished to marry her." He was to tell Chief Mococo that he should protect Ortiz "in consideration of her." Ortiz cast himself at his lady's feet in gratitude. What else transpired between the young man and his noble rescuer that night is not reported by El Inca. Perhaps they shook hands in the European way, or embraced in a pledge of eternal friendship and nothing more. This was an early meeting of cultures, and the rules of the game must have been a mystery to both sides.

Chief Mococo gave asylum to Juan Ortiz in the name of the woman he loved. And, on hearing the story of how Ortiz had killed the lion to preserve the dignity of Chief Hirrihigua's tribal burial ground, Mococo treated him as a fellow warrior. When the old chief, his beloved's father, came to reclaim his slave, Chief Mococo invoked the sacred pact between host and guest, refusing to dishonor himself and his tribe by giving up a man who had been sentenced to death, claiming that he would rather "renounce his love than violate his faith."

From then on, Juan Ortiz was a full-fledged member of Chief Mococo's tribe. Assuming the clothing, lifestyle, and language of his adopted people, the cultural chameleon lived under his host's benevolent rule. That is, until General Hernando de Soto sails into this story ten years later. The encounter seems inevitable: de Soto would have noticed Ortiz's ability to communicate with, and even blend seamlessly into, the native population—and the general would have recognized this young man as an invaluable tool in his own quest for fame and treasure.

El Inca does not mention the fate of the princess, nor did I find anything else about her in other accounts I have read. Did she marry Chief Mococo, and did the three friends live peaceably in the same village for the next decade? Or did Chief Hirrihigua discover his daughter's role in the escape of Juan Ortiz and punish her in one of the many inventive ways he had practiced on the Spaniards? Women seem to have had some voice in the tribe's decisions, as shown by their power to save Juan Ortiz from the same fate as his fellow Spaniards in spite the chief's wishes. Perhaps the princess was protected by her mother and sisters, women like her, who understood Juan Ortiz's appeal and had been part of the chorus raised to save the handsome young man in the first place. I prefer to believe in this latter possibility.

Some modern historians, including William Coker, an emeritus professor of history at the University of West Florida, speculate that Juan Ortiz's rescue by the Indian princess may have been the historical inspiration for Captain John Smith's account of his own rescue by Pocahontas some sixty years later: the Ortiz narrative may have been familiar to Smith, passed down through lore and the written accounts and logs of the early explorations—the latter certainly available to a learned, inquisitive colonizer. However he may have come upon the report, John Smith might have seen it as a good story of love and heroism, and especially of contact and communication between races, a story that had the potential to ease the tensions afflicting the Jamestown settlers and the tribes led by Pocahontas's father, Chief Powhatan. Crucial discrepancies exist in Smith's story, different versions told at different times, which justify the speculation that he may have fabricated parts of his tale—leaving a few holes in America's birth story, holes whose mention may seem unpatriotic to those who view the Pocahontas–John Smith legend as a sacred text or early American history. But since the tale of Juan Ortiz and his Indian princess was not immortalized by American chroniclers, whose narrative of the colonizing competition prevails, and since no big-budget Disney movie is likely to be made from Juan Ortiz's life and times, I choose to reimagine history; I want Ortiz's spirit and that of his noble rescuer also to have attended the birth and christening of America, want to have the invisible couple of Spaniard and Indian princess hovering over John Smith as he put quill to paper and, in a few leaps of imagination, changed history. Perhaps like Smith, I feel the magnetic pull of the romance between cultures, the potent metaphor of the merging of cultures to create el Nuevo Mundo.

Is there *oro* in Ortiz? As my imagination runs wildly alongside Juan Ortiz deep in the old accounts, I seem to find myself back where I began, for it actually may have been a language problem that led to the liberation of Juan Ortiz.

The lure of Ortiz's story is integral to de Soto's saga also. Along with many others in the supply port of La Habana, de Soto and his men had heard the rumor of "Orotis" in La Florida, El Inca writes, reportedly from an Indian informant to whom Spanish was a second language: he was understood as saying that there was "oro" in Chief Hirrihigua's territory—gold—when he was actually giving an accented pronunciation of the Spanish captives last name.

> The Spaniards, notwithstanding their interpreters, believed that this barbarian asserted that his country abounded in gold, and they rejoiced to hear this word "Orotis," because their views did not extend beyond searching for gold in Florida.

De Soto may have come searching for *oro* and instead found Ortiz. In any case, the story of the young captive interested the conquistador enough that he decided to take time out from his search for treasure to "rescue" Ortiz from the "barbarians." De Soto's motives were more likely to be strategic than humanitarian. In unfamiliar and often hostile territory, a Spanish guide who was multilingual and who had assimilated into a tribe must have seemed like a godsend. I believe that de Soto sought Ortiz not so much to rescue him as to use him as one would a compass or a map.

El Inca describes how de Soto sent a Sergeant de Gallego, along with sixty lancers, to thank Chief Mococo for his kindness toward Ortiz, to request that the chief return the man to his people, and, while they were at it, to scout the area and report on the numbers and resources of the Indian tribes. In the meantime, having heard of de Soto's approach with a large army, and concerned about a possible attack, Chief Mococo had asked Ortiz to be his peace emissary and sent him along with fifty warriors to meet de Soto's lancers on the road. When the two forces met head on, Sergeant de Gallego immediately engaged the hostile Indians in combat, failing to recognize their leader, Juan Ortiz, as a white man—and no wonder:

> He was dressed as an Indian, with a cap covered with plumes, short drawers, a bow and arrow in his hand.

In the heat of the battle, Ortiz saved himself from a certain death at the hands of a fierce Spanish soldier named Nieto by managing to draw out a Spanish word from the deep place where he had buried his native tongue during all those years of his Indian life. "Xivilla!" he cried out, while at the same time making the sign of the cross with his bow. He was trying to say "Sevilla," the name of his hometown, and to prove that he was a Christian.

Here El Inca, half Peruvian Indian and an expatriate himself, in a moment of empathy for Juan Ortiz, injects his own nostalgia into his narrative:

> He had, to such a degree, lost the custom of speaking his language, since he was among the Indians, that he had so forgotten it that he could not even pronounce Sevilla, the proper name of the place where he was born. The same thing has happened to me, for not having found in Spain any one with whom I could converse in my native tongue, which is that of Peru, I have lost to such a degree the habit of speaking it, that, to make myself understood, I cannot speak six or seven words in succession. I had, notwithstanding, formerly known how to express myself in Indian, with so much grace, that, except the Incas who spoke the best, no others could express themselves more elegantly than I.

When Ortiz was delivered to him, General de Soto greeted the strange half-savage white man with kindness, although the creature before him had never been seen before, even by world travelers like himself: here was a Spaniard who had gone native to the point that he could not stand to wear civilized garments,

> because he was accustomed to go naked. He wore only a shirt, linen drawers, a cap, and slices [pantaloons]; and remained in this condition more than twenty days, until, by degrees, he recovered the habit of clothing himself.

Shifting costumes, customs, languages, and allegiances after his "rescue" from Mococo, Juan Ortiz served de Soto as interpreter and guide until de Soto's early death in 1542 on the banks of the Mississippi River, where his starved and diminished army had camped for respite from its long march toward the mythical "North Sea" from La Florida. Many of the men succumbed to exposure and illness, and Juan Ortiz was one of them. After twelve years of surviving on his wits and, with the help of generous strangers, not merely surviving but thriving in a strange land, Ortiz succumbed to the fate of the common army follower of his time, death by exposure and deprivation. Here Ortiz's story ends.

I cannot help but wonder if Juan Ortiz ever became a true Spaniard again, one who was comfortable in his pantaloons, breastplate, and helmet, and with the rigid discipline imposed by the relentless General de Soto. Did he retain his adopted Indian identity to the end, hidden in the same place within him where he had kept his Spanish all those years until he needed it? Did he die yearning for the only life he had known as a grown man?

I claim Juan Ortiz as my adopted forebear, part of a series of choices and circumstances that brought the two of us to the American South—creating, through time, a common ground. In Juan Ortiz I see myself as a young person brought across the ocean on a ship my parents called *El Destino* to a new world. Like him, I learned the language and the customs of the tribe, and I became a translator and a guide to my less adaptable parents. It is an old story that repeats itself in predictable cycles. The cyclical story of the chameleon goes around Ortiz and returns to me: Narváez and Cabeza de Vaca were lured to La Florida because the first governor or my native island of Puerto Rico, Juan Ponce de León, went there first on his quest for the "fountain of youth." Ponce de León did not find what he sought, but he explored and claimed the territories called La Florida for Spain; what is now the Deep South was for a time imagined in the mother country as another Mexico, Cuba, or Puerto Rico. One of Narváez's ships brought Juan Ortiz to La Florida, where he was tortured, loved by an Indian princess, given asylum by the noble Chief Mococo, and "rescued" by de Soto.

And de Soto, another of Ponce de León's disciples, took Juan Ortiz to the Mississippi River—the end of the road for both men. Ortiz followed his general toward El Río Grande de Mississippi, crossing the Chattahoochee River and trekking among the rivers, lakes, and villages of Indian country including Capachiqui, Kolomoki, Toa, Chisi, Ichisi, Altamaha, Ocute, Ocmulgee, Oconee, Ogechee, and Cofaqui—names that still echo within the geography of Georgia, along today's De Soto Trail that winds through the towns of Blakely, Edison, Dawson, and Louisville (Cofaqui). On the way the army "discovered" the original Georgia barbeque, the *barbacoa*, a grill where the meat of "hens of the land" (turkeys), venison, and other animals was transformed into the mouth-watering wonder that made the conquistadores forget gold for a while, at least while they were eating. The army may have continued with renewed energy on its trek, meandering through what are now Americus, Andersonville, Oglethorpe, Montezuma, Perry, Warner Robins, Fort Valley, Milledgeville, Sandersville, Davisboro, and Louisville, Georgia.

I trace the De Soto Trail on a map with my finger—there, at the point when they cross the Ocmulgee River into what is now Macon, my heart beats a little faster, for de Soto's ragged army and my adopted ancestor Juan Ortiz are approaching today's Sandersville, which is very close to where I live. Finally they arrive at my future hometown of Louisville, where Chief Cofaqui, "an old man with a full white beard," greets them with food and gifts. Did they rest in his village? Did Juan Ortiz lay his tired head on the red clay of the former Creek settlement where my home now sits? Did he eat out of earthen pots, like those whose fragments we occasionally find after a heavy rain? Did Chief Cofaqui show them the precious arrowheads his warriors had made from local stones? I know the art of these objects, their beauty. They are still here, where I live, turning up like the old chief himself, out of the mist. We accept them as gifts and care for them, until it is time to pass them forward into other hands. We are the guests on this land.

From what will become Louisville, they march on to what will become Augusta, the city where centuries later I will attend high school and college, where I will marry, and where my child will be born.

I leave Juan Ortiz here, on the banks of the Savannah River, within my home territory, for this is where I wish to complete our circle in time, Juan's and mine—although in reality he followed a cruelly determined, unyielding General de Soto further on. Hernando de Soto died having found neither his treasure of gold nor his "Ocean Sea passage to China, on which he had staked his reputation." His soldiers buried his body in the waters of the river to preserve the myth that their leader was an immortal, El Hijo del Sol, the Son of the Sun, temporarily away in his celestial realm gathering strength, supplies, and reinforcements to finish his conquest.

De Soto may have been as young as thirty-six years old. Juan Ortiz, his humble servant, guide, and translator, was perhaps thirty-one. The single line given to Ortiz's death in the old narrative calls him "un buen soldado," a good soldier, high praise for a man of his time. Was his heart broken? Did he yearn for his native Sevilla in the end, or for the place where he had earned his manhood, the land of his friend Chief Mococo and his heroic Indian princess? Were his final thoughts about the lush landscape of La Florida, our Deep South, the country he knew better than any other soldier in de Soto's doomed army, or about his native España? Or perhaps both? Had Juan Ortiz become the first Latino in America to love equally two homelands and two languages?

Proclamation of Appropriation of Kinship with Juan Ortiz

Juan Ortiz, by the powers vested in me by time and its effects on reported history, and by the right I claim as the teller of my version of your story, I proclaim you my kinsman and a direct ancestor of all Latinos in the South. I designate you forefather to those of us who have taken you as a model, learning from you to adopt and to adapt, to speak the language of the land while guarding our Spanish in case of emergency. Through you, Juan Ortiz, I claim our part in the creation myth of this land we now call home.

Author's disclaimer: The narrative is based on research, which in the case of the early accounts of the chroniclers meant reading a lot of highly creative interpretations of historical events, but it is mainly an attempt to imagine the inner life of an obscure young Spanish soldier, whom I appropriate for my own storytelling purposes as my ancestor and link to Georgia history. Further information regarding source materials can be found in the notes at the end of the essay.

Author's Notes

All quotations except one are taken from "El Inca" Garcilaso de la Vega's *History of the Conquest of Florida*, based on interviews with de Soto expedition survivors. This translation was made by Charmion Shelby in 1935 and published in *The De Soto Chronicles: The Expedition of Hernando de Soto to North America in 1536–1543*, edited by Lawrence A. Clayton, Vernon James Knight Jr., and Edward C. Moore (University of Alabama Press, 1993). The quotation about "Orotis," which begins "The Spaniards, notwithstanding their interpreters . . ." is taken from E. Barnard Shipp's translation of El Inca's "History" in *The History of Hernando de Soto and Florida; or, Record of the events of fifty-six years, from 1512 to 1568* (Robert M. Lindsay, 1881).

Much of the general historical information and—as in the case of the original chroniclers of the Spanish explorations—many of the imaginative accounts (that is, narratives collected from second- and third-party sources long after the events had taken place) incorporated into this essay were gleaned from general Internet sources on the Spanish explorers in North America, which themselves drew heavily on the early accounts. I relied on *The De Soto Chronicles* for the most accurate historical information.

As to speculation that Ortiz's rescue by the Indian princess may have inspired Captain John Smith's account of his own rescue by Pocahontas, sources include two writers separated by nearly one hundred years of history: F. P. Fleming writing in the *Florida Historical Quarterly* (vol. 1, no. 2, July 1908), recounts the Ortiz story, suggesting it as a precursor to the Smith narrative, and in an article by Associated Press writer Bill Kaczor that appeared in the *Los Angeles Times on* July 16 1995, "'Pocahontas' Tale Likened to Earlier Rescue of Spaniard in Florida," historian William Coker is quoted as saying, "It's something nobody can prove one way or the other. But on the other hand, the evidence, I think, leans pretty heavily in favor of [John Smith] borrowing the story." References to the story of Pocahontas and Jamestown are informed by the third book of the five-volume *The General History of Virginia, New England and the Summer Isles: Together with the True Travels, Adventures and Observations, and a Sea Grammar*, by Captain John Smith (London, 1624).

MY WORD HUNGER

According to legend, the first machine translation program was given the sentence "The flesh is weak, but the spirit willing." The translation (into Russian) was then translated back to English, yielding, "The meat is spoiled, but the vodka is good."

—Gary Marcus, *Kluge: The Haphazard Evolution of the Human Mind*

It can strike me anytime, but it usually happens summers when I'm reunited with my mother in Puerto Rico. Not when we embrace, and she tells me I'm too thin and gives me her blessing, "Dios te bendiga, Hija," and I respond automatically, "Gracias, Mami." Nor when I tell her she looks younger than ever, and she answers, "Gracias, Hija." And it doesn't happen over the much-anticipated traditional dinner she has prepared for my husband and me—arroz, habichuelas, pollo, plátanos dulces, followed by ultra-sweet café con leche and a budín, a small high-density square of such deeply satisfying sweetness that I suspect (but never want to confirm) it contains an entire day's worth of calories for most moderately active adults. It may not even happen while we are discussing the family gossip and health problems: my uncle with diabetes, aunts getting on in age, and the family curse of arthritis—the ailment that is slowly but certainly descending over most of us in the immediate and extended maternal side of my family. Diabetes, arthritis—di-ah-beh-tis, ar-tree-tis—both have cognates in Spanish.

It usually accosts me when the conversation takes a turn, entering any subject in Spanish that I live with only in English: politics; medical conditions that I have not encountered during my previous visits; the intricacies of topics such as cooking, house building, and sex (this subject hardly ever a problem unless my mother is reading about a sex-change operation or the sexual preferences of a celebrity in her *Vanidades* magazine); and many other areas of interest to her and my Spanish-only relatives. It is in those awkward pauses in conversation that I can now identify the beginning of my episodes; for example, if I am asked a question, or if it is my turn to comment on the high price of renovating a part of a house that I have never spoken of in Spanish. This is an area that, as a homeowner in Georgia, I have learned to communicate well in Southern English, my daily dialect: "And, Sir," I will say to the handyman assiduously avoiding my interference as he climbs up on the roof of our house, "Sir, will you be able to put in that new gutter lickety-split? It looks like this rain's going to be a gulley-washer."

In my mother's conversation groups, however, I am always the contestant, on the spot, playing *Double Jeopardy*, and the question is "¿Cómo se dice—?"

"¿Qué crees?" someone will invite me to offer my opinion, and I am muted by an invisible remote control aimed at me from above. I am suffering the first symptoms of *word hunger*. I search frantically through my brain files for an equivalent. Awkward moment of silence. Exchange of dubious looks, not subtle; Puerto Rican-style irony can become visual aggression. *La Profesora* cannot cough up a simple answer to a simple question? Usually my mother, a great improvisational dancer, both on the dance floor and off, makes her move to rescue me, translating the unknown into a synonymous concept.

"Prices here for una instalación de unos altos (an addition to the house) are twice as much as in the United States ¿No creen?"

Even with my desperate segues and my mother's conversational diversions, La Profesora loses face. I have an academic title (my area is creative writing and American literature) and teach at the University of Georgia, where I am only now encountering the occasional Latina/o student in my classrooms—and they usually want to speak in English. I rarely get to speak Spanish, even when I am asked to give readings to Latinos in the United States. My North American, Bolivia–raised son-in-law, who is teaching my two-year-old grandson Spanish, knows more words than I because he speaks it every day; currently his most extensive vocabulary entails baby concerns, not complex scientific terminology, in which I am sure he is also fluent. My excuse for ignorance in infant-care terminology is that I never had a reason to learn those words in Spanish: pañales, pediatra, andador, mecedora—not a difficult vocabulary, but these words are simply not on the tip of my brain. I keep a Spanish-English dictionary handy when my nieto and his papi are around. With language, it is a natural but frustrating process of use it or lose it, as it is with any human function: for most of my life since our move to the United States, I have been undergoing the change from being a primary Spanish speaker toward English becoming my first language—this is not a choice, any more than is having one arm stronger than the other because I use it more often. I have kept the Spanish vocabulary I use and have been losing the words I don't need. In the meantime, my English has grown and evolved as the language of my everyday concerns and of my professional life.

Occasionally, my mother lets me suffer through a word vacuum, at least for a minute or two, long enough to allow me to dig up la palabra—if it happens to still exist somewhere in the deep recesses of my brain area—for my own good, she claims; I can regain my Spanish, she insists. She lends me her *Buen Hogar* and *People en Español* magazines, so I can continue to acquire a conversational vocabulary. And it works. I can discuss the lives of celebrities with some competence, and if the topic of setting up a buffet meal for twenty comes up, I can probably get a few words into the conversation. I usually spend the time at her house reading books by contemporary Puerto Rican writers such as Rosario Ferré, Ana Lydia Vega, Carmen Lugo Filippi, and many others, and marveling at the beauty of my native tongue, especially when it sings at the hands of a talented wordsmith. I fall in love again with its cadences, its music. Spanish is a delicious language, miel en la boca, and I often feel like an onlooker at a banquet, kept out of the festivities mainly because of a speech impediment. Pero en mi vida, I had to choose a tongue to serve me, and it had to be English. But I can dream in Spanish. ¿No creen?

Yet there are times when the word hunger defeats me. It happens when I am trying to share with my mother or a relative or friend on the Island something that is both complicated and serious, and all the words I can come up with date back to the last stages in my life when I was more Spanish than English speaking, my adolescence. I stopped acquiring working vocabularies in what became my second language then; it is as if I became frozen within the boundaries of my native language at the point I had reached at age fifteen. During my formative years we lived mainly in Paterson, New Jersey, and it was a hard city for Puerto Rican kids who did not have a grasp of survival English—preferably in tough, street-wise, Italian-mafia affected cadences. I was also required to speak polite English at St. Joseph's Catholic School. Spanish became intrinsically related to our family's apartment interactions, and to visits to the homes of my relatives, where the children talked in English among themselves, while our parents discussed their luchas and travails in passionate Spanish. Mainly, in those years of rebellion, I used my Spanish with and against my mother. I had a good fighting vocabulary.

"No soy tu prisionera. Todos mis amigos salen en dates con muchachos. No vivimos en tu isla. Es el twentieth century, Mami. Estamos en America. Sí, voy a usar makeup. Está bien, no voy a usar makeup, for now. Mami, necesito dinero."

I never had a reason to discuss paradigms, dichotomies or dialectics, pedagogy or gender issues with my mother, unless it was the constant argument about what a good mujer should be, and when it was appropriate to wear makeup (never), date boys (never), or increase my allowance (that is for your father to decide). I could probably still defend myself well in these areas, but no longer have to.

But I exaggerate a bit, as is my cultural privilege. Mother taught us how to write in basic familial Spanish so we could correspond with our grandparents, and because I was her interpreter, I learned how to deal with doctors, clerks, the U.S. Navy, the Red Cross, and the occasional lawyer. But I was her recording device and her trained parrot; none of these matters were my causes; therefore, I forgot many words that did not interest me as I distanced myself from my childhood roles.

Recently I was in line at a gate in Hartsfield Airport in Atlanta. An irate airline employee was dealing with angry passengers experiencing many delays and missed connections. In front of me, a woman was desperately trying to find out why her flight to San Juan had been canceled. The attendant kept motioning her to move aside, telling her that he had requested a Spanish speaker to come talk to her. I normally do not get involved in airline disputes, as I have learned that next to the famously impassive New York City waiters, airline agents are the most adept public service personnel at avoiding your gaze and ignoring your presence at their counters (or supplicants' altars, as I think of these barriers to communication). You are made to wait until you have to declare temporary residency at the gate, or for the next shift to take over, then grovel and ingratiate yourself to them as best you can under the weight of travel fatigue and carry-on luggage. Travel is a humbling experience. Yet something in this woman's voice told me I needed to offer her my emergency Spanish. I asked her what the problem was. She told me she had to get home for her mother's funeral; she had been visiting her son at Fort Benning. He was soon to be deployed to Iraq, and as a result, she had missed being at her mamá's deathbed. Madre, morir—two of the most dramatic and connotative words in Spanish brought me to full attention. I could not understand any more of what she said as she broke down crying, but I knew I had to use my survival language to help her. I explained the situation to the attendant, who actually showed a small, measured sympathetic response. I also made sure that the fidgety people behind us heard me explaining the dire circumstances, which I described in my best lecturing mode. *Please understand, death in the family, a son, fighting for OUR country.* There was a palpable shift in attitudes, an almost imperceptible making of a bit of space for this suffering woman. Soon enough she was put on another airline's flight to the Island. My survival English had met the challenge and my emergency Spanish had sufficed. This time.

Not long after that, I faced a different, more frustrating situation. I was asked to give a talk at a Spanish-language academic conference. After all, I have various books about my experiences in two cultures, I was perfectly suited for the task; here was an opportunity to feature the Puerto Rican in my Puerto Rican American identity: could I deliver a paper? The time had come for me to admit that although I speak Spanish, I am not bilingual beyond a certain conversational level. I would have to ask my friend and translator of my books, Dr. Elena Olazagasti-Segovia, Vanderbilt University professor, PhD in Spanish, University of Puerto Rico, to translate my paper, and then learn to pronounce academese in Spanish (hard enough in English). I found the task not within my zone of Spanish-language comfort. It was hard to explain to my dominant-Spanish colegas in academia, many of whom seem to feel little or no embarrassment in speaking in heavily accented English and using translators for their work, that I am a Spanish-fluent, non-bilingual, English-dominant Latina, not out of choice, but due to circumstances I could not control when, as a pre-literate child, I was brought to the United States by my parents. Yet, it is as if it is my responsibility as the speaker of the language not of the minority group, which is English, to make the effort. But that is not how I see the situation. It was not my personal decision to become English-dominant. My formal education has been in English; my cultural education has been split between heart and mind, with Spanish remaining at the core of my identity, while English increasingly became the language of both my survival and my art. I use Spanish in my work to distinguish the English as that of a Latina, to dramatize and to emphasize my words. I use it to add humor and spice, as well as to indicate nuances of joy and pain. My Spanish flavors my writing as it does the most memorable meals of my life. Spanish is still the language de mi corazón. But I have to declare this in my best words, so I say it using my best English, with a little Spanish added, which is, I believe, the best language for expressing amor. English is my first language now. This is simply how it is, not how I decided it should be.

But on the surface, it must appear to the individuals who bind identity so strictly to the choice of a primary language that mine is betrayal of the mother tongue—a puertorriqueña who will not write or give a talk in her native language. Shame! ¡Qué vergüenza! I also did not mention this to distinguished colleagues—that, until recently, I too suffered from bilingualism-paradigm confusion; either you *is* bilingual *honey*, or you *ain't*. ¿Cómo se dice paradigm en español? I once heard two Latino academics practicing their paradigm insider joke at a conference. One asks, "What is a paradigm?" The other answers "Four nickels?" The conclusion I have come to is that the level of my bilingualism depends on my particular circumstances and needs—how much Spanish I will speak is a personal decision for me, one I will not make based on someone else's dogmatic views on ethnic identity.

There was a situation recently that left me feeling truly word-starved because it was a family matter of great importance to me, and yet I failed to find the words to meet the challenge. It had to do with my mother's decision to let me ask her many difficult questions about my father's long battle with depression and about the psychological traumas I suspected he had experienced during his lifetime career in the military, which I had only heard about in snatches and rumors, and which I suspected were at the root of his malady. But more significant to my understanding of the loss my family suffered, I needed to know more facts about his early death in a car accident during one of his worst bouts with what my mother has always referred to as la tristeza, the chronic sadness he wore daily like a heavy coat he could not or would not take off. I had always respected her reticence on this subject and had tried to piece together my father's story through other channels, such as questions I occasionally asked of his brothers and sisters, who, like me, only knew what he and my mother chose to reveal.

But one day, alone with her in her house on the Island, not long after she lost her beloved father to old age, after a prolonged bout with dementia and other agonies of the mind and body in his final years, we sat together in camaraderie. We sat and talked of many things, like friends, like what we are, two women in late middle age reminiscing about family times of joy, the birth of my grandson, her great-grandson, and the tristeza we will all experience in the end: birth and death, the bookends of all our lives. Here was my chance to ask the source, the keeper of our shared memories and the witness to my father's life story, to tell me what I needed to know about him. And I knew what questions I needed to ask, but they had to be phrased exactly right. We were both feeling emotional, and I could not very well run out of the room to find a dictionary, or power up my laptop to google translations when I could not come up with las palabras. In my desperate need to phrase it just right, the moment passed, the window closed. I had felt the pangs, the spiritual hunger, but I had been unable to make the right sentences out of the wordless pain. Now it would have to wait until another time, when all the elements were aligned again. When I came home to my English-language life, I wrote everything out and laboriously translated it, committing the right words to memory, preparing my passionate Spanish, the dream tongue I will always need, for when the time comes. I will be ready.

Do I speak Spanish? Yes, I speak Spanish. I speak survival Spanish. I speak yearning Spanish, I speak nostalgic Spanish. I dream in Spanish. The dream-Spanish trickles down into my poems, stories, and essays. And en mi vida, el español de mis sueños y mi corazón suffices.

OUT OF THE DARKNESS

Writing to Survive La Lucha[1]

Touch the page at your peril: it is you who are blank and innocent. Nevertheless, you want to know, nothing will stop you. You touch the page, it's as if you've drawn a knife across it, the page has been hurt now, a sinuous wound opens, a thin incision. Darkness wells through.

—Margaret Atwood

The page, the page, that eternal blankness, the blankness of eternity which you cover slowly, affirming time's scrawl as a right and your daring as necessity.

—Annie Dillard

A Visit to Hades

Hades, the ancient Greek underworld, is not to be confused with our modern hell; it's rather a place of shadows where the spirits of the dead congregate neither in a state of joy nor of torment, but of mild dissatisfaction, an eternal limbo. They are always hungry for what they no longer have—life—yet they do not despair. When, on his way home to Ithaca, Odysseus visits Hades looking for the prophet Tiresias, he brings the fresh blood of an animal sacrifice. The parched shades gather around him. The kings, queens, philosophers, and warriors are all famished for company and warm blood, their hunger equal in measure to that of the beggars and criminals. The shade of Odysseus' own mother won't talk to him until she's had her taste of blood.

When I write, I am bribing the shades to speak to me. I am visiting the place where the patient, hungry ones gather. They do not envy the living, for we are all

1. La lucha: The phrase literally translates to "the struggle." When I heard it used idiomatically by my Puerto Rican relatives, it seemed to mean not only the work of daily survival, but the gradual wearing down of the immigrant's constantly embattled psyche. Under such circumstances I found little room for the artist; what he or she could offer was not considered a primary need. So to me, surviving la lucha meant making writing necessary, in fact, vital, to my life.

on our way to join them. With trepidation, I take the ride down the river Styx, hoping it's a round-trip ticket I have purchased, and offer my warm blood to them in exchange for their visions.

The offering has to be fresh every day, and the questions have to be phrased carefully. In this place of shadows and nuance, the right question is a beam of light; the wrong question throws you into darkness. The writer learns that the darkness of writing gone wrong doesn't have to be eternal. But it often feels like it. Once you find your way back to the light, if you do, you start again with what you believe is a better question. One of the spirit voices speaks up. It is not always the one you summoned, but it is the hungriest one in the group today, the one willing to trade with you for a bit of your living blood.

An odyssey is what you have if, at the end of a long trip, real or symbolic, you have learned something about the world, human nature, and most importantly, yourself. The writer's journey is the one I know best, but anyone who leads a thoughtful life is on a journey, one in which you are the driver, not merely a passenger. In following the way of the creative, the movement is internal and the progress is towards self-discovery. The ultimate goal: to impose some order on the random patterns, to give some meaning to our chaotic lives.

When I write, each word I set down on a blank sheet of paper adds to the internal map of the world I am constructing. Since I am doing it freehand, since I am using recollection and imagination as the basis for my directions, I am always risking falling off the edge of a flat landscape. I am the one responsible for making it round, for giving it depth and dimension. If I fail, then I am left here, at the X. *You are here*, is what I say to myself sometimes after hours of work on a poem or story. And "here" is unfortunately either right where I started or a little off the page.

As a young immigrant girl, uncomfortable with my sense of myself in a strange world, I needed to be precise in my language, certain of my facts. I was, had to be, the scholarship kid. Awards and recognition assured me that I was on the right road, not about to fall off some edge I didn't know existed. I developed the ability to memorize entire chapters in my textbooks, could eventually write solid essays that were sometimes put on the overhead projectors by my teachers to show the class that even a Puerto Rican girl, just up from a U.S. territorial possession, an island so small it wasn't even a speck on the classroom globe, knew what a thesis statement was, how to close a report on the U.S. Bill of Rights with just the right quote: "No taxation without representation!" Oh, God. How hard I labored to meet my teachers' and my parents' expectations, which later became my own until I gave myself a stomach ulcer for my twenty-fifth birthday while still trying to be the perfect student in graduate school as well as a mother, wife, and more. I also discovered poetry that year of the ulcer. No, I don't think it was poetry that cured my ulcer. In fact, my ulcer is still adorning my stomach wall like the portrait of the tyrant that hangs in the houses of his most oppressed subjects. Poetry did not heal my body, it just allowed me to free myself from a fate that many of us fall into early in our lives, and that is, to deny yourself the right to create, to make art for its own sake, to pursue your own idea of beauty and truth.

The sense of liberation I felt when I began writing to meet my own need for a creative life I can only compare to what people describe who have undergone psychoanalysis for many years, or who have found or regained religious faith: it is an actual spiritual revival. To live as a writer is to discover your real self underneath the layers of indoctrination and programming that the well-meaning people who reared and educated you poured into you, trying to mold you into a "normal" person.

When I was a freshman in college, my world-weary humanities professor told the class that his job was to provide us with "a thin veneer of culture." I have carried that image with me ever since. On bad days I have felt that my public persona is a fragile, ordinary object like a hen's egg that I must transport through a crowded world. All that is keeping it safe from cracking under the jostling and the pressures is a thin coating of something like shellac provided by that kind professor and others whose noses would turn up at the messy sight of our inner selves. I have also assumed that the others around me, who don't seem worried about their shells, are able to access some esoteric material that makes their veneer invulnerable to outside forces. When I am writing, my shell is as hard as the earth's core, either that or as soft and vulnerable, resilient and pliable as a soft-boiled egg.

God, Truth, Beauty, and La Lucha

> More and more mankind will discover that we have to turn to poetry to interpret life for us, to console us, to sustain us. Without poetry our science will appear incomplete.
>
> —Matthew Arnold

Once I had religious ritual. Now I have writing ritual. I feel like I am doing penance every time I face the blank page. If I succeed in making a poem, or in composing a few lines of prose that are better than ordinary, I feel saved, but only for that day. Writing is a daily quest for redemption.

I remember when I was preparing for my First Communion and my mother used to drill me in the Catechism. She would sit with me at the kitchen table before school. Then she and I would go over our plans for the day. From as early as I can remember, I had to take one or another religion class at our parish church at the end of the school day.

"*Hija*, I will be waiting for you after school to take you to Sister María Josefa's catechism class today. Have you memorized your lesson?"

"Yes," I would answer, "but don't make me say it." I found the repetitious nature of the pamphlets I had to take home and learn offensively simple. It was mindless rote: "Do you believe in God?" *Yes, I believe in God*. "Do you believe in the one, holy, catholic, and apostolic church?" *Yes, I believe in the one, holy, catholic, and apostolic church*. And so on. We children would memorize and repeat for our mothers, memorize and repeat in church basement classrooms, until the droning of the old nun's monotone voice and the chorus of bored future Catholics would get stuck like a record in my head. *I believe, I believe, I believe!*

Mami always waited patiently until I said my lesson, going to the next one only when I had recited the last. It was a stand-off: if I played my part correctly, the time left before she walked me to school was mine to read for pleasure. Even comic books were allowed.

And so I learned the terms: pay now, fly later. Reading was a privilege I had to earn. In my life, books have always been a reward for hard work.

All my young adulthood, I read and read and read. I acquired words and took some home with me in books. I built a little fortress of language so that when the Simon and Garfunkel song came out, the one that says "I have my books and my poetry to protect me," I imagined Rhyming Simon had written it for me.

Mine is an unexceptional story of initiation into a new culture. After living outside the Puerto Rican community for years, I found a way to keep a conversation going with myself about the connections I was discovering between my past and present life. I became a writer. While in college, I had tried ignoring everything that had happened before my American life began. New knowledge filled me. I concentrated on acquiring information that would prepare me for la lucha outside. The past seemed inconsequential. After I left the walled city of the university, where it was possible to feel protected from the past, I saw that it would be impossible for me to live a fulfilling life without the recourse of writing to help me catalogue my days.

More important than the random scenes and fragments of events I have recorded, working on poems and stories has deepened my knowledge of myself and my awareness of my right to autonomy. Placing my observations neatly in lines on blank pages, which follow one another in a sequence like hours, days, months, and years, makes me feel that my life, like a book, is an act of reason and will, not merely a leaf caught in the winds of *El Destino*. I choose to believe that its patterns will become clearer to me as I turn each page of my story as both creator and active participant in my own American history.

By the simple choice of leaving the Puerto Rican community of my childhood and going to college on a scholarship, I became another kind of *Puertorriqueña* from the girls and women I grew up with in the barrio and from other women in my family who had stayed on the Island. I believed that my *abuelas*, my mother and her sisters, had demarcation lines around their world: *la casa, la Isla*, the city blocks of a barrio. When I say that I became different, I mean that, as I soon discovered, I had chosen a different arena for my lucha. My vehicle, my weapon of choice, my tool for survival is language. Possessing the tongue of the mainstream gives me the power to navigate between worlds. I learned early that when we open our mouths to speak we give away who we are, both our strengths and our weaknesses. Our personal history is in the syntax of the first sentence we speak to a stranger. That is why Pygmalion continues to be the classic Cinderella tale, but the prize is not Professor Higgins, it is the gift of language. By mastering the intricacies of the King's English, Eliza made herself a worthy competitor in la lucha, a participant in her domain, rather than the marginalized little person she had been when she could not speak effectively for herself. She gained stature every time she got those vowels to open and close just right. Long live the rain in Spain!

As a literature student, I learned that the written word contains humankind's accumulated knowledge. And that libraries are our treasure vaults. Yet our individual brains have infinite stacks, more than any man-made structure can hold, some locked behind secret panels you sometimes may stumble into. Nothing is thrown away; all is filed in a system more complicated than the Dewey decimal, or the Congressional, or even the cosmic internet, one accessed only through a lifetime of introspection. And that is what I mean when I say that studying made me different from the barrio Puertorriqueñas, whose daily lucha left them little time or energy in which to examine their lives.

They, the ones I got to know, were wise in ways I cannot aspire to, wily about survival and the eternal lucha against poverty, inequality, and often, abuse. I can only compare them—these women who were skilled at obtaining what they needed each day for themselves and their families—to the pioneer women of the early history of any New World country. These women of the barrio marched every day like urban warriors to the front lines. They worked in factories all day, then returned to their tiny apartments to work some more, taking care of children and their sometime-husbands—for many of the younger men of the barrio were the mercenary troops in this war—who made their brief appearances, left a swollen belly here and there, then were quickly gone to new adventures.

The women of the barrio partied as hard as they worked. On weekends their celebrations rocked our apartment building. Bits of plaster sometimes rained on our heads from the feet pounding out their *cumbias, pachangas, and mambos,* as they worked la lucha out of their systems. Sadly, I did not find many poets among these women. Weary after years of work and disappointments, some either dropped out into dissolute lives of welfare checks and daily TV, or they endured with the fortitude of the shipwrecked and accepted their lives as domestic martyrs. Many of them, of my mother's generation and older, could not see other choices. These women had wisdom and will, but not the words necessary to make combat outside the borders of the barrio. "Broken English Spoken Here" proudly stated a sign on the door of the bodega, the grocery store haven where people gathered to shun the English-speaking world, to comfort each other in their native tongue or through the power of their neolanguage, the witty, juxtaposed dialect of a juxtaposed life, Spanglish. It is a poetic blend, but not acceptable on college or job application forms. Of course, there were exceptions. Some of us escaped to tell the tale. In almost every case I have heard about, of the Latina writer, scholar, activist, and professional, books came into our lives early and stayed to guide us. Words saved us from the despair of living only to work, working only to live.

Yet, growing up in a New Jersey neighborhood of old immigrants and new migrants prepared me to fall in love with language. I delighted in the new language being made up as improvisational comedy, Spanglish, then adopted as the dialect of the barrio, later made famous by the Nuyorican poets in their odes and laments to lives lived between languages, in the middle of new meanings. In my childhood, it was part of the ritual of *El Gufeo* (Spanglish for goofing-around) to make up new combinations of Spanish and English to make and have fun at the expense of one another. One year I became the object of the block's sidewalk banter when I let my neighbors know that I was going to be a literature student, a teacher, maybe a writer.

"*Pues mira*, the *chica* thinks she can learn about *la vida* from books." I was supposed to overhear their stage whispers as I walked past the stoops of buildings where the women sat watching their children play hopscotch on the sidewalk.

"Ay hija, women *comelibros* all end up *jamonas*. Anyway, that's what I heard."

I would become jamona, a spinster, a lonely *comelibros* (literally, a book-eater), is what they predicted. They were 50% correct. For years, I fed my hunger for words, accepting the lonely future that awaited me. I had decided to take the veil of the scholar. It was not too hard to do my last two years of high school after we moved to Georgia and I found myself, shall we say, not in with the in crowd. I was the outsider, the dark foreigner in a school just being "desegregated." A Latina from the Yankee North was a negligible factor in a decidedly tense milieu. So my dedication to the examined life intensified, especially on weekends when I practiced being a jamona at sixteen. Later, I lost myself for awhile in the monasterial university library. I almost missed the excitement of the late sixties and early seventies because I was busy reading about ancient centers of civilization and the salvaged manuscripts the medieval monks laboriously copied, thus keeping the small pilot light burning for future generations while the world sank into the Dark Ages. My sophomoric dream was to keep the small light burning while the world fell apart around me.

But college was different. Finally, my socialization into the American life I had read about but never fully experienced began. Boys asked me out on dates. I met people from all over the country and the world, who actually valued individuality and diversity. I studied with them, partied with them, and got married, too. So I did not become a jamona (in those days a single woman past twenty five would have been an object of pity in my old neighborhood), but the barrio women were right about the loneliness of choosing the examined life. I have always missed, and tried in my work to pay tribute to, the vitality of life in the barrio. The salsa tune of my childhood lives in my blood and feeds my imagination, but I don't dance nearly enough.

Making Your Mark

I once watched an illiterate man in a courthouse make his mark on a document. I believe I was waiting for my turn to request a notarized copy of my birth certificate. I saw the man, obviously nervous, dressed in a dark suit as if for a funeral, the uniform of the insecure and unsophisticated (I myself wore my most conservative outfit for protection against the pre-judgements of bureaucrats). His hand visibly trembled as he made his deliberate X, which the eye-contact-avoiding clerk quickly countersigned with a flourish I found despicable. The man left the building with his document. He, too, avoided looking into the eyes of the witnesses to his shameful inability to make an appropriate individual mark. At least, that is the way I saw it. Maybe I was the one who misjudged it all, maybe the man felt no shame at not knowing how to make words with letters, and maybe the clerk was not showing off his superiority through his penmanship and body language. I am doing what a reader does when she enters my books, bringing into my dramas all of her experiential baggage. My writing is my way of leaving my mark on the world, and I neither want to make an X for my name, nor leave behind a pictograph of my ego every time I write a check or leave a note. I want it to read I WAS HERE, though, in a way that is unique and original.

"Making Your Mark" is a phrase that is as individually defined as each person's handwriting. To writers it can mean attaining fame and fortune or the other prize we seek along with just about everyone else on the planet: immortality. Freud defined immortality as being remembered by a lot of anonymous people, but since most of us want to be known and remembered by our contemporaries, we try for that ultimate human goal while we are still on the planet. Defining our need to leave something of ourselves for posterity is hard since immortality can only be discussed theoretically. So, when we hear the claim that someone has attained immortality, it is the same as accepting the lifetime guarantee that comes with some products.

I have trouble with both concepts. Vague wording is the problem. And so, I have decided that my goal in making my mark will be a more modest goal than the attainment of immortality. I found the word that best describes what I wish for my art in a textbook I was using, and I reveled at the Renaissance concept of *virtu*: to create for yourself a life's work that you can take pride in simply because it represents the full expression of your ability and potential, not because it will make you rich or famous. It's a wonderfully flexible concept that applies both to the Queen of England and her dressmaker, and to the President of the United States and his chauffeur. For a time in human history, if you were the village shoemaker and you possessed the quality of virtu, it gave you a certain standing in the community: people knew that every pair of shoes you made were your best possible effort. It is easy to see why this lovely idea could not survive the Industrial Revolution, especially not Henry Ford's stroke of genius in devising the assembly line. But in our world there is still evidence of the products of virtu. The things we value for their quality and beauty are usually the results of someone's virtu. All serious artists practice virtu. The poet (who was originally called a Maker) is a master of the best possible work. If you settle for nearly the best, you will not be a poet for long. Whether we know the word or not, we recognize virtu when we witness it. I decided long ago that virtu was the religion for me. To do one thing as well as my abilities allowed. *Basta, suficiente.* It would be enough.

¿Cómo se dice?: It's Like This

The discovery of any surprising likeness is one more clue to the suspicion that there seems to be an order, however deep and mysterious, in the universe.

—John Frederick Nims

Over the years, I've kept up my connections to Spanish through correspondence and conversations with my mother, who returned to the Island twenty-five years ago and reinvented herself as an Island Puertorriqueña. In writing to her and about her, I have discovered that we *newcomers* to America are morphers rather than assimilationists, at least those of us who cannot or will not melt into the American pot. We shift our shapes, learn new vocabularies, move ourselves or our modes to a climate that better suits our skin-types or personality-types. I stayed with English, she returned to Spanish, and we live with our choice of mother-tongue, very different lives.

Like the poet, the immigrant is primarily a metaphor-maker, a translator of experience. Struggling between languages, I learned this skill early—how to answer the question ¿Cómo se dice?—by making a comparison, trying to access the unfamiliar road by following the familiar *camino* first. The poem is the vehicle.

Where You Need to Go
(A VISIT HOME TO PUERTO RICO)
My life began here in this pueblo
now straining against its boundaries
and still confused about its identity:
Spanish village or tourist rest-stop,
with its centuries-old church
where pilgrims on their knees beg
a dark madonna for a miracle,
then go to lunch at Burger King.
Here is the place
where I first wailed for life
in a pre-language understood by all
in the woman-house where I was born,
where absent men in military uniform
paraded on walls alongside calendars
and crosses; and telegrams were delivered
by frightened adolescent boys
who believed all coded words from Korea
were about death. But sometimes
they were just a "*Bueno, Mujer*,"
to the women who carried on
their blood duties on the home-front.

I know this place,
although I've been away most of my life.
I've never really recovered
from my plunge, that balmy February day,
into the unsteady hands
of the nearly blind midwife,
as she mumbled prayers in Latin
to the Holy Mother, who had Herself
been spared the anguish
this old woman witnessed all those years;
to the aroma of herbal teas
brewed for power in *la lucha*, and the haunting
of the strangely manic music
that accompanies both beginnings
and endings here. I absorbed it all
through my pores. It remains
with me still, as a vague urge
to reconnect.

Today, opening my eyes again
in my mother's house,
I know I will experience certain things
that come to me in dreams, and déjá vu,
and memory: the timeless tolling of bells,
because time must be marked for mortal days
in seconds and in measured intervals,
to remind them as they drink their morning *café*
that they will die; the rustling of palm fronds
against venetian blinds, kitchen sounds
from my childhood; and muffled words
I cannot quite decipher, spoken in a language
I now have to translate, like signs
in a foreign airport you recognize
as universal symbols, and soon
their true meaning will come to you. It must.
For this is the place where you decide
where you need to go.[2]

2. "Where You Need to Go" first appeared in *The Chattahoochee Review*, 16.4 (Summer 1996): 21–23.

Los Sueños and Poetry

One year I was having troubling dreams of highly confusing content. I was also having difficulty writing poems. My mother sent me a book of dream interpretations in Spanish to help me decipher the secrets that my unconscious mind was trying to communicate to my reluctant brain. The book fascinated me by its total disregard of scientific facts. It did not refer once to Freud, or to neuroscience. I loved its poetic approach to the nightly flights of our souls to a realm as substantive as that of *el mundo* of our daily lives. From these interpretations (which I in turn translated and in the process re-interpreted for myself), which are to me a metaphor for my life between cultures, poems came.

Here are variations from the book of dreams in Spanish:

Agua

Water in your dreams reveals that there is much you must still plumb from your secret depths before you can know yourself. Agua rises from the womb of la tierra. If you dream that you are diving or fishing, you are really seeking an answer from your own self. Are you exposed to the elements of el mar? Is the wind buffeting you and you fear falling in? You must take control of your life. The elements are not your enemies; the danger is your powerlessness in their face. If water is falling in the form of rain, it may portend a renaissance for your weary soul, yet beware, if you are blinded by the water, if it drives you to hide, then you are afraid of the baptism, the near drowning that is required to be truly alive.

Fuego

If you dream of fire, a consuming fuego, you should not doubt that you are ready to give yourself over to passion. Beware. It is never a purifying flame that licks your body like a huge tongue, inflaming you, but does not turn you to ashes. The ancients called fire, el hijo del sol, the son of the sun. He was a god with a *corazón fogoso*—a hungry, fiery entity. It was reckless lovers who prayed to el hijo del sol. A dream of fire may mean a threat to your heart. ¿Ardes de pasión? Are you burning with desire? Do you smell smoke in your dream? Try to awaken yourself if the dream seems too real, and check the house for signs of fire.

My mother's book of dreams, with its insistent thesis that life, both in its conscious and unconscious manifestations, is elemental and decipherable, led me back to the wellspring of my subconscious life, poetry. The poems and the dreams blended together into a workable reality. I saw that my dreams were ingredients from which to make gold in my alchemy laboratory, or they were magical condiments—the eye of toad, the scale of dragon—tossed into my witch's cauldron. Metaphor-making is both science and magic, and it is my main means of surviving la lucha. If I can make the ordinary new through language, then I can see the world as interesting and full of potential for myself. This gives me a glimpse of a meaningful life after the lucha of today; I guess you could call it hope. And if I'm really an artist, my virtu may also result in something of value to a few others. On the other hand, if the day ever dawns when I cannot look for truth through language, if words will no longer yield beauty, then the darkness will surely swallow me.

The Need for Poetry

Comes upon you with the sweet urgency
of first love, a sudden need to enter
another consciousness, another self;
a longing to slip into the white embrace
of the blank page; to suspend
the arbitration of calendar and clock
in a short, vivid dream, to explore
the yet unimagined life on the other side
of whatever in you stirs, struggles
and flies, and in a sublime instant
surrenders to the attenuation of desire—
that is the making of a poem.

THE MYTH OF THE LATIN WOMAN

I Just Met a Girl Named María

On a bus trip to London from Oxford University where I was earning some graduate credits one summer, a young man, obviously fresh from a pub, spotted me and as if struck by inspiration went down on his knees in the aisle. With both hands over his heart he broke into an Irish tenor's rendition of "María" from *West Side Story*. My politely amused fellow passengers gave his lovely voice the round of gentle applause it deserved. Though I was not quite as amused, I managed my version of an English smile: no show of teeth, no extreme contortions of the facial muscles—I was at this time of my life practicing reserve and cool. Oh, that British control, how I coveted it. But María had followed me to London, reminding me of a prime fact of my life: you can leave the Island, master the English language, and travel as far as you can, but if you are a Latina, especially one like me who so obviously belongs to Rita Moreno's gene pool, the Island travels with you.

This is sometimes a very good thing—it may win you that extra minute of someone's attention. But with some people, the same things can make you an island—not so much a tropical paradise as an Alcatraz, a place nobody wants to visit. As a Puerto Rican girl growing up in the United States and wanting like most children to "belong," I resented the stereotype that my Hispanic appearance called forth from many people I met.

Our family lived in a large urban center in New Jersey during the sixties, where life was designed as a microcosm of my parents' casas on the island. We spoke in Spanish, we ate Puerto Rican food bought at the bodega, and we practiced strict Catholicism complete with Saturday confession and Sunday mass at a church where our parents were accommodated into a one-hour Spanish mass slot, performed by a Chinese priest trained as a missionary for Latin America.

As a girl I was kept under strict surveillance, since virtue and modesty were, by cultural equation, the same as family honor. As a teenager I was instructed on how to behave as a proper señorita. But it was a conflicting message girls got, since the Puerto Rican mothers also encouraged their daughters to look and act like women and to dress in clothes our Anglo friends and their mothers found too "mature" for our age. It was, and is, cultural, yet I often felt humiliated when I appeared at an American friend's party wearing a dress more suitable to a semi-formal than to a playroom birthday celebration. At Puerto Rican festivities, neither the music nor the colors we wore could be too loud. I still experience a vague sense of letdown when I'm invited to a "party" and it turns out to be a marathon conversation in hushed tones rather than a fiesta with salsa, laughter, and dancing—the kind of celebration I remember from my childhood.

I remember Career Day in our high school, when teachers told us to come dressed as if for a job interview. It quickly became obvious that to the barrio girls, "dressing up" sometimes meant wearing ornate jewelry and clothing that would be more appropriate (by mainstream standards) for the company Christmas party than as daily office attire. That morning I had agonized in front of my closet, trying to figure out what a "career girl" would wear because, essentially, except for Marlo Thomas on TV, I had no models on which to base my decision. I knew how to dress for school: at the Catholic school I attended we all wore uniforms; I knew how to dress for Sunday mass, and I knew what dresses to wear for parties at my relatives' homes. Though I do not recall the precise details of my Career Day outfit, it must have been a composite of the above choices. But I remember a comment my friend (an Italian-American) made in later years that coalesced my impressions of that day. She said that at the business school she was attending the Puerto Rican girls always stood out for wearing "everything at once." She meant, of course, too much jewelry, too many accessories. On that day at school, we were made the negative models by the nuns who were themselves not credible fashion experts to any of us. But it was painfully obvious to me that to the others, in their tailored skirts and silk blouses, we must have seemed "hopeless" and "vulgar." Though I now know that most adolescents feel out of step much of the time, I also know that for the Puerto Rican girls of my generation that sense was intensified. The way our teachers and classmates looked at us that day in school was just a taste of the culture clash that awaited us in the real world, where prospective employers and men on the street would often misinterpret our tight skirts and jingling bracelets as a come-on.

Mixed cultural signals have perpetuated certain stereotypes—for example, that of the Hispanic woman as the "Hot Tamale" or sexual firebrand. It is a one-dimensional view that the media have found easy to promote. In their special vocabulary, advertisers have designated "sizzling" and "smoldering" as the adjectives of choice for describing not only the foods but also the women of Latin America. From conversations in my house I recall hearing about the harassment that Puerto Rican women endured in factories where the "boss men" talked to them as if sexual innuendo was all they understood and, worse, often gave them the choice of submitting to advances or being fired.

It is custom, however, not chromosomes, that leads us to choose scarlet over pale pink. As young girls, we were influenced in our decisions about clothes and colors by the women—older sisters and mothers who had grown up on a tropical island where the natural environment was a riot of primary colors, where showing your skin was one way to keep cool as well as to look sexy. Most important of all, on the island, women perhaps felt freer to dress and move more provocatively, since, in most cases, they were protected by the traditions, mores, and laws of a Spanish/Catholic system of morality and machismo whose main rule was: *You may look at my sister, but if you touch her I will kill you.* The extended family and church structure could provide a young woman with a circle of safety in her small pueblo on the island; if a man "wronged" a girl, everyone would close in to save her family honor.

This is what I have gleaned from my discussions as an adult with older Puerto Rican women. They have told me about dressing in their best party clothes on Saturday nights and going to the town's plaza to promenade with their girlfriends in front of the boys they liked. The males were thus given an opportunity to admire the women and to express their admiration in the form of *piropos*: erotically charged street poems they composed on the spot. I have been subjected to a few piropos while visiting the Island, and they can be outrageous, although custom dictates that they must never cross into obscenity. This ritual, as I understand it, also entails a show of studied indifference on the woman's part; if she is "decent," she must not acknowledge the man's impassioned words. So I do understand how things can be lost in translation. When a Puerto Rican girl dressed in her idea of what is attractive meets a man from the mainstream culture who has been trained to react to certain types of clothing as a sexual signal, a clash is likely to take place. The line I first heard based on this aspect of the myth happened when the boy who took me to my first formal dance leaned over to plant a sloppy overeager kiss painfully on my mouth, and when I didn't respond with sufficient passion said in a resentful tone: "I thought you Latin girls were supposed to mature early"—my first instance of being thought of as a fruit or vegetable—I was supposed to *ripen*, not just grow into womanhood like other girls.

It is surprising to some of my professional friends that some people, including those who should know better, still put others "in their place." Though rarer, these incidents are still commonplace in my life. It happened to me most recently during a stay at a very classy metropolitan hotel favored by young professional couples for their weddings. Late one evening after the theater, as I walked toward my room with my new colleague (a woman with whom I was coordinating an arts program), a middle-aged man in a tuxedo, a young girl in satin and lace on his arm, stepped directly into our path. With his champagne glass extended toward me, he exclaimed, "Evita!"

Our way blocked, my companion and I listened as the man half-recited, half-bellowed "Don't Cry for Me, Argentina." When he finished, the young girl said: "How about a round of applause for daddy?" We complied, hoping this would bring the silly spectacle to a close. I was becoming aware that our little group was attracting the attention of the other guests. "Daddy" must have perceived this too, and he once more barred the way as we tried to walk past him. He began to shout-sing a ditty to the tune of "La Bamba"—except the lyrics were about a girl named María whose exploits all rhymed with her name and gonorrhea. The girl kept saying "Oh, Daddy" and looking at me with pleading eyes. She wanted me to laugh along with the others. My companion and I stood silently waiting for the man to end his offensive song. When he finished, I looked not at him but at his daughter. I advised her calmly never to ask her father what he had done in the army. Then I walked between them and to my room. My friend complimented me on my cool handling of the situation. I confessed to her that I really had wanted to push the jerk into the swimming pool. I knew that this same man—probably a corporate executive, well educated, even worldly by most standards—would not have been likely to regale a white woman with a dirty song in public. He would perhaps have checked his impulse by assuming that she could be somebody's wife or mother, or at least somebody who might take offense. But to him, I was just an Evita or a María: merely a character in his cartoon-populated universe.

Because of my education and my proficiency with the English language, I have acquired many mechanisms for dealing with the anger I experience. This was not true for my parents, nor is it true for the many Latin women working at menial jobs who must put up with stereotypes about our ethnic group such as: "They make good domestics." This is another facet of the myth of the Latin woman in the United States. Its origin is simple to deduce. Work as domestics, waitressing, and factory jobs are all that's available to women with little English and few skills. The myth of the Hispanic menial has been sustained by the same media phenomenon that made "Mammy" from *Gone with the Wind* America's idea of the black woman for generations; María, the housemaid or counter girl, is now indelibly etched into the national psyche. The big and the little screens have presented us with the picture of the funny Hispanic maid, mispronouncing words and cooking up a spicy storm in a shiny California kitchen.

This media-engendered image of the Latina in the United States has been documented by feminist Hispanic scholars, who claim that such portrayals are partially responsible for the denial of opportunities for upward mobility among Latinas in the professions. I have a Chicana friend working on a Ph.D. in philosophy at a major university. She says her doctor still shakes his head in puzzled amazement at all the "big words" she uses. Since I do not wear my diplomas around my neck for all to see, I too have on occasion been sent to that "kitchen," where some think I obviously belong.

One such incident that has stayed with me, though I recognize it as a minor offense, happened on the day of my first public poetry reading. It took place in Miami in a boat-restaurant where we were having lunch before the event. I was nervous and excited as I walked in with my notebook in my hand. An older woman motioned me to her table. Thinking (foolish me) that she wanted me to autograph a copy of my brand new slender volume of verse, I went over. She ordered a cup of coffee from me, assuming that I was the waitress. Easy enough to mistake my poems for menus, I suppose. I know that it wasn't an intentional act of cruelty, yet of all the good things that happened that day, I remember that scene most clearly, because it reminded me of what I had to overcome before anyone would take me seriously. In retrospect I understand that my anger gave my reading fire, that I have almost always taken doubts in my abilities as a challenge—and that the result is, most times, a feeling of satisfaction at having won a convert when I see the cold, appraising eyes warm to my words, the body language change, the smile that indicates that I have opened some avenue for communication. That day I read to that woman and her lowered eyes told me that she was embarrassed at her little faux pas, and when I willed her to look up at me, it was my victory, and she graciously allowed me to punish her with my full attention. We shook hands at the end of the reading, and I never saw her again. She has probably forgotten the whole thing but maybe not.

Yet I am one of the lucky ones. My parents made it possible for me to acquire a stronger footing in the mainstream culture by giving me the chance at an education. And books and art have saved me from the harsher forms of ethnic and racial prejudice that many of my Hispanic *compañeras* have had to endure. I travel a lot around the United States, reading from my books of poetry and my novel, and the reception I most often receive is one of positive interest by people who want to know more about my culture. There are, however, thousands of Latinas without the privilege of an education or the entrée into society that I have. For them life is a struggle against the misconceptions perpetuated by the myth of the Latina as whore, domestic or criminal. We cannot change this by legislating the way people look at us. The transformation, as I see it, has to occur at a much more individual level. My personal goal in my public life is to try to replace the old pervasive stereotypes and myths about Latinas with a much more interesting set of realities. Every time I give a reading, I hope the stories I tell, the dreams and fears I examine in my work, can achieve some universal truth which will get my audience past the particulars of my skin color, my accent, or my clothes.

I once wrote a poem in which I called us Latinas "God's brown daughters." This poem is really a prayer of sorts, offered upward, but also, through the human-to-human channel of art, outward. It is a prayer for communication, and for respect. In it, Latin women pray "in Spanish to an Anglo God / with a Jewish heritage," and they are "fervently hoping/ that if not omnipotent, / at least He be bilingual."

THE SIGN

"Give us a sign," my friend says, and for a second I am back in my childhood of rosaries, candles, and incense, kneeling next to Mother and Grandmother, who are pelting God with petitions: *Por favor, Dios mío. Dame, Dame, Dame.* They are asking Him to prove Himself through a sign: a healing, a stray husband's return, relief from their female burdens. *Show us proof, a small miracle, Papá Dios, of your love for us.* My friend is joking: The signs we are looking for are the neon-colored YARD SALE markers. We are hunting and gathering for the sheer pleasure of the drive and each other's company, and certainly for the pre-owned treasures we don't yet know we need, but will, as soon as we spot them. Today we are also talking motherhood, specifically the impending birth of my first grandchild, my joy tempered with concern for my daughter, so far from home. Deep into our woman wisdom, we fail to notice we are in unfamiliar territory. No surprise. We are invariably lost on these Georgia roads that change names apparently at someone's whim, as Gaines School Road turns to Barnett Shoals, and a little farther ahead, Whitehall; or they don't change names often enough: Milledge Drive, Milledge Circle, Milledge Way. On this crisp autumn Saturday, we have wandered far off. We see only woods circled with trees, still green but tipped with gold, and a field of soil so rich-red it looks like velvet cake—appetizing? The word comes to mind out of stories I've heard about cravings for clay that drive some pregnant women in rural Georgia to seek iron in the soil, drawn like dousing wands to water.

"Give us a sign," says Kathryn, and we come upon a field of cotton, snow in September, and just beyond the last row, an old barn. We see it at the same time—I put my hand on Kathryn's arm instinctively, as I used to do in church, grasping my mother's hand when the hypnotizing Latin and the clouds of candle smoke and incense made me feel as if I would drift up to the cherubim-rimmed cupola like a lost balloon. Painted on the side of that dilapidated barn, the Virgin of Guadalupe floats on her cotton cloud, a brown woman with long black hair and brilliant robes of gold, red, and blue green, crushing the feathered snake, Quetzalcoatl, with bare feet, her slightly swollen belly cinched by the black Aztec maternity belt. Serene and majestic, she is with child, always. The painting is crude, perhaps done with house paint, yet this apparition over a cotton field in Georgia is the kind of happenstance that empties your head of the mundane, that filters all brain processes down dark passages and into a room you thought you had sealed off long ago, the storing place for questions you no longer need to answer.

We slow down but do not stop. We laugh at ourselves, our awestruck faces. Who would take the time to bring the Virgin of Guadalupe to this place, and why? I imagine a pregnant young woman handing cans of paint and brushes to her man, working after a day in the fields to keep *una promesa* they made to the *Virgencita*, for the safe delivery of their child who will be born in a strange land. We will never be able to retrace our route to this field that will be harvested by workers under the gaze of the Queen of Heaven. Or more likely, the mural will be whitewashed or torn down and this land will revert to just another cotton field in the Georgia countryside. On this day, we say no more about apparitions. We keep moving down a road we hope will lead us back to the familiar. We follow the signs, and we are lost no more.

CHAPTER 4

Revamped Puerto Rican Fables as Repositories of Cultural Legacy

I wanted to make it a story so that little Puerto Rican or American girls read and say what I said when I went to the library in Paterson, "You can be Chinese and be Cinderella, African and be Cinderella." You don't even need to have a prince!

—*Judith Ortiz Cofer in Ocasio, An Interview with Judith Ortiz Cofer* 11

In her essays exploring the folklore of her native Hormigueros, Judith Ortiz Cofer often embedded or reinterpreted traditional Puerto Rican folktales and international fairy tales. Indeed, Ortiz Cofer was interested in exploring how Puerto Rican oral folklore contributed to a broader and rich Latin American culture. Speaking to me on August 10, 1993, she referred to a recent trip to Yucatan, Mexico, in heightened terms: "I had what English teachers call an epiphany, an awakening while I was there, that I think has led me to study the native cultures of Puerto Rico." She underscored the effect of that experience as the beginning of a new literary project: "I sort of made myself a promise that I would dig into Puerto Rican culture and, if I could, I would write about it in English so that people could understand that the history of Puerto Rico did not start with the Spaniard. It began long before that; and that Africans also enriched our culture."

Local folktales were also the source of a personal connection with her maternal grandmother, Mamá, whom Ortiz Cofer often recognized as an innate short story teller. In 1990, during her first formal interview for a Puerto Rican newspaper, she proudly introduced her not only as her literary muse but also as an outstanding storyteller: "Tengo una abuela en Hormigueros que debió haber sido novelista por la capacidad extraordinaria que tiene para contar historias. Muchas de ellas aparecen en mis libros" (Trelles 22; My grandmother in Hormigueros should have been a novelist for her extraordinary ability to tell stories. Many of them appear in my books). She often entertained family members with dramatic family anecdotes or popular folk stories, "cuentos that would seed my imagination" (*Cruel Country* 12). Ortiz Cofer remembered Mamá's stories as effective didactic narratives, frequently intended to be lessons for her married daughters and their small children: "She tells a simple little story, and the story is more powerful in its simplicity than anything that I could lecture about" (Bartkevicius 64). While underscoring the role of storytelling in cultures worldwide as a way to "preserve [their] memories and to teach lessons for the same reason that artists write their stories" (Kavane 116), Ortiz Cofer noted her grandmother's unique oral techniques: "What my grandmother liked to do that made her, at least I thought, different and unique was that she didn't mind changing the story for her audience. So I would hear her tell one story for my aunts in a particular way and assure us that it was absolutely true and then tell it to us in a different way to make a different point" (116).

Ortiz Cofer also came to know oral folklore formally as a *fábula*. The fable was a popular literary publication in Puerto Rico easily accessible in various formats. Children had access to cheap serial publications (often only one story) or collections that gathered several stories with common themes or highlighted characters as protagonists. Puerto Rican and international fables were also part of reading primers written specifically for the Puerto Rican public school system for elementary and secondary levels in classes such as Spanish, social sciences, or Puerto Rican history. These books highlight native folk characters, such as the well-known picaresque Juan Bobo, the youth who always manages to overcome adversities through well-planned tricks, and his counterpart, the know-it-all María Sabida. That rich cultural background was of utmost importance: "I am indebted to my heritage for the material that it has provided me with; it is enriching to my imagination to have the cuentos [tales], the Spanish language, and the history of this rich place" (qtd. in Ocasio, "Infinite Variety" 738).

Another type of classic reading for children widely available to Ortiz Cofer was the fairy tale. Ortiz Cofer often recalled how she escaped into a magical world away from the grim reality of the inner city in Paterson, New Jersey. In her own words, "I became addicted to reading the world's folktales and fairy tales" (qtd. in Bartkevicius 59). The contribution of fairy tales is fully documented in her creative nonfiction essay "Paterson Public Library": "I am still fascinated by the idea that fairy tales and fables are part of humankind's collective unconscious—a familiar theory that acquires concreteness in my own writing today, when I discover over and over that the character I create or the themes that I recur in my poems and in my fiction are my own versions of the 'types' I learned to recognize very early in my life in fairy tales" (132). A testament to her strong liking for oral folklore was her extensive personal collection of books on folklore and fairy tales from Puerto Rican and international traditions.

Readings in this chapter illustrate Ortiz Cofer's frequent documentation of native Puerto Rican folktales as prime examples of her interest in preserving Puerto Rico's rich oral folklore legacy. This recovery project also included updating key oral folk stories in English translations, which in our correspondence she described as "translations of fábulas criollas with lots of poetic license involved." The stories reflect recognizable, although highly symbolic settings, often the Puerto Rican countryside, where peculiar characters face and overcome insurmountable difficulties. For Ortiz Cofer, their didactic nature remained relevant and applicable to the modern world, as she described to me: "One of the reasons for these translations is to make wisdom available in a new form."

The creative nonfiction essays "*Casa*: A Partial Remembrance of a Puerto Rican Childhood" and "Tales Told Under the Mango Tree" recreate formal storytelling sessions like many of those that Ortiz Cofer heard as a child from her grandmother, a remarkable storyteller and repository of key Puerto Rican fables. These creative nonfiction essays introduce María la Loca and María Sabida, protagonists who are meant to represent opposite survival strategies available to women. María la Loca, a true personage, is a homeless woman who crazily wanders around Hormigueros after being left standing at the altar the day of her wedding. After this traumatic event, La Loca regressed to her childhood, thus ignoring reality.

María la Loca's counterpart, María Sabida, is a mischievous girl, a fictional character who was the protagonist of many of Mamá's stories: "I first heard the one about María Sabida from my grandmother, and she changed it over the years. Sometimes it was bloody, or other times sanitized depending on what point she was making" (qtd. in Ocasio, "Latina in the Piney Woods" 11). Ortiz Cofer was also exposed to versions of María Sabida stories in a more formal manner. In her acknowledgments to the short story collection *Silent Dancing*, she recognized versions of María Sabida that Puerto Rican folklorist Rafael Ramírez de Arellano (1854–1921) had published in his collection *Folklore portorriqueño: Cuentos y adivinanzas recogidos de la tradición oral* (1926; Puerto Rican folklore: stories and conundrums collected from an oral tradition). Ramírez de Arellano's folk stories were available to Ortiz Cofer as part of her schooling in reading primers intended as tools for basic literary analysis.

It was clearly María Sabida, not María la Loca, who became Ortiz Cofer's role model, as she wrote to me: "I saw myself as María Sabida as a little girl because I wanted to go on a quest to save my brother. That was the beginning of my interest in María Sabida and, as I say in the essay, I wanted to see what the subtext was. My grandmother did not always refer to her as María Sabida, but whenever I would 'show off,' she would say, 'Mira, la Sabida.' Later I discovered that she was getting this from the folk tale" (unpublished interview). In the formal essay "The Woman Who Slept with One Eye Open," Ortiz Cofer turned María Sabida into her own godmother, a mentor whose clever ways of taming a bloodthirsty bandit, forcing him to take her as a bride, become an unusual lesson: "My comadre taught me how to defend my art, how to conquer the villain by my wits" (Ortiz Cofer and Kallet 4).

Witty characters are central protagonists in the creative nonfiction essays "Marina" and "The Witch's Husband." An "insatiable curiosity about the history and the people of the Island which have become prominent features in my work" inspires "Marina," the story of yet another unusual protagonist who defied cultural expectations, including strict gender roles. Similarly, "The Witch's Husband" makes Mamá the smart protagonist and designer of a plan to overcome societal expectations as a young mother and devoted wife. Through the story of a "witch's husband," Mamá reveals to an adult Ortiz Cofer the reason for her mysterious trip to New York City in the early stages of her marriage, which are directly connected to the reasons she remains fully devoted to her husband even in his advanced stages of dementia.

The last stories are Ortiz Cofer's tributes to Puerto Rican folk stories. "La Jurga: A Puerto Rican Folktale," "Aunty Misery," and "Cenizosa" underscore ingenious ways to survive seemingly insurmountable life situations. While "La Jurga"—a witch-like character turned into a bird—supports the evil means of an oppressive landowner, both of them are ultimately defeated by a more clever campesino. Yet in the story "Aunty Misery," even the most clever of the tricksters, who thwarts death by trapping her in a tree and rendering her unable to kill any more, must understand it is not always a good idea to go against the established order.

Ortiz Cofer's rendition of a Puerto Rican Cinderella story is a sample from the literary project of recovery that she introduced to me as her translations of *fábulas criollas*; a handful of them, including this version, remain unpublished. She drafted several renditions of a rural Cinderella, renamed Cenizosa, or someone covered in ashes, a character she mentioned to me in the following way: "I am working on a Puerto Rican Cinderella *cuento* with no prince but rather with mondongo at its core" (unpublished 2008 interview). As a young peasant woman, Cenizosa is subjected to the domestic tasks of the Puerto Rican countryside, such as washing tripes beside a river as part of concocting the delicious mondongo stew. Nonetheless, as Ortiz Cofer commented, Cenizosa frees herself from the tyranny of an evil stepmother while aided by fairies who appear without a prince: "The fairy tales allowed me to see that sometimes by the use of wit and intelligence a girl could leave her allotted place in the ashes and come out into the sunlight!" (Kallett 71).

Animal protagonists in tropical settings constitute a second phase of Ortiz Cofer's creative fables. "The Parrot Who Loved Chorizos" is a type of warning tale that highlights the daring thefts of a clever parrot as it dared to outwit its owners for its own egotistical benefit. Nonetheless, his wit was no match for its mistress's rural cook, who found a way to control the bird's insatiable habit of stealing chorizos from her delicious stews.

Finally, "A Cockroach Named Martina," an unpublished fable, is Ortiz Cofer's homage to one of the most popular children's characters in Puerto Rican literary history. With her rendition of the love story of two unusual animal characters, La Cucarachita (Little Cockroach) Martina and El Ratoncito (Little Mouse) Pérez, Ortiz Cofer signaled her interest in incorporating a cornerstone fábula criolla alongside other well-known animal folk characters in Latin America and Latinx popular oral cultures.

CASA

A Partial Remembrance of a Puerto Rican Childhood

At three or four o'clock in the afternoon, the hour of *café con leche*, the women of my family gathered in Mamá's living room to speak of important things and retell familiar stories meant to be overheard by us young girls, their daughters. In Mamá's house (everyone called my grandmother Mamá) was a large parlor built by my grandfather to his wife's exact specifications so that it was always cool, facing away from the sun. The doorway was on the side of the house so no one could walk directly into her living room. First, they had to take a little stroll through and around her beautiful garden where prize-winning orchids grew in the trunk of an ancient tree she had hollowed out for that purpose. This room was furnished with several mahogany rocking chairs, acquired at the births of her children, and one intricately carved rocker that had passed down to Mamá at the death of her own mother.

It was on these rockers that my mother, her sisters, and my grandmother sat on these afternoons of my childhood to tell their stories, teaching each other, and my cousin and me, what it was like to be a woman, more specifically, a Puerto Rican woman. They talked about life on the island, and life in *Los Nueva Yores*, their way of referring to the U.S. from New York City to California: the other place, not home, all the same. They told real life stories though, as I later learned, always embellishing them with a little or a lot of dramatic detail. And they told *cuentos*, the morality and cautionary tales told by the women in our family for generations: stories that became a part of my subconscious as I grew up in two worlds, the tropical island and the cold city, and that would later surface in my dreams and in my poetry.

One of these tales was about the woman who was left at the altar. Mamá liked to tell that one with histrionic intensity. I remember the rise and fall of her voice, the sighs, and her constantly gesturing hands, like two birds swooping through her words. This particular story usually would come up in a conversation as a result of someone mentioning a forthcoming engagement or wedding. The first time I remember hearing it, I was sitting on the floor at Mamá's feet, pretending to read a comic book. I may have been eleven or twelve years old, at that difficult age when a girl was no longer a child who could be ordered to leave the room if the women wanted freedom to take their talk into forbidden zones, nor really old enough to be considered a part of their conclave. I could only sit quietly, pretending to be in another world, while absorbing it all in a sort of unspoken agreement of my status as silent auditor. On this day, Mamá had taken my long, tangled mane of hair into her ever busy hands. Without looking down at me and with no interruption of her flow of words, she began braiding my hair, working at it with the quickness and determination that characterized all her actions. My mother was watching us impassively from her rocker across the room. On her lips played a little ironic smile. I would never sit still for *her* ministrations, but even then, I instinctively knew that she did not possess Mamá's matriarchal power to command and keep everyone's attention. This was never more evident than in the spell she cast when telling a story.

"It is not like it used to be when I was a girl," Mamá announced. "Then, a man could leave a girl standing at the church altar with a bouquet of fresh flowers in her hands and disappear off the face of the earth. No way to track him down if he was from another town. He could be a married man, with maybe even two or three families all over the island. There was no way to know. And there were men who did this. Hombres with the devil in their flesh who would come to a pueblo, like this one, take a job at one of the haciendas, never meaning to stay, only to have a good time and to seduce the women."

The whole time she was speaking, Mamá would be weaving my hair into a flat plait that required pulling apart the two sections of hair with little jerks that made my eyes water; but knowing how grandmother detested whining and *boba* (sissy) tears, as she called them, I just sat up as straight and stiff as I did at La Escuela San José, where the nuns enforced good posture with a flexible plastic ruler they bounced off of slumped shoulders and heads. As Mamá's story progressed, I noticed how my young aunt Laura lowered her eyes, refusing to meet Mamá's meaningful gaze. Laura was seventeen, in her last year of high school, and already engaged to a boy from another town who had staked his claim with a tiny diamond ring, then left for Los Nueva Yores to make his fortune. They were planning to get married in a year. Mamá had expressed serious doubts that the wedding would ever take place. In Mamá's eyes, a man set free without a legal contract was a man lost. She believed that marriage was not something men desired, but simply the price they had to pay for the privilege of children and, of course, for what no decent (synonymous with "smart") woman would give away for free.

"María La Loca was only seventeen when *it* happened to her." I listened closely at the mention of this name. María was a town character, a fat middle-aged woman who lived with her old mother on the outskirts of town. She was to be seen around the pueblo delivering the meat pies the two women made for a living. The most peculiar thing about María, in my eyes, was that she walked and moved like a little girl though she had the thick body and wrinkled face of an old woman. She would swing her hips in an exaggerated, clownish way, and sometimes even hop and skip up to someone's house. She spoke to no one. Even if you asked her a question, she would just look at you and smile, showing her yellow teeth. But I had heard that if you got close enough, you could hear her humming a tune without words. The kids yelled out nasty things at her, calling her *La Loca*, and the men who hung out at the bodega playing dominoes sometimes whistled mockingly as she passed by with her funny, outlandish walk. But María seemed impervious to it all, carrying her basket of *pasteles* like a grotesque Little Red Riding Hood through the forest.

María La Loca interested me, as did all the eccentrics and crazies of our pueblo. Their weirdness was a measuring stick I used in my serious quest for a definition of normal. As a Navy brat shuttling between New Jersey and the pueblo, I was constantly made to feel like an oddball by my peers, who made fun of my two-way accent: a Spanish accent when I spoke English, and when I spoke Spanish I was told that I sounded like a *Gringa*. Being the outsider had already turned my brother and me into cultural chameleons. We developed early on the ability to blend into a crowd, to sit and read quietly in a fifth story apartment building for days and days when it was too bitterly cold to play outside, or, set free, to run wild in Mamá's realm, where she took charge of our lives, releasing Mother for a while from the intense fear for our safety that our father's absences instilled in her. In order to keep us from harm when Father was away, Mother kept us under strict surveillance. She even walked us to and from Public School No. 11, which we attended during the months we lived in Paterson, New Jersey, our home base in the states. Mamá freed all three of us like pigeons from a cage. I saw her as my liberator and my model. Her stories were parables from which to glean the *Truth*.

"María La Loca was once a beautiful girl. Everyone thought she would marry the Méndez boy." As everyone knew, Rogelio Méndez was the richest man in town. "But," Mamá continued, knitting my hair with the same intensity she was putting into her story, "this *macho* made a fool out of her and ruined her life." She paused for the effect of her use of the word "macho," which at that time had not yet become a popular epithet for an unliberated man. This word had for us the crude and comical connotation of "male of the species," stud; a macho was what you put in a pen to increase your stock.

I peeked over my comic book at my mother. She too was under Mamá's spell, smiling conspiratorially at this little swipe at men. She was safe from Mamá's contempt in this area. Married at an early age, an unspotted lamb, she had been accepted by a good family of strict Spaniards whose name was old and respected, though their fortune had been lost long before my birth. In a rocker Papá had painted sky blue sat Mamá's oldest child, Aunt Nena. Mother of three children, stepmother of two more, she was a quiet woman who liked books but had married an ignorant and abusive widower whose main interest in life was accumulating wealth. He too was in the mainland working on his dream of returning home rich and triumphant to buy the *finca* of his dreams. She was waiting for him to send for her. She would leave her children with Mamá for several years while the two of them slaved away in factories. He would one day be a rich man, and she a sadder woman. Even now her life-light was dimming. She spoke little, an aberration in Mamá's house, and she read avidly, as if storing up spiritual food for the long winters that awaited her in *Los Nueva Yores* without her family. But even Aunt Nena came alive to Mamá's words, rocking gently, her hands over a thick book in her lap.

Her daughter, my cousin Sara, played jacks by herself on the tile porch outside the room where we sat. She was a year older than I. We shared a bed and all our family's secrets. Collaborators in search of answers, Sara and I discussed everything we heard the women say, trying to fit it all together like a puzzle that, once assembled, would reveal life's mysteries to us. Though she and I still enjoyed taking part in boys' games—chase, volleyball and even *vaqueros*, the island version of cowboys and Indians involving cap-gun battles and violent shoot-outs under the mango tree in Mamá's backyard—we loved best the quiet hours in the afternoon when the men were still at work, and the boys had gone to play serious baseball at the park. Then Mamá's house belonged only to us women. The aroma of coffee perking in the kitchen, the mesmerizing creaks and groans of the rockers, and the women telling their lives in *cuentos* are forever woven into the fabric of my imagination, braided like my hair that day I felt my grandmother's hands teaching me about strength, her voice convincing me of the power of storytelling.

That day Mamá told how the beautiful María had fallen prey to a man whose name was never the same in subsequent versions of the story; it was Juan one time, José, Rafael, Diego, another. We understood that neither the name nor any of the facts were important, only that a woman had allowed love to defeat her. Mamá put each of us in María's place by describing her wedding dress in loving detail: how she looked like a princess in her lace as she waited at the altar. Then, as Mamá approached the tragic denouement of her story, I was distracted by the sound of my Aunt Laura's violent rocking. She seemed on the verge of tears. She knew the fable was intended for her. That week she was going to have her wedding gown fitted, though no firm date had been set for the marriage. Mamá ignored Laura's obvious discomfort, digging out a ribbon from the sewing basket she kept by her rocker while describing María's long illness, "a fever that would not break for days." She spoke of a mother's despair: "that woman climbed the church steps on her knees every morning, wore only black as a *promesa* to the Holy Virgin in exchange for her daughter's health." By the time María returned from her honeymoon with death, she was ravished, no longer young or sane. "As you can see, she is almost as old as her mother already," Mamá lamented while tying the ribbon to the ends of my hair, pulling it back with such force that I just knew I would never be able to close my eyes completely again.

"That María is getting crazier every day." Mamá's voice would take a lighter tone now, expressing satisfaction, either for the perfection of my braid, or for a story well told—it was hard to tell. "You know that tune María is always humming?" Carried away by her enthusiasm, I tried to nod, but Mamá still had me pinned between her knees.

"Well, that's the wedding march." Surprising us all, Mamá sang out. "Da, da, dara . . . da, da, dara." Then lifting me off the floor by my skinny shoulders, she would lead me around the room in an impromptu waltz—another session ending with the laughter of women, all of us caught up in the infectious joke of our lives.

TALES TOLD UNDER THE MANGO TREE

María Sabida

Once upon a time there lived a girl who was so smart that she was known throughout Puerto Rico as María Sabida. María Sabida came into the world with her eyes open. They say that at the moment of her birth she spoke to the attending midwife and told her what herbs to use to make a special *guarapo*, a tea that would put her mother back on her feet immediately. They say that the two women would have thought the infant was possessed if María Sabida had not convinced them with her descriptions of life in heaven that she was touched by God and not spawned by the Devil.

María Sabida grew up in the days when the King of Spain owned Puerto Rico, but had forgotten to send law and justice to this little island lost on the map of the world. And so thieves and murderers roamed the land terrorizing the poor people. By the time María Sabida was of marriageable age, one such *ladrón* had taken over the district where she lived.

For years people had been subjected to abuse from this evil man and his henchmen. He robbed them of their cattle and then made them buy their own cows back from him. He would take their best chickens and produce when he came into town on Saturday afternoons riding with his men through the stalls set up by farmers. Overturning their tables, he would yell, "Put it on my account." But, of course, he never paid for anything he took. One year several little children disappeared while walking to the river, and although the townspeople searched and searched, no trace of them was ever found. That is when María Sabida entered the picture. She was fifteen then, and a beautiful girl with the courage of a man, they say.

She watched the chief *ladrón* the next time he rampaged through the pueblo. She saw that he was a young man: red skinned, and tough as leather. *Cuero y sangre, nada más*, she said to herself, a man of flesh and blood. And so, she prepared herself to either conquer or to kill this man.

María Sabida followed the horses' trail deep into the woods. Though she left the town far behind she never felt afraid or lost. María Sabida could read the sun, the moon, and the stars for direction. When she got hungry, she knew which fruits were good to eat, which roots and leaves were poisonous, and how to follow the footprints of animals through a waterhole. At nightfall, María Sabida came to the edge of a clearing where a large house, almost like a fortress, stood in the forest.

"No woman has ever set foot in that house," she thought, "no *casa* is this, but a man-place." It was a house built for violence, with no windows on the ground level, but there were turrets on the roof where men could stand guard with guns. She waited until it was nearly dark and approached the house through the kitchen side. She found it by smell.

In the kitchen, which she knew would have to have a door or window for ventilation, she saw an old man stirring a huge pot. Out of the pot stuck little arms and legs. Angered by the sight, María Sabida entered the kitchen, pushed the old man aside, and picking up the pot threw its horrible contents out of the window.

"Witch, witch, what have you done with my master's stew!" yelled the old man. "He will kill us both when he gets home and finds his dinner spoiled."

"Get, you filthy viejo." María Sabida grabbed the old man's beard and pulled him to his feet. "Your master will have the best dinner of his life if you follow my instructions."

María Sabida then proceeded to make the most delicious *asopao* the old man had ever tasted, but she would answer no questions about herself, except to say that she was his master's fiancée.

When the meal was done, María Sabida stretched and yawned and said that she would go upstairs and rest until her *prometido* came home. Then she went upstairs and waited.

The men came home and ate ravenously of the food María Sabida had cooked. When the chief *ladrón* had praised the old man for a fine meal, the cook admitted that it had been *la prometida* who had made the tasty chicken stew.

"My what?" the leader roared, "I have no *prometida*." And he and his men ran upstairs. But there were many floors, and by the time they were halfway to the room where María Sabida waited, many of the men had dropped down unconscious and the others had slowed down to a crawl until they too were overcome with irresistible sleepiness. Only the chief *ladrón* made it to where María Sabida awaited him holding a paddle that she had found among his weapons. Fighting to keep his eyes open, he asked her, "Who are you, and why have you poisoned me?"

"I am your future wife, María Sabida, and you are not poisoned, I added a special sleeping powder that tastes like oregano to your *asopao*. You will not die."

"Witch!" yelled the chief ladrón, "I will kill you. Don't you know who I am?" And reaching for her, he fell on his knees, whereupon María Sabida beat him with the paddle until he lay curled like a child on the floor. Each time he tried to attack her, she beat him some more. When she was satisfied that he was vanquished, María Sabida left the house and went back to town.

A week later, the chief *ladrón* rode into town with his men again. By then everyone knew what María Sabida had done and they were afraid of what these evil men would do in retribution. "Why did you not just kill him when you had a chance, *muchacha*?" many of the townswomen had asked María Sabida. But she had just answered mysteriously, "It is better to conquer than to kill." The townspeople then barricaded themselves behind closed doors when they heard the pounding of the thieves' horses approaching. But the gang did not stop until they arrived at María Sabida's house. There the men, instead of guns, brought out musical instruments: a *cuatro*, a *güiro*, *maracas*, and a harmonica. Then they played a lovely melody.

"María Sabida, María Sabida, my strong and wise María," called out the leader, sitting tall on his horse under María Sabida's window, "come out and listen to a song I've written for you—I call it *The Ballad of María Sabida*."

María Sabida then appeared on her balcony wearing a wedding dress. The chief *ladrón* sang his song to her: a lively tune about a woman who had the courage of a man and the wisdom of a judge, who had conquered the heart of the best bandido on the island of Puerto Rico. He had a strong voice and all the people cowering in their locked houses heard his tribute to María Sabida and crossed themselves at the miracle she had wrought.

One by one they all came out and soon María Sabida's front yard was full of people singing and dancing. The *ladrones* had come prepared with casks of wine, bottles of rum, and a wedding cake made by the old cook from the tender meat of coconuts. The leader of the thieves and María Sabida were married on that day. But all had not yet been settled between them. That evening, as she rode behind him on his horse, she felt the dagger concealed beneath his clothes. She knew then that she had not fully won the battle for this man's heart.

On her wedding night María Sabida suspected that her husband wanted to kill her. After their dinner, which the man had insisted on cooking himself, they went upstairs. María Sabida asked for a little time alone to prepare herself. He said he would take a walk but would return very soon. When she heard him leave the house, María Sabida went down to the kitchen and took several gallons of honey from the pantry. She went back to the bedroom and there she fashioned a life-sized doll out of her clothes and poured the honey into it. She then blew out the candle, covered the figure with a sheet and hid herself under the bed.

After a short time, she heard her husband climbing the stairs. He tip-toed into the dark room thinking her asleep in their marriage bed. Peeking out from under the bed, María Sabida saw the glint of the knife her husband pulled out from inside his shirt. Like a fierce panther he leapt onto the bed and stabbed the doll's body over and over with his dagger. Honey splattered his face and fell on his lips. Shocked, the man jumped off the bed and licked his lips.

"How sweet is my wife's blood. How sweet is María Sabida in death—how sour in life and how sweet in death. If I had known she was so sweet, I would not have murdered her." And so declaring, he kneeled down on the floor beside the bed and prayed to María Sabida's soul for forgiveness.

At that Moment María Sabida came out of her hiding place. "Husband, I have tricked you once more, I am not dead." In his joy, the man threw down his knife and embraced María Sabida, swearing that he would never kill or steal again. And he kept his word, becoming in later years an honest farmer. Many years later he was elected mayor of the same town he had once terrorized with his gang of ladrones.

María Sabida made a real *casa* out of his thieves' den, and they had many children together, all of whom could speak at birth. But, they say, María Sabida always slept with one eye open, and that is why she lived to be one hundred years old and wiser than any other woman on the Island of Puerto Rico, and her name was known even in Spain.

"Colorín, colorado este cuento se ha acabado." Mamá would slap her knees with open palms and say this little rhyme to indicate to the children sitting around her under the giant mango tree that the story was finished. It was time for us to go play and leave the women alone to embroider in the shade of the tree and to talk about serious things.

I remember that tree as a natural wonder. It was large, with a trunk that took four or five children holding hands to reach across. Its leaves were so thick that the shade it cast made a cool room where we took refuge from the hot sun. When an unexpected shower caught us there, the women had time to gather their embroidery materials before drops came through the leaves. But the most amazing thing about that tree was the throne it had made for Mamá. On the trunk there was a smooth seat-like projection. It was perfect for a storyteller. She would take her place on the throne and lean back. The other women—my mother and her sisters—would bring towels to sit on; the children sat anywhere. Sometimes we would climb to a thick branch we called "the ship," to the right of the throne, and listen there. "The ship" was a thick limb that hung all the way down to the ground. Up to three small children could straddle this branch while the others bounced on the end that sat near the ground making it sway like a ship. When Mamá told her stories, we sat quietly on our crow's nest because if anyone interrupted her narrative she should stop talking and no amount of begging would persuade her to finish the story that day.

The first time my mother took my brother and me back to Puerto Rico, we were stunned by the heat and confused by a houseful of relatives. Mamá's *casa* was filled to capacity with grandchildren, because two of the married daughters had come to stay there until their husbands sent for them: my mother and the two of us and her oldest sister with her five children. Mamá still had three of her own children at home, ranging in age from a teenage daughter to my favorite uncle who was six months older than me.

Our solitary life in New Jersey, where we spent our days inside a small dark apartment watching television and waiting for our father to come home on leave from the Navy, had not prepared us for life in Mamá's house or for the multitude of cousins, aunts and uncles pulling us into their loud conversations and rough games. For the first few days my little brother kept his head firmly buried in my mother's neck, while I stayed relatively close to her; but being nearly six, and able to speak as loudly as anyone, I soon joined Mamá's tribe.

In the last few weeks before the beginning of school, when it was too hot for cooking until it was almost dark and when mothers would not even let their boys go to the playgrounds and parks for fear of sunstroke, Mamá would lead us to the mango tree, there to spin the web of our *cuentos* over us, making us forget the heat, the mosquitos, our past in a foreign country, and even the threat of the first day of school looming just ahead.

It was under that mango tree that I first began to feel the power of words. I cannot claim to have always understood the point of the stories I heard there. Some of these tales were based on ancient folklore brought to the colonies by Spaniards from their own versions of even older myths of Greek and Roman origins—which, as I later discovered through my insatiable reading, had been modified in clever ways to fit changing times. María Sabida became the model Mamá used for the "prevailing woman"—the woman who "slept with one eye open"—whose wisdom was gleaned through the senses: from the natural world and from ordinary experiences. Her main virtue was that she was always alert and never a victim. She was by implication contrasted to María La Loca, that poor girl who gave it all up for love, becoming a victim of her own foolish heart.

The mango tree was located at the top of a hill, on land that belonged to "The American," or at least to the sugar refinery that he managed. *La Central*, as it was called, employed the majority of the pueblo's men. Its tall chimney stacks loomed over the town like sentinels, spewing plumes of gray smoke that filled the air during cane season with the syrupy thick aroma of burnt sugar.

In my childhood the sugarcane fields bordered both sides of the main road, which was like a part on a head of spiky, green hair. As we approached the pueblo on our way coming home, I remember how my mother sat up in the back seat of the *carro público*, the taxi we had taken from the airport in San Juan. Although she was pointing out the bell tower of the famous church of La Monserrate, I was distracted by the hypnotizing motion of men swinging machetes in the fields. They were shirtless, and sweat poured in streams down their backs. Bathed in light reflected by their blades, these laborers moved as on a ballet stage. I wondered whether they practiced like dancers to perfect their synchronicity. It did not occur to me that theirs was "survival choreography"—merely a safety measure—for wild swinging could lead to lost fingers and limbs. Or, as I heard one of the women say once, "there are enough body parts in the cane fields to put one whole man together."

And although trucks were already being used in most *centrales*, in our town, much of the cane harvest was still transported from the fields to the mill in oxen-drawn carts which were piled so high with the stalks, that, when you followed one of them you could see neither the cart driver nor the beasts in front: It was a moving haystack.

To car drivers they were a headache and a menace on the road. A good wind could blow the cane off the top of the cart and smash a windshield. But what most drivers hated was getting stuck behind one that would take up the whole road traveling at five miles per hour and ignore the horn, the mad hand waving and the red-faced man shouting incentives. In later years this vehicle would be almost totally replaced by the open bed trucks that were also loaded to the limit traveling the roads of the island at sixty or seventy miles per hour, granting no other vehicle (except police cars) right-of-way. The driver would keep his hand on the horn and that was all the warning a passenger car received. Pulling over as if for an emergency vehicle, was usually the best plan to follow.

We sucked on little pieces of sugar cane Mamá had cut for us under the mango tree. Below us a pasture rolled down to the road and the cane fields could be seen at a distance; the men in their perpetual motion were tiny black ants to our eyes. You looked up to see the red roof of the American's house. It was a big white house with a large porch completely enclosed by mosquito screens (on the Island at that time this was such a rarity that all houses designed in that way were known as "American"). At Mamá's house we slept cozily under mosquito nets, but during the day we fought the stinging, buzzing insects with bare hands and, when we lost a battle, we soothed our scratched raw skin with calamine lotion.

During the first few weeks of our visits both my brother and I, because we were fresh, tender meat, had skin like a pink target, dotted with red spots where the insects had scored bulls-eyes. Amazingly, either we built up natural resistance, or the mosquitoes gave up, but it happened every time: a period of embarrassment as pink "turistas," followed by brown skin and immunity. Living behind screens the American couple would never develop the tough skin needed for Island survival.

When Mamá told stories about kings and queens and castles, she would point to the big house on the hill. We were not supposed to go near the place. In fact, we were trespassing when we went to the mango tree. Mamá's backyard ended at the barbed-wire fence that led to the American's pasture. The tree stood just on the other side. She had at some point before my time, placed a strong stick under the barbed wire to make an entrance; but it could only be pulled up so much, so that even the children had to crawl through. Mamá seemed to relish the difficulty of getting to our special place. For us children it was fun to watch our mothers get their hair and clothes caught on the wire and to listen to them curse.

The pasture was a magical realm of treasures and secret places to discover. It even had a forbidden castle we could look at from a distance.

While the women embroidered, my girl-cousins and I would gather leaves and thorns off a lemon tree and do some imaginative stitch work of our own. The boys would be in the "jungle" gathering banana leaves they built teepees with. Imitating the grownups who were never without a cigarette hanging from their mouths, we would pick the tightly wrapped buds of the hibiscus flowers, which, with their red tips, looked to us like lighted cigarettes. We glued wild flower petals to our fingernails and, although they did not stay on for long, for a little while our hands, busy puncturing the leaves into patterns with lemon tree thorns, looked like our mother's with their red nail polish, pushing needle and thread through white linen, creating improbable landscapes of trailing vines and flowers, decorating the sheets and pillowcases we would sleep on.

We picked ripe guavas in their season and dumped them on Mamá's capacious lap for her to inspect for worms before we ate them. The sweetness of a ripe guava cannot be compared to anything else: its pink, gooey inside can be held on the tongue and savored like a caramel.

During mango season we threw rocks at the branches of our tree, hanging low with fruit. Later in the season, a boy would climb to the highest branches for the best fruit—something I always yearned to do, but was not allowed to: too dangerous.

On days when Mamá felt truly festive she would send us to the store with three dollars for ten bottles of Old Colony pop and the change in assorted candies: Mary Janes, Bazooka gum, lollipops, tiny two-piece boxes of Chicklets, coconut candy wrapped in wax paper, and more—all kept in big glass Jars and sold two for one penny. We would have our reckless feast under the mango tree and then listen to a story. Afterwards, we would take turns on the swing that touched the sky.

My grandfather had made a strong swing from a plank of heavy wood and a thick length of rope. Under Mamá's supervision he had hung it from a sturdy lower branch of the mango tree that reached over the swell of the hill. In other words, you boarded the swing on level ground, but since the tree rose out of the summit, one push and you took off for the sky. It was almost like flying. From the highest point I ever reached, I could see the big house, as a bird would see it, to my left; the church tower from above the trees to my right; and far in the distance, below me, my family in a circle under the tree, receding, growing smaller; then as I came back down to earth, looming larger, my mother's eyes glued on me, reflecting the fear for my safety that she would not voice in her mother's presence and thus risk overriding the other's authority. My mother's greatest fear was that my brother or I would hurt ourselves while at Mamá's, and that she would be held accountable by my excessively protective father when he returned from his tour of duty in Europe. And one day, because fear invites accident, I did fall from a ride up to the clouds.

I had been catapulting myself higher and higher, when out of the corner of my eye I saw my big cousin, Javier, running at top speed after his little brother, swinging a stick in front as if to strike the younger boy. This happened fast. The little boy, Roberto, ran towards Mamá, who at that moment, was leaning towards my mother in conversation. Trying to get to his brother before he reached safe haven, Javier struck, accidentally hitting my mother square on the face. I saw it happening. I saw it as if in slow motion. I saw my mother's broken glasses fly off her face, and the blood began to flow. Dazed, I let go of the swing ropes and flew down from the clouds and the treetops and onto the soft cushion of pasture grass and just rolled and rolled. Then I lay there stunned, tasting grass and dirt until Mamá's strong arms lifted me up. She carried me through the fence and down to her house where my mother was calling hysterically for me. Her glasses had protected her from serious injury. The bump on her forehead was minor. The nosebleed had already been contained by the age-old method of placing a copper penny on the bridge, between the eyes. Her tears upset me, but not as much as the way she made me stand before her, in front of everyone, while she examined my entire body for bruises, scratches, and broken bones. "What will your father say," she kept repeating, until Mamá pulled me away. "Nothing," she said to my mother, "if you don't tell him." And, leaving her grown daughters to comfort each other, she called the children out to the yard where she had me organize a game of hide-and-seek that she supervised, catching cheaters right and left.

When it rained, the children were made to take naps or play quietly in the bedroom. I asked for Mamá's monumental poster bed, and, when my turn came, I got it. There I lay four or five feet above ground inhaling her particular smells of coconut oil, (which she used to condition her thick black hair) and Palmolive soap. I would luxuriate in her soft pillows and her mattress which was covered with gorgeously embroidered bed linens. I would get sleepy listening to the drone of the women's conversation out of the parlor.

Beyond the double doors of her peacock blue room I could hear Mamá and her older daughters talking about things that, at my age, would not have interested me: They read letters received from my father traveling with the navy in Europe, or letters from any of the many relatives making their way in the barrios of New York and New Jersey, working in factories and dreaming of returning "in style" to Puerto Rico.

The women would discuss the new school year, and plan a shopping trip to the nearest city, Mayagüez, for materials to make school uniforms for the children, who by September had to be outfitted in brown and white and marched off to the public school looking like Mussolini's troops in our dull uniforms. Their talk would take on more meaning for me as I got older, but that first year back on the Island I was under María Sabida's spell. To entertain myself, I would make up stories about the smartest girl in all of Puerto Rico.

When María Sabida was only six years old, I began, she saved her little brother's life. He was dying of a broken heart, you see, for he desperately wanted some sweet guavas that grew at the top of a steep, rocky hill near the lair of a fierce dragon. No one had ever dared to climb that hill though everyone could see the huge guava tree and the fruit, as big as pears, hanging from its branches. María Sabida's little brother had stared at the tree until he had made himself sick from yearning the forbidden fruit.

Everyone knew that the only way to save the boy was to give him one of the guavas. María Sabida's parents were frantic with worry. The little boy was fading fast. The father tried climbing the treacherous hill to the guava tree but the rocks were loose and for every step forward he took, he slipped back three. He returned home. The mother spent her days cooking delicious meals with which to tempt her little son to eat, but he just turned his sad eyes to the window in his room from where he could see the guava tree loaded with the only food he wanted. The doctor came to examine the boy and pronounced him as good as gone. The priest came and told the women they should start making their black dresses. All hope seemed lost when María Sabida, whose existence everyone seemed to have forgotten, came up with an idea to save her brother one day while she was washing her hair in the special way her grandmother had taught her.

Her mamá had shown her how to collect rainwater—water from the sky—into a barrel, and then, when it was time to wash her hair, how to take a fresh coconut and draw the oil from its white insides. You then took a bowl of clear rainwater and added the coconut oil, using the mixture to rinse your hair. Her mamá had shown her how the rainwater, coming as it did from the sky, had little bits of starshine in it. This star stuff was what made your hair glossy, the oil was to make it stick.

It was while María Sabida was mixing the starshine that she had the brilliant idea which saved her brother. She ran to her father who was in the stable feeding the mule and asked if she could borrow the animal that night. The man, startled by his daughter's wild look (her hair was streaming wet and she still held the coconut scraps in her hands) at first just ordered his daughter into the house, thinking that she had gone crazy with grief over her brother's imminent death. But María Sabida could be stubborn, and she refused to move until her parents heard what she had to say. The man called his wife to the stable, and when María Sabida had finished telling them her plan, he still thought she had lost her mind. He agreed with his desperate wife that at this point anything was worth trying. They let María Sabida have the mule to use that night.

María Sabida then waited until it was pitch black. She knew there would be no moon that night. Then she drew water from her rain barrel and mixed it with plenty of coconut oil and plastered her mule's hooves with it. She led the animal to the bottom of the rocky hill where the thick sweet smell of ripe guavas was irresistible. María Sabida felt herself caught in the spell. Her mouth watered and she felt drawn to the guava tree. The mule must have felt the same thing because it started walking ahead of the girl with quick, sure steps. Though rocks came tumbling down, the animal found footing, and in doing so, left a shiny path with the bits of starshine that María Sabida had glued to its hoofs. María Sabida kept her eyes on the bright trail because it was a dark, dark night.

As she approached the guava tree, the sweet aroma was like a liquid that she drank through her nose. She could see the fruit within arms-reach when the old mule stretched her neck to eat one and a horrible scaly arm reached out and yanked the animal off the path. María Sabida quickly grabbed three guavas and ran down the golden trail all the way back to her house.

When she came into her little brother's room, the women had already gathered around the bed with their flowers and their rosaries, and because María Sabida was a little girl herself and could not see past the crowd, she thought for one terrible minute that she was too late. Luckily her brother smelled the guavas from just this side of death and he sat up in bed. María Sabida pushed her way through the crowd and gave him one to eat. Within minutes the color returned to his cheeks. Everyone rejoiced remembering other wonderful things that she had done, and why her middle name was "Sabida."

And yes, María Sabida ate one of the enchanted guavas herself and was never sick a day in her long life. The third guava was made into a jelly that could cure every childhood illness imaginable, from a toothache to the chicken pox.

"Colorín, colorado . . ." I must have said to myself, "Colorín Colorado . . . este cuento se ha acabado" as I embroidered my own fable, listening all the while to that inner voice which, when I was very young, sounded just like Mamá's when she told her stories in the parlor or under the mango tree. And later, as I gained more confidence in my own ability, the voice telling the story became my own.

THE WOMAN WHO SLEPT WITH ONE EYE OPEN

Notes on Being a Writer

As a child caught in that lonely place between two cultures and two languages, I wrapped myself in the magical veil of folktales and fairy tales. The earliest stories I heard were those told by the women of my family in Puerto Rico, some of the tales being versions of Spanish, European and even ancient Greek and Roman myths that had been translated by time and by each generation's needs into the *cuentos* that I heard. They taught me the power of the word. These centos have been surfacing in my poems and my prose since I decided to translate them for myself and to use them as my palette, the primary colors from which all creation begins.

The stories that have become the germinal point for not only my work as a creative artist but also my development as a free woman are those of two women. One is María Sabida, "the smartest woman on the whole Island"—who conquered the heart of a villain who would murder his own bride in their wedding bed—and who "slept with one eye open." And the other is María Sabida's opposite, María La Loca: the woman who was left at the altar, the tragic woman who went crazy as a result of a broken heart. Once a beautiful girl, María La Loca ends up, in my grandmother's cuento, a pitiful woman who retreats into insanity because she is shamed by a man, cheated out of the one option she allowed herself to claim: marriage.

The crude and violent tale of María Sabida, which I have found in collections of folktales recorded from the oral telling of old people at the turn of the century, revealed to me the amazing concept that a woman can have "macho"—that quality that men in certain countries, including my native island, have claimed as a male prerogative. The term *macho*, when divested of gender, to me simply means the arrogance to assume that you belong where you choose to stand, that you are inferior to no one, and that you will defend your domain at whatever cost. In most cases, I do not recommend this mode as the best way to make room for yourself in a crowded world. But I grew up in a place and time where modesty and submissiveness were the qualities a girl was supposed to internalize. So, the woman who slept with one eye open intrigued me as a possible model in my formative years as a creative artist. Of course, it would be a long time before I articulated what I knew then instinctively: María Sabida's "macho" was what I myself would need to claim for my art. It is almost bravado to say "I am a writer" in a society where that condition usually means "I am unemployed,"

"I live on the fringes of civilization," "I am declaring myself better/different," and so forth. I know writers who will put anything else under "occupation" on a passport or job application form rather than call up a red flag of distrust that the word "writer" has come to have for many people.

When I feel that I need a dose of "macho," I follow a woman's voice back to María Sabida. I have come to believe that she was the smartest woman on the island because she learned how to use the power of words to conquer her fears; she knew that this was what gave men their aura of power. They knew how to convince themselves and others that they were brave. Of course, she still had to sleep with one eye open because when you steal secrets, you are never again safe in your bed. María Sabida's message may be entirely different to me from what it was to the generations of women who heard and told the old tale. As a writer I choose to make her my alter ego, my *comadre*. In Catholic cultures two women otherwise unrelated can enter into a sacred bond, usually for the sake of a child, called the *comadrazgo*. One woman swears to stand in for the other as a surrogate mother if the need arises. It is a sacrament that joins them, more sacred than friendship, more binding than blood. And if these women violate the trust of their holy alliance, they will have committed a mortal sin. Their souls are endangered. I feel similarly about my commitment to the mythical María Sabida. My *comadre* taught me how to defend my art, how to conquer the villain by my wits. If I should ever weaken my resolve, I will become María La Loca, who failed herself, who allowed herself to even be left at the altar.

> *Comadres y compadres*, let me tell you the *cuento* of María Sabida, the smartest woman on the whole island.
>
> Once upon a time, there was a widower merchant who had no other children, only a daughter. He often had to leave her alone while he traveled on business to foreign lands. She was called María Sabida because she was smart and daring and knew how to take care of herself. One day, the merchant told her that he would be away on a trip for a long time and left María Sabida in the company of her women friends.
>
> One moonless night when she and her compañeras were sitting on the veranda of her father's house talking, María Sabida saw a bright light in the distance. Since the house was far away from the pueblo, she was very curious about what the light could be. She told her friends that they would investigate the source of light the very next morning.
>
> As planned, early the next day, María Sabida and her friends set out through the woods in the direction where they had seen the light. They arrived at a house that seemed to be unoccupied. They went in and peered into each room. It looked like a man's place. But they smelled cooking. So, they followed their noses to the kitchen, where an old man was stirring a huge cauldron. He welcomed them and

asked them to stay and eat. María Sabida looked in the pot and saw that it was filled with the arms and legs of little children. Then she knew that this was the house of a gang of killers, kidnappers, and thieves that had been terrorizing the countryside for years. Sickened by the sight, María Sabida picked up the pot and threw its contents out of the window. The old man screamed at her: "You will pay for this, woman! When my master comes home, he will kill you and your compañeras!" Then at gunpoint he led them upstairs where he locked them up.

When the leader of the thieves arrived with his gang, María Sabida heard him conspiring with his men to trick the women. Bearing a tray of *higos de sueño*, sleep-inducing figs, the *jefe* came up to the bedroom where the women were being kept. In a charming voice he persuaded the women to eat the fruit. María Sabida watched her friends fall deeply asleep one by one. She helped the jefe settle them in beds as she planned. Then she pretended to eat a fig and lay down yawning. To test how well the potion in the fruit had worked, the jefe of the thieves lit a candle and dripped a few drops of hot wax on the women's faces. María Sabida bore the pain without making a sound.

Certain now that the women were deeply asleep, the jefe went to the second-floor veranda and whistled for his comrades to come into the house. María Sabida leaped from the bed as he was leaning over the rail, and she pushed him off. While his men were tending to their injured leader, María Sabida awakened the women and they followed her to safety.

When María Sabida's father returned from his journey days later, she told him that she had decided to marry the leader of the thieves. The father sent a letter to the man asking him if he would marry his daughter. The jefe responded immediately that he had been unable to forget the smart and brave María Sabida. Yes, he would marry her. The wedding took place with a great fiesta. Everyone in the pueblo hoped that María Sabida would reform this criminal and they could stop fearing his gang. But as soon as the couple had arrived at the thieves' house, the new husband told his bride that now she would pay for having humiliated him in front of his men. He told her to go to the bedroom and wait for him. María Sabida knew that he was going to murder her. She had an idea. She asked her husband if he would let her take some honey to eat before she went to bed. He agreed. And while he drank his rum and celebrated her death with his gang, María Sabida worked in the kitchen making a life-size honey-doll out of burlap sacks. She filled the doll with honey, cutting off some of her own hair to glue on its head. She even tied a string to its neck so that she could make the doll move from where she planned to hide under the marriage bed. She took the honey-doll upstairs and placed it on the bed. Then she slid underneath the bed where she could see the door.

It was not long before the husband came in drunk and ready for blood. He struck the honey-doll, thinking that it was María Sabida. He insulted her and asked if she thought she was smart now. Then he plunged a dagger into the doll's heart. A stream of honey hit him on the face. Tasting the sweetness on his mouth and tongue, the assassin exclaimed: "María Sabida, how sweet you are in death, how bitter in life. If I had known your blood contained such sweetness, I would not have killed you!"

María Sabida then came out from under the bed. In awe that María Sabida had outsmarted him again, the leader of the thieves begged her to forgive him. María Sabida embraced her husband. They lived happily together, so they say. But on that night of her wedding, and every other night, María Sabida slept with one eye open.

I have translated the tale of María Sabida several times for different purposes, and each time the story yields new meanings. Time and again the words I use to roughly equate the powerful Spanish change meanings subtly as if the story were a Ouija board, drawing letters out of my mind to form new patterns. This is not hocus-pocus. It is the untapped power of creativity. When a writer abandons herself to its call, amazing things happen. On the surface the cuento of María Sabida may be interpreted as a parable of how a good woman conquers and tames a bad man. In the Spanish cultures, with their Holy Mother Mary mystique, the role of the woman as spiritual center and guide in a marriage is a central one. Men were born to sin; women, to redeem. But as a writer, I choose to interpret the tale of the woman who outmaneuvers the killer, who marries him so that she does not have to fear him, as a metaphor for the woman/creator. The assassin is the destroyer of ambition, drive, and talent—the killer of dreams. It does not have to be a man. It is anything or anyone who keeps the artist from her work. The smartest woman on the island knows that she must trap the assassin so that he/she/it does not deprive her of her creative power. To marry the killer means to me that the artist has wedded the negative forces in her life that would keep her from fulfilling her mission and, furthermore, that she has made the negative forces work for her instead of against her.

Her sweetness is the vision of beauty that the artist carries within her, that few see unless she sacrifices herself. Does she have to be destroyed, or destroy herself so that the world can taste her sweet blood? Woolf, Plath, Sexton may have thought so. I would rather believe that the sweetness may be shared without total annihilation, but not without pain or sacrifice: that is part of the formula for the honey-filled burlap sack that will save your life. The transaction that took place between María Sabida and her assassin-husband was a trade-off on macho. She took on his macho. He understood that. So they embraced. The artist and the world struck a compromise, albeit an uneasy one on her part. She had to sleep with one eye open and watch what was offered her to eat. Remember the sleep-inducing figs.

Some women eat sleep-inducing figs early in their lives. At first, they are unwitting victims of this feminine appetizer. Later they reach for the plate. It is easier to sleep while life happens around you. Better to dream while others *do*. The writer recognizes the poisoned fruit. She may pretend to sleep and bear the pain of hot wax as she prepares herself for battle. But she knows what is happening around her at all times. And when she is ready, she will act. Occasionally my comadre will try to save other women who have eaten the higos de sueño. She will try to rouse them, to wake them up. And sometimes, the sleepers will rise and follow her to freedom. But very often, they choose to remain unconscious. They rise briefly, look around them. They see that the world goes on without them. They eat another fig and go back to sleep.

There is another kind of woman that my comadre cannot save: María La Loca, the woman who was left at the altar. I first heard my grandmother tell this cuento when I was a child in Puerto Rico. I later wrote this poem:

The Woman Who Was Left at the Altar
She calls her shadow Juan,
looking back often as she walks.
She has grown fat, breasts huge
as reservoirs. She once opened her blouse
in church to show the silent town
what a plentiful mother she could be.
Since her old mother died, buried in black,
she lives alone. Out of the lace
she made curtains for her room,
doilies out of the veil. They are now
yellow as malaria.
She hangs live chickens from her waist to sell,
walks to the silent town swinging her skirts of flesh.
She doesn't speak to anyone. Dogs follow
the scent of blood to be shed. In their hungry,
yellow eyes she sees his face.
She takes him to the knife time after time.

Again, this is a tale that is on the surface about the harsh lessons of love. But even my Mamá knew that it had a subtext. It was about failing oneself and blaming it on another. In my book *Silent Dancing*, I wrote around my Mamá's cuento, showing how she taught me about the power of storytelling through the tale of María La Loca. Mamá told it as a parable to teach her daughters how love can defeat you, if you are weak enough to let it.

There is a woman who comes to my comadre and complains that she knows that she has talent, that she has poetry in her, but that her life is too hard, too busy; her husband, her children, are too demanding. She is a moral, responsible person and cannot in good conscience allow herself the luxury of practicing art. My comadre takes the time to tell this woman that she can choose to "learn to sleep with one eye open," to conjure up some female macho and claim the right to be an artist. But the woman is always prepared with an arsenal of reasons, all bigger than her needs, as to why she will die an unfulfilled woman, yearning to express herself in lyrical lines. She will, if pressed, imply that my comadre cannot possibly be a nurturing mother or caring partner, if she can find the time to write. In my culture, this type of woman who has perfected one art—that of self-abnegation, sometimes even martyrdom—is called *la sufrida*, the suffering one. There is much more admiration and respect for la sufrida in our society than there is for the artist.

The artist, too, suffers—but selfishly. She suffers mainly because the need to create torments her. If she is not fortunate enough to be truly selfish (or doesn't have enough macho in her to do as men have always done and claim the right, the time, and the space she needs), then she is doomed to do a balancing act, to walk the proverbial line that is drawn taut between the demands of her life—which may include choices that were made *before* she discovered her calling, such as marriage and children, and her art. The true artist will use her creativity to find a way, to carve the time, to claim a kitchen table, a library carrel, if a room of her own is not possible. She will use subterfuge, if necessary, write poems in her recipe book, give up sleeping time or social time, and write.

Once I was asked to teach an evening writing class for a group of working-class Latinas who had taken the initiative to ask a community arts organization for a workshop they could attend. These women toiled at mind-numbing jobs eight or more hours each day, and most of them had several small children and a tired husband at home waiting for them to cook at the end of the workday. Yet somehow the women had found one another as artists. Perhaps on a lunch break one of them had dared to mention that she wrote poems or kept a journal. In any case, I met a determined group of tired women that first night, many nervously make complex arrangements to leave their homes on a weeknight. Perceiving that the needs of this class would be different from those of my usual writing students, I asked these women to write down their most pressing artistic problem. I read the slips of paper during the break and confirmed my intuition about them. Almost unanimously they had said that their main problem was no time and no place to write. When we came together again, I told them about my method of writing: how I had developed it because, by the time I knew I had to write, I was a young mother and wife and was teaching full-time. At the end of the day, after giving my child all the attention I *wanted* to give her, grading papers, and doing the normal tasks involved with family life, I was done for. I could not summon a thought into my head, much less try to create. After trying various ways of finding time for myself, short of leaving everyone I loved behind for the sake of *Art*, I decided on the sacrifice I had to make—and there is always one: I had to give up some of my precious sleep-time. In order to give myself what I needed, I had to stop eating the delicious sleep-inducing figs that also make you good at finding excuses for not becoming who you need to be. I started going to bed when my daughter did and rising at 5:00 A.M. And in the two hours before the household came alive and the demands on me began, I wrote and I wrote and I wrote. Actually, I usually had just enough time, after drinking coffee and bringing order to the chaos in my head, to write a few lines of a poem, or one or two pages on my novel—which took me, at that pace, three and one half years to complete. But I was working, at a rate that many unencumbered writers would probably find laughably slow. But I wrote, and I write. And I am not left at the altar. Each line that I lay on a page points me toward my comadre María Sabida and takes me farther away from falling into the role of la sufrida.

The first assignment I gave that group of women was this: to go home and create a place to write for themselves. It had to be a place that could be cordoned off somehow, a place where books and notes could be left without fear of someone disturbing them and ruining a thought left unfinished; and, also important, a place where no one would feel free to read a work-in-progress—to ridicule and perhaps inhibit the writer. Their second assignment: to come up with a plan to make time to write every day.

As I expected, this latter injunction caused an uproar. Each of them claimed that her situation was impossible: no room, no privacy, no time, no time, no time. But I remained firm. They were going to write their version of Virginia Woolf's *A Room of One's Own* to fit their individual lives.

Two evenings later I met them again. I recall the faces of those weary women on that night. They were tired but not beaten, as they were used to challenges and to dealing with nearly impossible odds. I had dared them to use the strength of character that allowed them to survive in a harsh world of barrio and factory and their endless *lucha*. The struggle for survival was familiar to them. One by one they read their cuentos of how they had made a writing corner for themselves, the most fortunate among them having a guest room which her mother-in-law often occupied. She turned it into her study and bought a lock;

permission for other uses would have to be requested. Others had appropriated a corner here and there, set up table and chair, and screened off a space for themselves, The *No Trespassing* rules had been discussed with family members; even mild threats had been issued to nosy teenage children: you mess with my papers, I'll make free with your things. It was a celebration, minor declarations of independence by women used to yielding their private territory to others.

That night I saw that the act of claiming a bit of space and time for themselves was the beginning of something important for some of these women. Of course, not all of them would succeed against the thief of time. Some would find it easier to revert to the less fatiguing norm of the usual daily struggle. It takes a fierce devotion to defend your artistic space, and eternal vigilance over it because the needs of others will grow like vines in your little plot and claim it back for the jungle. Finally, we came to the last writer in the circle. This was a young woman who always looked harried and disheveled in her old jeans and man's shirt. She had two sons, little hellions, both under six years of age, and an absent husband. The story she had brought to class the first night had made us cry and laugh. She had the gift, no doubt about it, but had been almost angry about the writing space and time assignment. She lived in a cramped apartment where the only table had to be used to store groceries, change babies, iron. The story she had read to us had been written during a hospital stay. What was she to do, cut her wrists so that she could find time to write? We waited in respectful silence for her to begin reading. She surprised us by standing up and announcing that she had brought her writing place with her that night. Out of the back pocket of her jeans she pulled out a handmade notebook. It had a sturdy cardboard covering, and within it was paper cut to fit and stitched together. There was also a small pencil that fit just right in the groove. She flipped the notebook open and began to read her essay. She had nearly given up trying to find a place to write. Everywhere she laid down her papers the kids had gotten to them. It became a game for them. At first she had been angry, but then she had decided to use her imagination to devise a way to write that was childproof. So she had come up with the idea of a portable room of her own. Since she could not leave her children and lock herself up in a room to write, she constructed a notebook that fit her jeans pocket precisely. It had a hard back so that she could write on it while she went around the house or took the kids to the park, or even while grocery shopping. No one thought anything of it because it just looked like a housewife making a laundry list. She had even written this essay on her son's head while he leaned on her knees, watching television.

Again, there was laughter and tears. We had all learned a lesson that night about the will to create. I often think about this woman carrying her writing room with her wherever she went, and I have told her story often to other women who claim that the world keeps them from giving themselves to art. And I have put this young woman, who knew the meaning of *being* an artist, in my little pantheon of women who sleep with one eye open, the clapboard temple where I visit my storytelling comadre, María Sabida, to seek her counsel.

There are no altars in this holy place, nor women who were left at one.

MARINA

Again it happened between my mother and me. Since her return to Puerto Rico after my father's death ten years before, she had gone totally "native," regressing into the comfortable traditions of her extended family and questioning all of my decisions. Each year we spoke more formally to each other, and each June, at the end of my teaching year, she would invite me to visit her on the Island—so I could see for myself how much I was missing out on.

These yearly pilgrimages to my mother's town where I had been born also, but which I had left at an early age, were for me symbolic of the clash of cultures and generations that she and I represent. But I looked forward to arriving at this lovely place, my mother's lifetime dream of home, now endangered by encroaching "progress."

Located on the west coast, our pueblo is a place of contrasts: the original town remains as a tiny core of ancient houses circling the church, which sits on a hill, the very same where the woodcutter claimed to have been saved from a charging bull by a lovely dark Lady who appeared floating over a treetop. There my mother lives, at the foot of this hill; but surrounding this postcard scene there are shopping malls, a Burger King, a cinema. And where the sugar cane fields once extended like a green sea as far as the eye could see: condominiums, cement blocks in rows, all the same shape and color. My mother tries not to see this part of her world. The church bells drown the noise of traffic, and when she sits on her back porch and looks up at the old church built by the hands of generations of men whose last names she would not recognize, she feels safe—under the shelter of the past.

During the twenty years she spent in "exile" in the U.S. often alone with two children, waiting for my father, she dedicated her time and energy to creating a "reasonable facsimile" of a Puerto Rican home, which for my brother and me meant that we led a dual existence: speaking Spanish at home with her, acting out our parts in her traditional play, while also daily pretending assimilation in the classroom, where in the early sixties, there was no such thing as bilingual education. But, to be fair, we were not the only Puerto Rican children leading a double life, and I have always been grateful to have kept my Spanish. My trouble with Mother comes when she and I try to define and translate key words for both of us, words such as "woman" and "mother." I have a daughter too, as well as a demanding profession as a teacher and writer. My mother got married as a teenager and led a life of isolation and total devotion to her duties as mother. As a Penelope-like wife, she was always waiting, waiting, waiting, for the return of her sailor, for the return to her native land.

In the meantime, I grew up in the social flux of the sixties in New Jersey, and although I was kept on a steady diet of fantasies about life in the tropics, I liberated myself from her plans for me, got a scholarship to college, married a man who supported my need to work, to create, to travel and to experience life as an individual. My mother rejoices at my successes, but is often anxious at how much time I have to spend away from home, although I keep assuring her that my husband is as good a parent as I am, and a much better cook. Her concern about my familial duties is sometimes a source of friction in our relationship, the basis for most of our arguments. But, in spite of our differences, I miss her, and as June approaches, I yearn to be with her in her tiny house filled with her vibrant presence. So I pack up and go to meet my loving adversary in her corner of the rapidly disappearing "paradise" that she waited so long to go home to.

It was after a heated argument one afternoon that I sought reconciliation with my mother by asking her to go with me for a walk down the main street of the pueblo. I planned to request stories about the town and its old people, something that we both enjoy for different reasons: she likes recalling the old days, and I have an insatiable curiosity about the history and the people of the Island which have become prominent features in my work.

We had been walking around the church when we saw a distinguished looking old man strolling hand-in-hand with a little girl. My mother touched my arm and pointed to them. I admired the pair as the old man, svelte and graceful as a ballet dancer, lifted the tiny figure dressed up in pink lace onto a stool at an outdoor cafe.

"Who is he?" I asked my mother, trying not to stare as we pretended to examine the menu taped on the window.

"You have heard his story at your grandmother's house."

She took my elbow and led me to a table at the far end of the cafe. "I will tell it to you again, but first I will give you a hint about who he is: he has not always been the man he is today."

Though her "hint" was no help, I suddenly recalled the story I had heard many years earlier as told by my grandmother, who had started the tale with similar words, "People are not always what they seem to be, that is something we have all heard, but have you heard about the one who ended up being what he was but did not appear to be?" Or something like that. Mamá could turn any story—it did not have to be as strange and fascinating as this one—into an event. I told my guess to my mother.

"Yes," she nodded, "he came home to retire. You know he has lived in Nueva York since before you were born. Do you remember the story?"

As we continued our walk, my mother recounted for me her mother's dramatic tale of a famous incident that had shaken the town in Mamá's youth. I had heard it once as a child, sitting enthralled at my grandmother's knee.

In the days when Mamá was a young girl, our pueblo had not yet been touched by progress. The cult of the Black Virgin had grown strong as pilgrims traveled from all over the island to visit the shrine, and the Church preached chastity and modesty as the prime virtues for the town's daughters. Adolescent girls were not allowed to go anywhere without their mothers or *dueñas*—except to a certain river that no man was allowed to approach.

Río Rojo, the river that ran its course around the sacred mountain where the Virgin had appeared, was reserved for the maidens of the pueblo. It was nothing but a stream, really, but crystalline, and it was bordered by thick woods, where the most fragrant flowers and herbs could be found. This was a female place, a pastoral setting where no true *macho* would want to be caught swimming or fishing.

Nature had decorated the spot like a boudoir—royal poincianas extended their low branches for the girls to hang their clothes, and the mossy grass grew like a plush green carpet all the way down to the smooth stepping-stones where they could sun themselves like *favoritas* in a virginal harem.

As a "grown" girl of fifteen, Mamá had led her sisters and other girls of the pueblo to bathe there on hot summer afternoons. It was a place of secret talk and rowdy play, of freedom from mothers and chaperones, a place where they could talk about boys, and where they could luxuriate in their bodies. At the río, the young women felt free to hypothesize about the secret connection between their two concerns: their changing bodies and boys.

Sex was the forbidden topic in their lives, yet these were the same girls who would be given to strangers in marriage before they were scarcely out of childhood. In a sense, they were betrayed by their own protective parents who could bring themselves to explain neither the delights, nor the consequences of sex to their beloved daughters. The prevailing practice was to get them safely married as soon after puberty as possible—because nature would take its course one way or another. Scandal was to be avoided at all costs.

At the río, the group of girls Mamá grew up with would squeal and splash away their last few precious days as children. They would also wash each other's hair while sitting like brown Naiads upon the smooth rocks in the shallow water. They had the freedom to bathe nude, but some of them could not break through a lifetime of training in modesty and would keep their chemises and bloomers on. One of the shyest girls was Marina. She was everyone's pet.

Marina was a lovely young girl with her *café-con-leche* skin and green eyes. Her body was willowy and her thick black Indian hair hung down to her waist. Her voice was so soft that you had to come very close to hear what she was saying during the rare times when she did speak. Everyone treated Marina with special consideration, since she had already known much tragedy by the time she reached adolescence. It was due to the traumatic circumstances of her birth, as well as her difficult life with a reclusive mother, all the girls believed, that Marina was so withdrawn and melancholy as she ended her fifteenth year. She was surely destined for convent life, they all whispered when Marina left their company, as she often did, to go sit by herself on the bank, and to watch them with her large, wet, melancholy eyes.

Marina had fine hands and all the girls liked for her to braid their hair at the end of the day. They argued over the privilege of sitting between her legs while Marina ran her long fingers through their hair like a cellist playing a soothing melody. It caused much jealousy that last summer before Mamá's betrothal (which meant it was the last summer she could play at the río with her friends) when Marina chose to keep company only with Kiki, the mayor's fourteen-year-old daughter who had finally won permission from her strict parents to bathe with the pueblo's girls at the river.

Kiki would be a pale fish among the golden tadpoles in the water. She came from a Spanish family who believed in keeping the bloodlines pure, and she had spent all of her childhood in the cool shade of mansions and convent schools. She had come to the pueblo to prepare for her debut into society, her *quinceañera*, a fifteenth birthday party where she would be dressed like a princess and displayed before the Island's eligible bachelors as a potential bride.

Lonely for the company of girls her age, and tired of the modulated tones of afternoons on the verandah with her refined mother, Kiki had pressured her father to give her a final holiday with the other girls, whom she would see going by the mansion, singing and laughing on their way to the río. Her father began to see the wisdom of her idea when she mentioned how democratic it would seem to the girls' parents for the mayor's daughter to join them at the river. Finally, he agreed. The mother took to her bed with a sick headache when she thought of her lovely daughter removing her clothes in front of the uncouth spawn of her husband's constituents: rough farmers and their sun-darkened wives.

Kiki removed all her clothes with glee as soon as the group arrived at the river. She ran to the water tossing lace, satin, and silk over her head. She behaved like a bird whose cage door had been opened for the first time. The girls giggled at the sight of the freckles on her shoulders, her little pink nipples, like rosebuds, her golden hair. But since she was the mayor's daughter, they dared not get too close. They acted more like her attendants than her friends. Kiki would have ended up alone again if it had not been for Marina.

Marina was awestruck by the exuberant Kiki; and Kiki was drawn to the quiet girl who watched the others at play with such yearning. Soon the two girls were inseparable. Marina would take Kiki's wet hair, like molten gold, into her brown hands and weave it into two perfect plaits which she would pin to the girl's head like a crown. It was fascinating to watch how the two came together wordlessly, like partners in a *pas de deux*.

It was an idyllic time, until one afternoon Marina and Kiki did not return to the river from an excursion into the woods where they had ostensibly gone to gather flowers. Mamá and her friends searched for them until nearly dark, but did not find them. The mayor went in person to notify Marina's mother of the situation. What he found was a woman who had fallen permanently into silence: secluded in a secret place of shadows where she wished to remain.

It was the events of one night long ago that had made her abandon the world.

Marina's mother had lost her young husband and delivered her child prematurely on the same night. The news that her man had been drowned in a fishing accident had brought on an agonizing labor. She had had a son, a tiny little boy, perfect in his parts, but sickly. The new mother, weakened in body and mind by so much pain, had decided that she preferred a daughter for company. Hysterically, she had begged the anxious midwife to keep her secret. And as soon as she was able to walk to church, she had the child dressed in a flowing gown of lace and had her christened Marina. Living the life of a recluse, to which she was entitled as a widow, and attended by her loyal nurse, and later, by her quiet obedient Marina, the woman had slipped easily out of reality.

By the time Marina was old enough to discover the difference between her body and the bodies of her girlfriends, her mother had forgotten all about having borne a son. In fact, the poor soul would have been horrified to discover a man under her roof. And so Marina kept up appearances, waiting out her body's dictates year by year. The summer that Kiki joined the bathers at the río, Marina had made up her mind to run away from home. She had been in torment until the blonde girl had appeared like an angel, bringing Marina the balm of her presence and the soothing touch of her hands.

The mayor found the woman sitting calmly in a rocking chair. She looked like a wax figure dressed in widow's weeds. Only her elegant hands moved as she crocheted a collar for a little girl's dress. And although she smiled deferentially at the men speaking loudly in her parlor, she remained silent. Silence was the place she had inhabited for years, and no one could draw her out now.

Furious, the mayor threatened to have her arrested. Finally, it was the old nurse who confessed the whole sad tale—to the horror of the mayor and his men. She handed him an envelope with *Papá y Mamá* written on its face in Kiki's hand. In a last show of control, the mayor took the sealed letter home to read in the privacy of the family mansion where his wife was waiting, still under the impression that the two girls had been kidnapped for political reasons.

Kiki's letter explained briefly that she and *Marino* had eloped. They had fallen in love and nothing and no one could change their minds about getting married. She had sold her pearl necklace—the family heirloom given to her by her parents to wear at her quinceañera, and they were using the money for passage on the next steamship out of San Juan to New York.

The mayor did not finish his term in office. He and his wife, now a recluse, exiled themselves to Spain.

"And Marina and Kiki?" I had asked Mamá, eager for more details about Kiki and Marino, "What happened to them?"

"What happens to *any* married couple?" Mamá had replied, putting an end to her story. "They had several children, they worked, they got old . . ." She chuckled gently at my naiveté.

On our way back through town from our walk, Mother and I again saw Marino with his pretty granddaughter. This time he was lifting her to smell a white rose that grew from a vine entangled on a tree branch. The child brought the flower carefully to her nose and smelled it. Then the old man placed the child gently back on the ground and they continued their promenade, stopping to examine anything that caught the child's eye.

"Do you think he made a good husband?" I asked my mother.

"He would know what it takes to make a woman happy," she said as she turned to face me, and winked in camaraderie.

As I watched the gentle old man and the little girl, I imagined Marina sitting alone on the banks of a river, his heart breaking with pain and wild yearnings, listening to the girls asking questions he could have answered; remaining silent; learning patience, until love would give him the right to reclaim his original body and destiny. Yet he would never forget the lessons she learned at the río—or how to handle fragile things. I looked at my mother and she smiled at me; we now had a new place to begin our search for the meaning of the word *woman*.

THE WITCH'S HUSBAND

My grandfather has misplaced his words again. He is trying to find my name in the kaleidoscope of images that his mind has become. His face brightens like a child's who has just remembered his lesson. He points to me and says my mother's name. I smile back and kiss him on the cheek. It doesn't matter what names he remembers anymore. Every day he is more confused, his memory slipping back a little further in time. Today he has no grandchildren yet. Tomorrow he will be a young man courting my grandmother again, quoting bits of poetry to her. In months to come, he will begin calling her Mamá.

I have traveled to Puerto Rico at my mother's request to help her deal with the old people. My grandfather is physically healthy, but his dementia is severe. My grandmother's heart is making odd sounds again in her chest. Yet she insists on taking care of the old man at home herself. She will not give up her house, though she has been warned that her heart might fail in her sleep without proper monitoring, that is, a nursing home or a relative's care. Her response is typical of her famous obstinacy: "Bueno," she says, "I will die in my own bed."

I am now at her house, waiting for my opportunity to talk "sense" into her. As a college teacher in the United States, I am supposed to represent the voice of logic: I have been called in to convince la abuela, the family's proud matriarch, to step down—to allow her children to take care of her before she kills herself with work. I spent years at her house as a child but have lived in the U.S. for most of my adult life. I learned to love and respect this strong woman, who with five children of her own had found a way to help many others. She was a legend in the pueblo for having more foster children than anyone else. I have spoken with people my mother's age who told me that they had spent up to a year at Abuela's house during emergencies and hard times. It seems extraordinary that a woman would willingly take on such obligations. And frankly, I am a bit appalled at what I have begun to think of as "the martyr complex" in Puerto Rican women, that is, the idea that self-sacrifice is a woman's lot and her privilege: a good woman is defined by how much suffering and mothering she can do in one lifetime. Abuela is the all-time champion in my eyes: her life has been entirely devoted to others. Not content to bring up two sons and three daughters as the Depression raged on, followed by the war that took one of her sons, she had also taken on other people's burdens. This had been the usual pattern with one exception that I knew of: the year that Abuela spent in New York, apparently undergoing some kind of treatment for her heart while she was still a young woman. My mother was five or six years old, and there were three other children who had been born by that time too. They were given into the care of Abuela's sister, Delia. The two women traded places for the year. Abuela went to live in her sister's apartment in New York City while the younger woman took over Abuela's duties at the house in Puerto Rico. Grandfather was a shadowy figure in the background during that period. My mother doesn't say much about what went on during that year, only that her mother was sick and away for months. Grandfather seemed absent too, since he worked all of the time. Though they missed Abuela, they were well taken care of.

I am sitting on a rocking chair on the porch of her house. She is facing me from a hammock she made when her first baby was born. My mother was rocked on that hammock. I was rocked on that hammock, and when I brought my daughter as a baby to Abuela's house, she was held in Abuela's sun-browned arms, my porcelain pink baby, and rocked to a peaceful sleep too. She sits there and smiles as the breeze of a tropical November brings the scent of her roses and her herbs to us. She is proud of her garden. In front of the house she grows flowers and lush trailing plants; in the back, where the mango tree gives shade, she has an herb garden. From this patch of weedy looking plants came all the remedies of my childhood, for anything from a sore throat to menstrual cramps. Abuela had a recipe for every pain that a child could dream up, and she brought it to your bed in her own hands smelling of the earth. For a moment I am content to sit in her comforting presence. She is rotund now; a small-boned brown-skinned earth mother—with a big heart and a temper to match. My grandfather comes to stand at the screen door. He has forgotten how the latch works. He pulls at the knob and moans softly, rattling it. With some effort Abuela gets down from the hammock. She opens the door, gently guiding the old man to a chair at the end of the porch. There he begins anew his constant search for the words he needs. He tries various combinations, but they don't work as language. Abuela pats his hand and motions for me to follow her into the house. We sit down at opposite ends of her sofa.

She apologizes to me as if for a misbehaving child.

"He'll quiet down," she says. "He does not like to be ignored."

I take a deep breath in preparation for my big lecture to Grandmother. This is the time to tell her that she has to give up trying to run this house and take care of others at her age. One of her daughters is prepared to take her in. Grandfather is to be sent to a nursing home. Before I can say anything, Abuela says: "Mi amor, would you like to hear a story?"

I smile, surprised at her offer. These are the same words that stopped me in my tracks as a child, even in the middle of a tantrum. Abuela could always entrance me with one of her tales. I nod. Yes, my sermon can wait a little longer, I thought.

"Let me tell you an old, old story I heard when I was a little girl.

"There was once a man who became worried and suspicious when he noticed that his wife disappeared from their bed every night for long periods of time. Wanting to find out what she was doing before confronting her, the man decided to stay awake at night and keep guard. For hours he watched her every movement through half-closed eyelids with his ears perked up like those of a burro.

"Then just about midnight, when the night was as dark as the bottom of a cauldron, he felt his wife slipping out of bed. He saw her go to the wardrobe and take out a jar and a little paintbrush. She stood naked by the window, and when the church bells struck twelve, she began to paint her entire body with the paintbrush, dipping it into the jar. As the bells tolled the hour, she whispered these words: *I don't believe in the church, or in God, or in the Virgin Mary.* As soon as this was spoken, she rose from the ground and flew into the night like a bird.

"Astounded, the man decided not to say anything to his wife the next day, but to try to find out where she went. The following night, the man pretended to sleep and waited until she had again performed her little ceremony and flown away, then he repeated her actions exactly. He soon found himself flying after her. Approaching a palace, he saw many other women circling the roof, taking turns going down the chimney. After the last had descended, he slid down the dark hole that led to the castle's bodega, where food and wine were stored. He hid himself behind some casks of wine and watched the women greet each other.

"The witches, for that's what they were, were the wives of his neighbors and friends, but he at first had trouble recognizing them, for like his wife, they were all naked. With much merriment, they took the meats and cheeses that hung from the bodega's rafters and laid a table for a feast. They drank the fine wines right from the bottles, like men in a cantina, and danced wildly to eerie music from invisible instruments. They spoke to each other in a language that he did not understand, words that sounded like a cat whose tail has been stepped on. Still, horrible as their speech was, the food they prepared smelled delicious. Cautiously placing himself in the shadows near one of the witches, he extended his hand for a plate. He was given a steaming dish of stewed tongue. Hungrily, he took a bite: it was tasteless. The other witches had apparently noticed the same thing, because they sent one of the younger ones to find some salt. But when the young witch came back into the room with a saltshaker in her hand, the man forgot himself and exclaimed: 'Thank God the salt is here.'

"On hearing God's name, all the witches took flight immediately, leaving the man completely alone in the darkened cellar. He tried the spell for flight that had brought him there, but it did not work. It was no longer midnight, and it was obviously the wrong incantation for going up a chimney. He tried all night to get out of the place, which had been left in shambles by the witches, but it was locked up as tight as heaven is to a sinner. Finally, he fell asleep from exhaustion, and slept until dawn, when he heard footsteps approaching. When he saw the heavy door being pushed open, he hid himself behind a cask of wine.

"A man in rich clothes walked in, followed by several servants. They were all armed with heavy sticks as if out to kill someone. When the man lit his torch and saw the chaos in the cellar, broken bottles strewn on the floor, meats and cheeses half-eaten and tossed everywhere, he cried out in such a rage that the man hiding behind the wine cask closed his eyes and committed his soul to God. The owner of the castle ordered his servants to search the whole bodega, every inch of it, until they discovered how vandals had entered his home. It was a matter of minutes before they discovered the witch's husband, curled up like a stray dog and, worse, painted the color of a vampire bat, without a stitch of clothing.

"They dragged him to the center of the room and beat him with their sticks until the poor man thought that his bones had been pulverized and he would have to be poured into his grave. When the castle's owner said that he thought the wretch had learned his lesson, the servants tossed him naked onto the road. The man was so sore that he slept right there on the public *camino*, oblivious to the stares and insults of all who passed him. When he awakened in the middle of the night and found himself naked, dirty, bloody, and miles from his home, he swore to himself right then and there that he would never, for anything in the world, follow his wife on her nightly journeys again."

"Colorín, colorado," Abuela claps her hands three times, chanting the childhood rhyme for ending a story, "Este cuento se ha acabado." She smiles at me, shifting her position on the sofa to be able to watch Grandfather muttering to himself on the porch. I remember those eyes on me when I was a small child. Their movements seemed to be triggered by a child's actions, like those holograms of the Holy Mother that were popular with Catholics a few years ago—you couldn't get away from their mesmerizing gaze.

"Will you tell me about your year in New York, Abuela?" I surprise myself with the question. But suddenly I need to know about Abuela's lost year. It has to be another good story.

She looks intently at me before she answers. Her eyes are my eyes, same dark brown color, almond shape, and the lids that droop a little: called by some "bedroom eyes": to others they are a sign of a cunning nature. "Why are you looking at me that way?" is a question I am often asked.

"I wanted to leave home," she says calmly, as though she had been expecting the question from me all along.

"You mean abandon your family?" I am really taken aback by her words.

"Yes, Hija. That is exactly what I mean. Abandon them. Never to return."

"Why?"

"I was tired. I was young and pretty, full of energy and dreams." She smiles as Grandfather breaks into song standing by himself on the porch. A woman passing by with a baby in her arms waves at him. Grandfather sings louder, something about a man going to his exile because the woman he loves has rejected him. He finishes the song on a long note and continues to stand in the middle of the tiled porch as if listening for applause. He bows.

Abuela shakes her head, smiling a little, as if amused by his antics then she finishes her sentence, "Restless, bored. Four children and a husband all demanding more and more from me."

"So you left the children with your sister and went to New York?" I say, trying to keep the mixed emotions I feel out of my voice. I look at the serene old woman in front of me and cannot believe that she once left four children and a loving husband to go live alone in a faraway country.

"I had left him once before, but he found me. I came back home, but on the condition that he never follow me anywhere again. I told him the next time I would not return." She is silent, apparently falling deep into thought.

"You were never really sick," I say, though I am afraid that she will not resume her story. But I want to know more about this woman whose life I thought was an open book.

"I *was* sick. Sick at heart. And he knew it," she says, keeping her eyes on Grandfather, who is standing as still as a marble statue on the porch. He seems to be listening intently for something.

"The year in New York was his idea. He saw how unhappy I was. He knew I needed to taste freedom. He paid my sister Delia to come take care of the children. He also sublet her apartment for me, though he had to take a second job to do it. He gave me money and told me to go."

"What did you do that year in New York?" I am both stunned and fascinated by Abuela's revelation. "I worked as a seamstress in a fancy dress shop. And . . . y, pues, Hija." She smiles at me as if I should know some things without being told, "I lived."

"Why did you come back?" I ask.

"Because I love him," she says, "and I missed my children."

He is scratching at the door. Like a small child he has traced the sound of Abuela's voice back to her. She lets him in, guiding him gently by the hand. Then she eases him down on his favorite rocking chant. He begins to nod; soon he will be sound asleep, comforted by her proximity, secure in his familiar surroundings. I wonder how long it will take him to revert to infantilism. The doctors say he is physically healthy and may live for many years, but his memory, verbal skills, and ability to control his biological functions will deteriorate rapidly. He may end his days bedridden, perhaps comatose. My eyes fill with tears as I look at the lined face of this beautiful and gentle old man. I am in awe of the generosity of spirit that allowed him to give a year of freedom to the woman he loved, not knowing whether she would ever return to him. Abuela has seen my tears and moves over on the sofa to sit near me. She slips an arm around my waist and pulls me close. She kisses my wet cheek. Then she whispers softly into my ear, "and in time, the husband either began forgetting that he had seen her turn into a witch or believed that he had just dreamed it."

She takes my face into her hands. "I am going to take care of your grandfather until one of us dies. I promised him when I came back that I would never leave home again unless he asked me to: he never did. He never asked any questions."

I hear my mother's car pull up into the driveway. She will wait there for me. I will have to admit that I failed in my mission. I will argue Abuela's case without revealing her secret. As far as everyone is concerned, she went away to recover from problems with her heart. That part is true in both versions of the story.

At the door she gives me the traditional blessing, adding with a wink, "Colorín, colorado." My grandfather, hearing her voice, smiles in his sleep.

LA JURGA

A Puerto Rican Folktale

Long ago there lived a landowning farmer who made his fortune by exploiting the campesinos. He was married to a woman many thought was a witch. She was said to be able to transform herself into a bitch-dog by day and into a large vulture-like bird everyone called "La Jurga" at night. When this bird perched on a tree near the landowner's house and screeched its terrifying song, it meant that the peasant last hired by him should be dismissed without pay.

In the same province lived three brothers who had fallen into dire poverty at their father's death. The oldest brother was obliged to find a job, so he went to the landowner who was married to La Jurga. On making his request for work, the young man was informed that he would first have to agree to all the conditions imposed on him by his employer. Anxious to make some money, the young peasant said that he was willing to do anything. The landowner, who was an avaricious man, then said:

"Any employee of mine must rise very early to go to work in the fields, and he may not return until my bitch-dog, who will always be by his side, starts for home. For lunch, he can have all the bread he wants—as long as he has some egg to go with it. He may not get angry with me no matter what I say. If he loses his temper, I will have the right to peel the skin off his back with my whip; if I get angry first, he will have the same privilege. When the Jurga sings, he will be dismissed without pay, since that always means that his work was not satisfactory."

The young man, thinking himself the winner in this bargain, accepted all the landowner's terms.

The following day, before the first ray of dawn, the bitch-dog started out for the fields. The boy, who had not been able to sleep a wink all night, heard the dog and followed her. The unhappy youth worked hard all morning waiting for the eleven o'clock break so he could eat and rest. He waited in vain, for the bitch-dog showed no signs of making for the house. Finally, at three in the afternoon, the dog rose. By that time the young man was so tired that he could hardly walk.

He was served his lunch upon arriving at the house. As expected it was an egg and a slice of bread. Since he was very hungry, he swallowed the entire egg in one gulp, therefore losing his right to eat any bread, which was taken from him according to the landowner's orders.

Distressed at what was happening to him, the young man told his boss that he could not continue to work there, that he was leaving immediately. The following exchange then took place between them:

"Does this mean that you are angry?" asked the landowner.

"No, I am not angry. But you must understand that a worker cannot sustain his strength on one egg. In other places, a laborer is fed plantains, sweet potatoes and codfish, sometimes even corn fritters and milk."

"I can see that you are upset that my bitch-dog came home late, and that you didn't get your bread for lunch. It's your fault for eating your egg first. Since you agreed to all of it, you are going to get your whipping, then you can leave this house."

And that is just what happened.

When the oldest brother got home, the middle brother got furious at the landowner's treatment of the eldest. He took a job at the same farm thinking that he could get revenge, but he too suffered the same fate as his older brother, and he too returned home defeated.

But the youngest brother had a plan. Though his two brothers begged him not to go, he was resolved to get revenge on the landowner and his Jurga.

He met the landowner and agreed to all the conditions.

The following morning, the dog was on her way to the fields even before all the stars had cleared the sky. The youngest brother followed her. He did his work, sowing the seeds of corn, until the clock struck ten. At that time, he began whipping the bitch-dog until she took off for the house, almost flying to get away from him.

The surprised landowner rushed out of his house. "Oh, you are here early!" he exclaimed in surprise.

The young man replied, "The bitch-dog wanted to come home, and I had no choice but to follow her. Does that upset you?"

"No, not me. But it is strange that she came home so early. Here's your lunch."

The boy ate his slice of bread, enjoying the smell of the egg that he had been served. When he finished eating his bread he called out, "More bread to eat with my egg!"

He did this until his hunger was nearly satisfied, then he ate his egg.

The landowner then spoke up, "I would have never believed that so much bread could have been eaten with only one egg. You have consumed an entire week's ration."

"Does that make you angry?" asked the boy.

"No, I am not angry. Eat all you want," replied the landowner.

That night the Jurga sang her terrible song. The young man was prepared for her. He took the rifle he had brought with him and he hunted her down. When the landowner heard the shot, he ran outside to see what had happened. He was confronted by the sight of his wife's body lying dead under the tree.

"You have killed my wife!" he yelled.

The young man calmly replied, "I did not kill your wife—I shot La Jurga."

"La Jurga was my wife," shouted the landowner, now out of control.

"This is what you deserve for making your wife a Jurga to sabotage the lives of honest workers. Are you angry now?"

"How can I not be angry—you have killed my wife."

"Then you owe me the skin off your back. It's what we agreed on."

The landowner was in a rage by now.

"What! Besides killing my wife, you are going to whip me too?"

Wrapping the whip around his hand, the young man calmly answered the frightened landowner, "You showed no compassion for my two older brothers, and since that was the treatment you gave us, you have to accept the conditions of the deal too. You have to give me what I've earned today."

And he gave the landowner a whipping he would never forget.

The youngest brother then returned home satisfied that he had avenged his family and also taught a lesson to the evil landowner.

AUNTY MISERY

Adapted and translated from Puerto Rican folktales collected from the oral tradition by Rafael Ramírez de Arellano, Madrid, 1926.

This is a story about an old, very old woman who lived alone in her little hut with no other company than a beautiful pear tree that grew at her door. She spent all her time taking care of her pear tree. But the neighborhood children drove the old woman crazy by stealing her fruit. They would climb her tree, shake its delicate limbs, and run away with armloads of golden pears, yelling insults at "Aunty Misery," as they called her.

One day, a pilgrim stopped at the old woman's hut and asked her permission to spend the night under her roof. Aunty Misery saw that he had an honest face and bade the traveler come in. She fed him and made a bed for him in front of her hearth. In the morning while he was getting ready to leave, the stranger told her that he would show his gratitude for her hospitality by granting her one wish.

"There is only one thing that I desire," said Aunty Misery.

"Ask, and it shall be yours," replied the stranger, who was a sorcerer in disguise.

"I wish that anyone who climbs up my pear tree should not be able to come back down until I permit it."

"Your wish is granted," said the stranger, touching the pear tree as he left Aunty Misery's house.

And so it happened that when the children came back to taunt the old woman and to steal her fruit, she stood at her window watching them. Several of them shimmied up the trunk of the pear tree and immediately got stuck to it as if with glue. She let them cry and beg her for a long time before she gave the tree permission to let them go, on the condition that they never again steal her fruit or bother her.

Time passed and both Aunty Misery and her tree grew bent and gnarled with age. One day another traveler stopped at her door. This one looked suffocated and exhausted, so the old woman asked him what he wanted in her village. He answered her in a voice that was dry and hoarse, as if he had swallowed a desert: "I am Death, and I have come to take you with me."

Thinking fast, Aunty Misery said, "All right, but before I go I would like to pluck some pears from my beloved pear tree to remember how much pleasure it brought me in this life. But, I am a very old woman and cannot climb to the tallest branches where the best fruit is; will you be so kind as to do it for me?"

With a heavy sigh like wind through a catacomb, Death climbed the pear tree. Immediately he became stuck to it as if with glue. And no matter how much he cursed and threatened, Aunty Misery would not give the tree permission to release Death.

Many years passed and there were no deaths in the world. The people who make their living from death began to protest loudly. The doctors claimed no one bothered to come in for examinations or treatments anymore, because they did not fear dying; the pharmacists' business suffered too because medicines are, like magic potions, bought to prevent or postpone the inevitable; the priests and undertakers were unhappy with the situation also, for obvious reasons. There were also many old folks tired of life who wanted to pass on to the next world to rest from the miseries of this one.

Aunty Misery realized all this, and not wishing to be unfair, she made a deal with her prisoner, Death: if he promised not ever to come for her again, she would give him his freedom. He agreed. And that is why so long as the world is the world, Aunty Misery will always live.

CENIZOSA

Once upon a time there was a nice widower and his young daughter, María, who lived across the road from a widow and her ill-tempered daughter. The widow's daughter hated María because she was known by everyone as a good girl and she was pretty too. But the widow wanted to marry María's father. So mother and daughter pretended to like María. The widow would invite María to her house and give her honey soup to eat.

"If your Papá marries me," the widow would say to María, "I will feed you honey every day."

María, who wanted a mother, would say to her father, "Marry our neighbor, dear Papá, she is good to me and makes me soup from honey."

María's father was not convinced of the widow's good intentions and he would answer: "Today she will give you honey, but tomorrow it may be bile you will taste."

But the widower loved his daughter, and since she insisted that she needed a mother, he married his neighbor.

When the widow and her daughter moved in, at first, she gave María the second-best room to sleep in. The next day she moved her to the third best room, saying that María was a restless sleeper and kept her up at night. On the third day she moved her to the smallest room in the house, way in the back. She said that she could still hear María and could not sleep well at night. Finally, she ordered María to sleep on the floor in the dining room. Still not satisfied she complained that María was not far away enough from her so that she could rest. From then on María slept in the kitchen in front of the fire.

Since she was usually covered in ashes, the widow started calling her "Cenizosa" and made her do all the heavy work around the house. Cenizosa had to clean floors, fetch water from the well, and cook. Her only friend was a little goat with whom she had learned to communicate.

One day the widow saw them together and decided that she wanted to eat goat stew. She told Cenizosa to kill her goat and cook it. Horrified, the girl told her goat that the widow wanted her killed and cooked for dinner.

But the goat answered that it was going to be fine.

"Please don't cry for me María. You must believe in my friendship and good things will happen to you. Go ahead and have me slaughtered and made for dinner. But make sure that you get my innards to eat."

So Cenizosa gave up her little goat and was given the tripe, called *mondongo*, for her dinner. She went down to the river to wash the meat before cooking it for herself. Some of the mondongo slipped out of her hands and was carried by the current into a cave. Cenizosa followed it in. Inside the cave, Cenizosa found a house. It was messy and dirty. She decided that since she had wandered into somebody's home, she should clean it and put it in order. As she was working, she found several little babies and a dog. So she washed the children and the dog and fed them too. Then she made dinner for whoever lived there.

While she was in another room, the three fairies who lived in the house arrived. They were amazed to see their home sparkling clean and dinner on the table. The first fairy said: "If I knew who the good sister was who took care of my home, I would place a golden star upon her forehead so that her way would always be bright."

The second fairy said: "If I knew who the good sister was who made me food to eat, I would wish that every time she opened her mouth to speak pearls and diamonds would flow from her lips."

The third fairy said: "If I knew who the good sister was who cared for my babies and my dog, I would give her a magic wand called Virtue that would help her get whatever she wished for in life."

Hearing her owners' voices, the little dog came out to greet them. In her own way, the dog told the fairies that they had a visitor in the house.

Hearing the small dog bark, Cenizosa emerged through a door into the room where the fairies were—a golden star appeared on her forehead and it lighted up the room. She started to speak and every word was a diamond or a pearl.

The wand called Virtue led her home.

As soon as the widow saw the changes in Cenizosa, she asked her sweetly where she had found them: "María, tell me how you got these treasures so that my daughter can go find some too."

María replied: "When I went to wash my little goat's innards to make mondongo for your dinner I lost some of it in the river. I followed it to a cave where I found someone's house. The house was sparkling clean and everything was in order. The children were clean and full and dog too was happy. So I broke the dishes, spread ashes over the whole house; I spanked the children, threw away the food, and kicked the dog. Then, I hid behind the door until the people who lived there arrived."

"They must have given you these gifts to get rid of you," said the widow. "Here is some money, María, go buy a little goat to cook for dinner. I will have my daughter take the innards to the river to wash and do just as you did."

And so, the widow's mean daughter was sent to the river where she let the current take the goat's innards to the cave. Once inside the fairy's house she did as Cenizosa said she had done. She destroyed everything she could find, spanked the children, and kicked the dog. Then she hid behind the door to wait for the people who lived there to arrive.

When the three fairies arrived, they could not believe the mess someone had made of their home.

The first fairy said: "If I knew who the evil sister is who destroyed my home, I would make a twisted horn grow out of her forehead so that she would bump into everything in her path."

The second fairy said: "If I knew who threw away my food and left me hungry, I would make garbage flow out of her mouth every time she said a word. And, furthermore, I would infest her hair with lice, fleas, and bugs of all kinds."

The third fairy said: "If I knew who has been so cruel to my babies and my dog, I would make her carry a stick that would beat her every time she asked for something she didn't deserve."

At that moment the little dog ran in and told the fairies that they had a visitor in the house. The widow's daughter came out from behind the door to claim her gifts. And everything the fairies had wished on her immediately came true.

She ran home to her mother who was horrified to see her daughter, and it was worse when the girl tried to speak and garbage came pouring out of her mouth.

"Don't speak," the widow screamed at her daughter, "You will make a mess in the house. You are to stay in the back of the house where no one will see you. God only knows what you did to deserve this."

The widow's daughter tried to say something but worms and toads came out instead of words. She tried to come close to her mother to whisper but the horn on her forehead got in the way. And every time she tried to tell anyone that she wanted something, the stick that followed her around beat her with her own hand.

And so Cenizosa, who was now known as María again, and her father lived peacefully in their own house since the widow and her daughter were not to be seen much anymore.

THE PARROT WHO LOVED CHORIZOS

Once upon a time, there was a Puerto Rican parrot named Señor Loro who loved the succulent chorizos his mistress's cook put into tasty stews on special occasions. He was a smart bird who would wait until the cook left the kitchen, then fly low over the pot to pick out a juicy sausage with his beak—quick enough so he wouldn't get a single feather scorched! Then Señor Loro would take it back to his cage in the dining room. There, he would drop it in his seed tray and eat it in secret. Señor Loro was a smart parrot.

The frustrated cook could never catch the chorizo thief since the culprit left no trace or clue behind. Who could be stealing the sausages without someone seeing or hearing something? Ghosts don't eat chorizos! She had to solve the mystery soon, or people would think that she was the one eating the missing chorizos!

Soon after, the cook came up with a plan to reveal the thief. She pretended to leave the kitchen, and instead she went to hide behind the door. Still and quiet, she waited and watched the pot of boiling stew, waiting for the thief to walk in. That's how she saw the parrot in action, hovering over the pot, his wings flapping so fast they were practically invisible, darting this way and that as he made his selection, then plucking out the plumpest chorizo with his beak. The tricky bird then buzzed out of the kitchen like a streak of green lightning.

The first time, the cook just watched Señor Loro in shock. She said nothing about it to anyone, for the bird was her mistress's darling pet. But soon, she had an idea for catching the chorizo burglar in the act. One day, she made sure to tell others in the house about a very special pot of chorizos she was cooking for dinner. Overhearing the word "chorizo," the parrot listened to the conversation around him while pretending to be cleaning his beak and preening his coat.

He kept his beady eyes on the kitchen. The cook saw how he stretched his wings and paced back and forth on his perch, muttering to himself—sure signs to her that devil of a parrot was very interested in the special chorizos everyone was talking about.

That night at dinnertime, the cook hid behind the door again. When Señor Loro saw that the coast was clear, he flew over the steaming pot, ready for his daring dive and quick get-away. But this time it was different. When he stuck his head into the pot to grab his treat, the cook was ready. She ran to the stove and grabbed him. Then she held him by his feet over the pot of boiling water, threatening to make a parrot chorizo out of him.

"I have you now, evil *loro*." She dangled him a little closer to his beloved chorizos, which now that Señor Loro saw them so close, seemed much less appetizing to him.

"¡*Socorro, ayuda*, help!" screeched the parrot, calling for help every way he could think of, for Señor Loro could speak Spanish as well as any native Puerto Rican. "*¡Por favor, Señora, rescáteme!*" he called out to his mistress in pitiful squeals. But the furious cook was not in the mood to listen to the thieving bird's pleas. Also, the lady of the house was away for the day. The crazy *loro* could scream himself hoarse in her kitchen, where no one would come his rescue.

The cook lifted the soggy, dazed bird with the tips of her fingers like a greenish sausage, and looked him right in the eye. "Do you promise never to steal my chorizos again, you rotten bird?"

Señor Loro was ready to promise her anything to escape the terrible fate of being cooked in the chorizo pot, for as much as he had once loved them, he now wanted to be as far away from them as possible.

"Sí, Señora. I promise you that from this day on I will only eat breadcrumbs that fall from my mistress's table. I will never steal your chorizos again!"

Before she released him, the cook made the bird repeat the promise several times while showing him the boiling pot of sausages from very close up.

The parrot promised her again and again, speaking eloquently in his perfect Spanish, that he would never steal chorizos again. Unfortunately, by the time the cook pulled his head out of the steaming pot, something terrible had happened—the parrot had lost all his head feathers. He was bald!

After this fateful day, feeling humiliated, Señor Loro kept to himself on his perch or in his cage. It was sad to see the once proud Puerto Rican parrot topped with a shiny bald pate where there should have been a crown of emerald feathers.

But let it be said, Señor Loro kept his promise. He never stole a sausage again. However now and then, he accepted treats from his mistress, who felt sorry for her bald parrot. She cried when he told her, in his perfect Spanish (which always delighted her and her guests), about his accident, how he nearly fell into a pot of boiling water one day while he was keeping the lonely cook company in the kitchen.

"*Sí*, Señora, I nearly drowned, but the good cook saved me."

"My poor little Señor Loro, I'm so glad you are still here to keep all of us company and to entertain us with your stories at dinner. You're a treasure. Here, have another little piece of cake."

Thank heavens that for as long as he had a tongue, Señor Loro did not have to survive on breadcrumbs alone!

But this is not where this story ends. There is still a little more to tell.

One day, there was a big dinner party given by the parrot's mistress for a very important man. Everyone sat at the table and began to eat and socialize, but Señor Loro, who had fixed his beady eyes on the guest of honor, kept interrupting the conversation. He flew around and around the table, as if fascinated by the gentleman, and muttering to himself. Everyone was amused by Señor Loro's odd behavior. The bird alighted on the man's shoulder and kept staring at him. Then, Señor Loro flew on top of the man's head, landing on a surface so smooth and shiny he could see himself on it. The man was as bald as he! The bird blurted out: "Important Señor, how marvelous! I see that you were caught stealing chorizos, too!"

Note: It may be of interest to young readers to know that there is a species of green parrot native to the island of Puerto Rico (*Amazona vittata*), and that it is an endangered species.

A COCKROACH NAMED MARTINA

Once upon a time a cockroach named Martina found a coin and wondered: "What shall I spend it on? If I buy bread, it will soon be gone, if I spend it on cheese or rice, it will soon disappear quickly also."

After thinking and thinking she said: "I will buy a little starch powder to make myself pretty. Maybe someone will ask me to marry him."

So, she spent the money on starch powder. She used it as makeup on her face. Then she went to sit on the porch.

A dog was the first to come by and he said to Martina:

"*Cucarachita*, you look pretty. Would you like to marry me?"

Martina asked the dog:

"What can you do that is special?"

The dog began howling and barking for Martina, but she sent him away saying:

"You frighten me, doggie. No, I will not marry you."

Then a goat came by Martina's house, and he too asked her to marry him. Martina asked him what he could do that was special, and the billy goat bucked his horns and said, "Bah! Bah!" But Martina was afraid of his horns, and she thought that his voice was ugly.

"No, thank you, Señor Chivo, I cannot marry you."

The cat came to Martina's house too. He sang "Meow" to her in a very high voice that hurt her head. She said, "Señor Gato, please go away. I will not marry you either."

Soon others who heard that Martina was looking for a husband also came to her porch to show off the special things that they could do.

An ox said:

"Moo, moo." He stomped his feet and raised dust on the road.

Martina said: "No, no. Thank you anyway, Señor Buey."

A rooster said: "Cock-a-doodle-doo," and "Good morning to you."

Martina said: "No, thank you, Señor Gallo. I do not like to get up so early. I will not marry you."

One by one, all of the suitors were sent away by Martina. She wanted someone very special for a husband.

Finally, a mouse named Pérez came by and said to Martina:

"My pretty Cucarachita, you have no idea how much I love you, please, marry me."

And Martina replied: "Before I answer you, tell me, what do you do that is special Señor Ratoncito Pérez?"

The mouse told her stories of his many adventures. He said that mice were brave and looked into everything. They found things that people lost such as buttons and pennies. He would bring many wonderful things home for her, even food that was left on the table after people went to bed!

"I will marry you with great pleasure." Martina said. And the Cucarachita Martina and Ratoncito Pérez were married.

They were very happy together. Until one day when Martina left a pot boiling in the kitchen. She was making a stew from grains of corn that Pérez had found on one of his nightly adventures.

Just then Ratoncito Pérez came home, and curious to see what she was cooking, he climbed up on the edge of the pot. He slipped and fell into the stew. There is where Martina found him.

Now when Martina powders her face and sits on her porch, she sings this little song of love:

"My Mouse Pérez fell in the stew, and your Cucarachita Martina sings and cries for you."

In Spanish: "El Ratoncito Pérez cayó en la olla y la Cucarachita Martina lo canta y lo llora."

WORKS CITED

Acevedo, Nicole. "Puerto Ricans Push Back on Kimberly Guilfoyle's 'First-Generation American' Remarks." NBC News, August 25, 2020. https://www.nbcnews.com/news/latino/puerto-ricans-push-back-kimberly-guilfoyle-s-first-generation-american-n1238042. Accessed August 19, 2021.

Acosta Belén, Edna. *"Adiós, Boriquén querida": The Puerto Rican Diaspora, Its History, and Contributions*. CELAC Comisión San Juan, 2000.

———. "A MELUS Interview: Judith Ortiz Cofer." *MELUS* 18: 3 (Autumn 1993): 83–97.

Acosta Belén, Edna, and Carlos E. Santiago. *Puerto Ricans in the United States*. Lynne Rienner Publishers, 2018.

Albino Plugues, Edwin. "Hormigueros." *Patrimonio* 5 (2012): 70–75.

Bartkevicius, Jocelyn. "An Interview with Judith Ortiz Cofer." *Speaking of the Short Story: Interviews with Contemporary Writers*. Edited by Farhat Iftekharuddin, Mary Rohrberger, and Maurice Lee. University Press of Mississippi, 2000. 57–74.

"A Capital Community." City of Louisville, Georgia. https://www.cityoflouisvillegeorgia.com/. Accessed February 15, 2023.

Castillo, Jorge. "Jasmine Camacho-Quinn Wins Gold for Puerto Rico, Sparking Another Identity Debate." *Los Angeles Times*, August 2, 2021. https://www.latimes.com/sports/olympics/story/2021-08-02/puerto-rico-identity-jasmine-camacho-quinn-tokyo-olympics. Accessed August 19, 2021.

Falconer, Blas, and Lorraine M. Lopez. "Introduction." *The Other Latin@: Writing Against a Singular Identity*. Edited by Blas Falconer and Lorraine M. López. University of Arizona Press, 2011. 1–7.

González, Christopher. *Permissible Narratives: The Promise of Latino/a Literature*. Ohio State University Press, 2017.

Gordon, Stephanie. "An Interview with Judith Ortiz Cofer." *AWP Chronicle* (October/November 1997): 1–9

Hidalgo, Hilda A. *The Puerto Ricans in Newark, New Jersey. (Aquí se habla español)*. Aspira, 1975.

Jiménez de Wagenheim, Olga. "From Aguada to Dover: Puerto Ricans Rebuild Their World in Morris County, New Jersey, 1948 to 2000." *The Puerto Rican Diaspora: Historical Perspectives*. Edited by Carmen Teresa Whalen and Víctor Vázquez-Hernández. Temple University Press, 2005. 106–127.

Jones, Isham B. *The Puerto Rican in New Jersey: His Present Status*. New Jersey State Department of Education Division Against Discrimination, 1955.

Kallett, Marilyn. "The Art of Not Forgetting: An Interview with Judith Ortiz Cofer." *Prairie Schooner* 68: 4 (Winter 1994): 68–75

Kavane, Bridget. "The Poetic Truth: An Interview with Judith Ortiz Cofer." *Latin Self-Portraits: Interviews with Contemporary Women Writers*. Edited by Bridget Kavane and Juanita Heredia. University of New Mexico Press, 2000. 109–123.

Lauria Santiago, Aldo. "Migration, Community, Labor, and Civil Rights: Puerto Rico's Department of Labor in New York-The Migration Division, 1945-1968." https://prac.rutgers.edu/managing-migration-labor-rights-and-community-civil-rights-puerto

-ricos-department-of-labor-in-new-york-the-migration-division-1945-1968/. Accessed January 28, 2025.

Lewis, John. *Carry On: Reflections for a New Generation.* Grand Central Publishing, 2021.

López, Lorraine M. "When We Were Spanish." *The Other Latin@: Writing Against a Singular Identity.* Edited by Blas Falconer and Lorraine M. López. University of Arizona Press, 2011. 39–45.

Lorrin, Thomas. *Puerto Rican Citizen: History and Political Identity in Twentieth-Century New York City.* University of Chicago Press, 2010.

Luis, William. "Foreword." *The Other Latin@: Writing Against a Singular Identity.* Edited by Blas Falconer and Lorraine M. Lopez. University of Arizona Press, 2011. vii–ix.

Mack, Will. "Paterson, New Jersey Uprising (1964)." *Black Past,* December 13, 2017. https://www.blackpast.org/african-american-history/1964-paterson-new-jersey-uprising-1964/. Accessed February 15, 2023.

Matías, Wanda Ivette. "Tesoro de gran valor histórico." *El Nuevo Día,* October 2, 2005, 54–55.

Meléndez, Edgardo. *Sponsored Migration: The State and Puerto Rican Postwar Migration to the United States.* Ohio State University Press, 2018.

Morales, Ed. *Fantasy Island: Colonialism, Exploitation, and the Betrayal of Puerto Rico.* Bold Type Books, 2019.

Moreno, Marisel. "Literary Representations of Migration". *The Oxford Encyclopedia of Latina and Latino Literature.* Edited by Louis G. Mendoza. Oxford University Press, 2020. Vol. 2, 1219–1240.

Noble, Don. "Interview with Judith Ortiz Cofer." Auburn University, 2013. https://vimeo.com/82295523. Accessed March 6, 2023.

Oberst, Lindsay. "Professor's Work Draws on Southern, Latin Roots." *The Red & Black,* February 20, 2008. https://www.redandblack.com/variety/professors-work-draws-on-southern-latin-roots/article_39ecf424-fbcd-59d1-9f68-58357fd85d46.html. Accessed February 26, 2023.

Ocasio, Rafael. "The Infinite Variety of the Puerto Rican Reality: An Interview With Judith Ortiz Cofer." *Callaloo* 17: 3 (Summer, 1994): 730–742.

———. "An Interview with Judith Ortiz Cofer: A Latina Writer in the Piney Woods of Georgia: The Landscape Has Changed Us." *Label Me Latina/o* VIII: 1 (2018): 1–12.

———. "Puerto Rican Literature in Georgia?: An Interview with Judith Ortiz Cofer." *The Kenyon Review* XIV: 4 (Fall 1992): 43–50.

———. "Quisiera ser recordada como alguien cuyas palabras sirvieron de puentes culturales." In *Ellas hablan de la isla. Interviews with Vitalina Alfonso.* Translated by Emilio Jorge Rodríguez. Ediciones Unión, 2002. 107–117.

———. "Words as Cultural Bridges." *Rituals of Movement in the Writing of Judith Ortiz Cofer.* Edited by Lorraine M. López and Molly Crumpton. Caribbean Studies Press, 2012. 27–35.

Ocasio, Rafael, and Rita Ganey, "Speaking in Puerto Rican: An Interview with Judith Ortiz Cofer." *Bilingual Review/Revista Bilingüe* XVII:2 (May-August, 1992): 143–146.

Ortiz Cofer, Judith. "The Aging of María: On the Value of Talismans and Amulets." *South Atlantic Review* 78: 3/4 (2013): 52–58.

———. *Among the Ancestors: Poems by Judith Ortiz Cofer.* Self-published, 1981.

———. *Animal Jamboree: Latino Folktales.* Piñata Books, Arte Público Press, 2012.

———. *Call Me María.* Orchard Books, 2004.

———. *The Cruel Country.* University of Georgia Press, 2016.

———. "I Find Myself a Latina Writer (Anywhere I Am)." *Brújula: Boletín del Instituto de Escritores Latinoamericanos/Compass: The Newsletter of the Latin American Writers Institute* 14 (Summer 1992): 25–26.
———. "First Class Back to the Summer of Love." *An Angle of Vision: Women Writers and Their Poor and Working-Class Roots*. Edited by Lorraine M. López. University of Michigan Press, 2009. 160–170.
———. *If I Could Fly*. Farrar, Straus and Giroux, 2011.
———. "Imagination Can Help You Invent the Self You Want to be in the World." *Lessons from a Writer's Life*. Heinemann, 2011. ix–x.
———. *Una isla como tú*. México: Fondo de Cultura, 1997.
———. *An Island Like You: Stories from the Barrio*. Orchard Books, 1995.
———. "It's Like This." *Lessons from a Writer's Life*. Heinemann, 2011. 29–31.
———. "Judith Ortiz Cofer." Poetry @ Tech. November 29, 2005. https://www.youtube.com/watch?v=IBvJaphIME4. Accessed April 2, 2022.
———. "Judith Ortiz Cofer at 2003 National Book Festival." October 4, 2003. https://www.loc.gov/item/webcast-3527/. Accessed May 16, 2023.
———. "Judith Ortiz Cofer at WCU's 2016 Literary Festival." April 5, 2016. https://vimeo.com/163724581. Accessed April 5, 2022.
———. *The Latin Deli: Prose and Poetry*. University of Georgia Press, 1993.
———. *Latin Women Pray*. The Florida Arts Gazette Press, 1980.
———. "A Life Boat." *Lessons from a Writer's Life*. Heinemann, 2011. 22–23.
———. *The Line of the Sun*. University of Georgia Press, 1989.
———. *The Meaning of Consuelo*. New York: Farrar, Straus, and Giroux, 2003.
———. *Mujer frente al sol*. University of Georgia Press, 2005.
———. *The Native Dancer*. A Pteranodon Chapbook, 1981.
———. "The Paterson Public Library." *The Latin Deli*. 130–134.
———. *Peregina*. Riverstone Press of the Foothills Art Center, 1986.
———. *The Poet Upstairs*. Piñata Books, 2012.
———. *Reaching for the Mainland*. Bilingual Press/Editorial Bilingüe, 1995.
———. *Silent Dancing: A Partial Remembrance of a Puerto Rican Childhood*. Arte Público Press, 1990.
———. *Terms of Survival*. Arte Público Press, 1995.
———. *The Year of Our Revolution: New and Selected Stories and Poems by Judith Ortiz Cofer*. Piñata Books, 1998.
———. "View From an Ivory Tower: An Interview with Luis Rafael Sénchez." *The San Juan Star* (September 25, 1983): 1–3.
———. "What I Know." *Lessons from a Writer's Life*. Heinemann, 2011. viii–ix.
———. "Who Is the Alien?" *Lessons from a Writer's Life*. Heinemann, 2011.
———. *Woman in Front of the Sun: On Becoming a Writer*. University of Georgia Press, 2000.
———. "12th Annual Calhoun Community College Writers' Conference." April 25, 2013. https://www.youtube.com/watch?v=PM9FMAxXzrw. Accessed April 2, 2022.
Ortiz Cofer, Judith, and Marilyn Kallet. *Sleeping With One Eye Open: Women Writers and the Art of Survival*. University of Georgia Press, 1999.
"Palante! A Brief History of the Young Lords." Libcom.com. https://libcom.org/article/palante-brief-history-young-lords. Accessed April 22, 2023.
Ramírez de Arellano, Rafael. *Folklore portorriqueño: Cuentos y adivinanzas recogidos de la tradición oral*. Madrid: Junta Para Ampliación de Estudios e Investigaciones Científicas, Centro de Estudios Históricos, 1926.

Rodríguez, Clara E. *Puerto Ricans: Born in the U.S.A.* Unwin Hyman, 1989.

Román-Odio, Clara. *Spiritist Women in Puerto Rico (1880–1920)*. Translated by Henry Hirschfeld. S.I.: s.n., 2022.

Romeu Toro, Carmen. *Espiritismo, transformación y compromiso social: Historia de la Escuela Magnético Espiritual de la Comuna Universal en Puerto Rico (1930–1980)*. Publicaciones Gaviota, 2015.

Ruppersburg, Hugh. "Literature: Overview." *The New Georgia Encyclopedia: Companion to Georgia Literature*. Edited by Hugh Ruppersburg and John C. Inscoe. University of Georgia Press, 2007. 1–11

Shea, Renee H. "Attempting Perfection: An Interview with Judith Ortiz Cofer." *Latina Writers*. Edited by Ilan Stavans. Greenwood Press, 2008. 94–105.

Socolovsky, Maya. *Troubling Nationhood in U.S. Latina Literature: Explorations of Place and Belonging*. Rutgers University Press, 2014.

Soto-Crespo, Ramón. *Mainland Passage: The Cultural Anomaly of Puerto Rico*. University of Minnesota Press, 2009.

Stavans, Ilan. "The New Latino: A Literary Renaissance." *Bendíceme, America: Latino Writers of the United States*. Edited by Harold Augenbraum, Terry Quinn, and Ilan Stavans. The Mercantile Library, 1993. 1–7.

Toro Sugrañes, José A. *Historia de los pueblos de Puerto Rico*. Editorial Edil, 1995.

Trelles, Carmen Dolores. "Judith Ortiz Cofer y su isla soñada." *El Nuevo Día,* July 1, 1990, 22.

Turner, Harry. "Judith Ortiz Cofer and the Third Nascent School of Island Writers." *The San Juan Star*, June 17, 1990,: n. p.

Whalen, Carmen Teresa. "Colonialism, Citizenship, and the Making of the Puerto Rican Diaspora: An Introduction." *The Puerto Rican Diaspora: Historical Perspectives*. Edited by Carmen Teresa Whalen and Víctor Vázquez-Hernández. Temple University Press, 2005.

PERMISSION CREDITS

The editor thanks the following rightsholders for permission to reprint Judith Ortiz Cofer's work and the various publications in which these works first appeared.

"More Room" originally appeared in *Puerto del Sol* 24: 2 (1989): 12–16 and later in *Silent Dancing* (Arte Público Press, 1990), 22–27, and is reprinted courtesy of the estate of Judith Ortiz Cofer.

"Talking to the Dead" originally appeared in *Puerto del Sol* 24: 2 (1989): 17–21 and later in *Silent Dancing* (Arte Público Press, 1990), 29–34, and is reprinted courtesy of the estate of Judith Ortiz Cofer.

"The Black Virgin" originally appeared in *The Americas Review* 17: 2 (1989): 11–17, and is reprinted by permission of the publisher. © 1998 Arte Público Press—University of Houston.

"The Aging María: On the Value of Talismans and Amulets" originally appeared in *South Atlantic Review* 78: 3–4 (2013): 52–58, and is reprinted courtesy of *South Atlantic Review*.

"Primary Lessons" appeared in *Riding Low on the Streets of Gold: Latino Literature for Young Adults* (Piñata Books, 2003), 186–193, and is reprinted by permission of the publisher. © 2003 Arte Público Press—University of Houston.

"¿La Verdad? Notes on the Writing of *Silent Dancing*, a Partial Remembrance of a Puerto Rican Childhood (a Memoir in Prose and Poetry)" appeared in *Truth in Nonfiction: Essays*, edited by David Lazar, 26–30, and is reprinted by permission of the publisher. © 2008 University of Iowa Press. Used with permission. All rights reserved.

"Silent Dancing" originally appeared in *Georgia Review* 44: 1–2 (Spring/Summer 1990): 51–59, and later in *Silent Dancing*, 83–93. Reprinted by permission of the publisher. © 1990 Arte Público Press—University of Houston.

"Nada" originally appeared in *Georgia Review* 46: 4 (Winter 1992): 754–62, and later in *The Latin Deli* (1993), 50–60. Reprinted by permission of the University of Georgia Press.

"Corazón's Café" appeared in *The Latin Deli* (1993), 93–116. Reprinted by permission of the University of Georgia Press.

"American History" appeared in *The Latin Deli* (1993), 7–15. Reprinted by permission of the University of Georgia Press.

"My Rosetta" is reproduced from *Prairie Schooner* 74: 2 (Summer 2000) by permission of the University of Nebraska Press. Copyright 1989 by the University of Nebraska Press.

"Las Muchachas" originally appeared in *South Atlantic Review* 82: 3 (Fall 2017): 120–123, and is reprinted courtesy of *South Atlantic Review*.

"The Year of Our Revolution" originally appeared in *The Year of Our Revolution* (Piñata Books, 1996), 75–87, and is reprinted by permission of the publisher. © 1998 Arte Público Press—University of Houston.

"American Beauty" is from *Call Me Maria* by Judith Ortiz Cofer. Copyright © 2004 by Judith Ortiz Cofer. Reprinted by permission of Orchard Books, an imprint of Scholastic Inc.

"In Search of My Mentors' Gardens" originally appeared in *Arts & Letters: A Journal of Contemporary Culture* 3 (Spring 2000): 39–44.

"Taking the Macho" is reproduced from *Prairie Schooner* 68: 4 (Winter 1994) by permission of the University of Nebraska Press. Copyright 1989 by the University of Nebraska Press.

"A Brief Account of the Adventures of My Appropriated Kinsman, Juan Ortiz, Indian Captive, Soldier, and Guide to General Hernando de Soto" originally appeared in *Georgia Review* 66, no. 3 (2012).

"My Word Hunger" appeared in *The Other Latin@: Writing Against a Singular Identity*, edited by Blas Falconer and Lorraine López (University of Arizona Press), 47–52. © 2011 The Arizona Board of Regents. Reprinting by permission of the University of Arizona Press.

"Out of the Darkness: Writing to Survive La Lucha" originally appeared in *Water Stone* 3 (Fall 2000): 65–79, and is reprinted courtesy of the estate of Judith Ortiz Cofer.

"The Myth of the Latin Woman: I Just Met a Girl Named María" appeared in *The Latin Deli* (1993), 148–54. Reprinted by permission of the University of Georgia Press.

"The Sign" originally appeared in *The Southern Review* 44: 1 (Winter 2008): 13–14, and is reprinted courtesy of the estate of Judith Ortiz Cofer.

"*Casa*: A Partial Remembrance of a Puerto Rican Childhood" is reproduced from *Prairie Schooner* 63: 3 (Fall 1989) by permission of the University of Nebraska Press. Copyright 1989 by the University of Nebraska Press.

"Tales Told Under the Mango Tree" appeared in *Silent Dancing*, 66–81. Reprinted by permission of the publisher. © 1990 Arte Público Press—University of Houston.

"The Woman Who Slept with One Eye Open: Notes on Being a Writer" originally appeared in *The American Voice* 32 (Fall 1993): 80–91, and later in *Women Writers and the Art of Survival: Sleeping with One Eye Open*, edited by Marilyn Kallet and Judith Ortiz Cofer (1999), 3–12. Reprinted by permission of the University of Georgia Press.

"Marina" appeared in *Silent Dancing*, 143–51. Reprinted by permission of the publisher. © 1990 Arte Público Press—University of Houston.

"The Witch's Husband" originally appeared in *Kenyon Review* 14: 4 (Autumn 1992): 56–61, and later in *The Latin Deli* (University of Georgia Press, 1993), 42–48, and is reprinted courtesy of the estate of Judith Ortiz Cofer.

"La Jurga: A Puerto Rican Folktale" originally appeared *Bilingual Review / La Revista Bilingüe* 17: 2 (May–August 1992): 147–149, and is reprinted courtesy of the estate of Judith Ortiz Cofer.

"Aunty Misery" is reprinted courtesy of the estate of Judith Ortiz Cofer.

"Cenizosa" was a previously unpublished manuscript, housed at Judith Ortiz Cofer's Special Collection, University of Georgia, and is reprinted courtesy of the estate of Judith Ortiz Cofer.

"The Parrot Who Loved Chorizos" appeared in *Animal Jamboree: Latino Folktales*, 29–34. Reprinted by permission of the publisher. © 2012 Arte Público Press—University of Houston.

"A Cockroach Named Martina" was a previously unpublished manuscript, and is reprinted courtesy of the estate of Judith Ortiz Cofer.

INDEX

Page numbers in italics represent reading selections.

www.ingramcontent.com/pod-product-compliance
Lightning Source LLC
Chambersburg PA
CBHW021315091025
33768CB00003B/11

* 9 7 8 0 8 2 0 3 7 4 1 1 6 *